THE LAWYER'S GUIDE TO
Records Management and Retention

George C. Cunningham

John C. Montaña

LawPracticeManagementSection

MARKETING • MANAGEMENT • TECHNOLOGY • FINANCE

Commitment to Quality: The Law Practice Management Section is committed to quality in our publications. Our authors are experienced practitioners in their fields. Prior to publication, the contents of all our books are rigorously reviewed by experts to ensure the highest quality product and presentation. Because we are committed to serving our readers' needs, we welcome your feedback on how we can improve future editions of this book.

Cover design by Jim Colao.

Nothing contained in this book is to be considered as the rendering of legal advice for specific cases, and readers are responsible for obtaining such advice from their own legal counsel. This book and any forms and agreements herein are intended for educational and informational purposes only.

The products and services mentioned in this publication are under or may be under trademark or service mark protection. Product and service names and terms are used throughout only in an editorial fashion, to the benefit of the product manufacturer or service provider, with no intention of infringement. Use of a product or service name or term in this publication should not be regarded as affecting the validity of any trademark or service mark.

The Law Practice Management Section of the American Bar Association offers an educational program for lawyers in practice. Books and other materials are published in furtherance of that program. Authors and editors of publications may express their own legal interpretations and opinions, which are not necessarily those of either the American Bar Association or the Law Practice Management Section unless adopted pursuant to the bylaws of the Association. The opinions expressed do not reflect in any way a position of the Section or the American Bar Association.

Library of Congress Cataloging-in-Publication Data

Cunningham, George C.
    The lawyer's guide to records management and retention / by George C. Cunningham, John C. Montaña.
        p. cm.
    Includes index.
    ISBN 1-59031-450-6
    1. Law offices—United States—Records and correspondence. 2. Legal ethics—United States. 3. Records retention—United States. I. Montaña, John C., 1955–
II. American Bar Association. Law Practice Management Division. III. Title.

KF320.R42C86 2006
340.068—dc22

                                                                                2006023914

Discounts are available for books ordered in bulk. Special consideration is given to state bars, CLE programs, and other bar-related organizations. Inquire at Book Publishing, American Bar Association, 321 North Clark Street, Chicago, Illinois 60610.

Contents

CHAPTER 1
Introduction   1

CHAPTER 2
Rationale and Benefits   15

CHAPTER 3
Ethics, Compliance, and Risk Management   33

CHAPTER 4
Records Retention Schedules   59

CHAPTER 7
Filing and Records Maintenance   137

CHAPTER 8
Filing and Managing Electronic Documents   163

CHAPTER 11
Record Management Program Implementation   221

APPENDIX 5
Legal-Specific Records Management Software Vendors   **253**

APPENDIX 6
Destruction Certification Memorandum   **255**

APPENDIX 7
Client Files Review and Documentation Procedures   **257**

APPENDIX 8
Client Files Review Announcement   **261**

APPENDIX 9
Client Files Review and Sign-Off Memo   **263**

APPENDIX 10
Client Notification Letter   **265**

Foreword

This book had its genesis in the late Leo Eisenstatt's pioneering work with the ABA Economics of Law Practice Section, predecessor to the present Law Practice Management Section. Leo was a visionary lawyer from Omaha who believed passionately that systems management techniques and the use of legal assistants could improve the practice of law and the quality of lawyers' lives. He was instrumental in the formation and success of the Section's Computer Division and its Publishing Board.

When the Section decided to publish a style manual for lawyers, Leo produced a practical guide for creating the most effective procedures for providing high-quality legal services. He also authored the Section's first book on the organization of law office files and file rooms. *The Style Manual* went through many editions after it left Leo's hands. Because Leo believed that law office systems should constantly improve and change with the times, he also lobbied for a revised and updated version of his filing book, one that would offer more complete and modern advice on law office information management. When Leo could not take on the job himself, we had to search for an author who was willing to fulfill Leo's vision—not an easy task, but a process involving many stops and starts over many years.

We finally found that author in the team of George Cunningham and John Montaña, noted experts in the field of information and records management. George and John have produced a book that will forever change how lawyers administer their workflow, retrieve information, fulfill their ethical responsibilities, and provide quality client service more profitably. Their guidance goes beyond the management of client files to more efficient administration of back office records. What's more, the authors provide comprehensive advice on a seemingly complex subject in a reader-friendly fashion.

We are proud to present this book as a memorial to Leo Eisenstatt and as a practical guide to a subject every law office must master.

Judith L. Grubner
LPM Publishing Board Chair Emeritus

Preface

Records management is about client service, attorney support, legal and ethics compliance, risk management, and cost control.

Those of us who labor in the field of records and information management have toiled for some time in something of a backwater, particularly as regards its prominence in the legal profession. Of late, this has changed—records and information management has become a high-profile topic as corporations become embroiled in accounting and other scandals in which records and information, and the management of them, are central. Law firms have been both called upon to render advice to clients that are involved in such matters and are concerned about avoiding related problems. Some firms have, as a result, become embroiled in controversies about their own records. Many lawyers who previously had little incentive to become interested in the topic have now been given that incentive.

This book is not about giving advice to clients about records and information management. Although many of the topics discussed here are germane to that advice, this book instead focuses on the management of records and information within a law firm. We do not intend to turn the lawyer who reads it into a records and information manager in the formal sense. It is unlikely that most lawyers are interested in any such thing, and in any event, this book is far too short to accomplish the job. The point is rather to introduce records management to lawyers, and provide them with an overview of it and its applicability to the practice of law.

In so doing, we have at some points in the book placed heavy emphasis on legal ethics and compliance as they relate to records and information management. We do this because the connection between records management and legal ethics is inescapable—like it or not, good or bad, a lawyer's records and information have a significant legal, ethics and compliance component, and one which is increasing over time, and every lawyer is well-advised to understand both the landscape within which they live, and the duties imposed upon them by it. But records and information are also important from a purely business and administrative sense—the practice of law is intimately tied to the creation and management of hard-copy and electronic records and information, and legal processes themselves are in a very real sense workflow processes involving creation, routing, and action upon hard-copy and electronic documents between the interested parties—litigants and court, parties to a transaction, or lawyer and testator.

This need for records and information management in a law firm environment does not require every lawyer to be an expert in the subject, but it does make it advisable that every lawyer have at least a passing familiarity with it. In a solo shop or small practice with few or no support personnel, the lawyers themselves may be intimately involved with recordkeeping activities. If so, it is incumbent upon them to learn it well—their records are just as important to them as are those of a large firm, and there is no one around to clean up after them if they do it poorly. Even in a large firm with records management staff, however, the lawyers should learn something about it. Just as with any other topic involving expertise, competent interaction with and supervision of your experts is best accomplished if you too know something of the topic. And since important decisions in a law firm, including those made concerning records and information will always be made by lawyers, the lawyers must have at least a high level user's understanding and overview of records management in order to make prudent choices about its structure and deployment in their offices.

This book is intended to provide that overview. Having read it, the lawyer should have an understanding of the basic concepts and building blocks of a records management program, of the activities and tools required to build it, and of the issues and difficulties they may encounter in rolling out their own records program. There is, to be sure, a level of detail and complexity with which the records management practitioner will have to deal that is not to be found in this book. Indices, for example, are the subject of whole books, and indeed a whole literature of their own. This is true of many other aspects of records management covered in this book as well. For that depth, we have provided citations to other books and resources. The lawyer interested in a more in-depth study of the topic of records and information management, or any sub-topic of it, is urged to consult them. They will provide a wealth of information and offer a wealth of resources, and permit the lawyer who really does want to be an expert, to commence that journey.

Acknowledgments

We would like to thank the many clients who have informed us of challenges and successes in their own law offices. Without their honest and capable feedback, our knowledge and experience would not amount to much and we would not have been able to share our combined fifty years of experience about law office culture, records management solutions that work, those that do not, and the challenges that are facing those who pursue records management in the legal environment.

We also want to thank the many vendors of the technology, goods, and services that are necessary components of good records management programs (you know who you are) who have answered our questions and have supported us and our clients in our endeavors.

Finally, we would like to thank those records management professionals in law offices who have labored, with great dedication, sometimes against great odds and often in obscurity, to push records management into the consciousness of the users and into the spectrum of lawyer and client service that makes a law office work and work well. We value and trust your insight and contributions to the records management discipline. Without you, good records management just would not be possible.

About the Authors

George Cunningham and John Montaña have been providing consulting services to clients for a combined 45-plus years. In 2002, with the merger of their separate consulting practices, they formed Cunningham & Montaña, with Mr. Cunningham acting as President and Mr. Montaña as General Counsel. Re-branded in 2006 as the Pelli Group, today they continue to lead the team that is recognized as the premier source for independent expertise, trusted advice, and meaningful guidance in the information and records management discipline.

In addition to his systems and strategic consulting work, Mr. Cunningham serves as an expert witness on information management, document management, and records management topics and is an advisor to venture capitalists and private equity placement groups about records management industry trends and investment opportunities. He has served on boards of directors of both technology and service organizations and has lectured in the United States and abroad to university audiences, professional groups, and bar associations. As an author, Mr. Cunningham's most recent work is a chapter on records management in *Nonprofit Governance and Management,* a joint publication of the ABA Section of Business Law and the American Society of Corporate Secretaries.

As a practicing lawyer, experienced litigator and trusted advisor, Mr. Montaña is uniquely qualified to provide guidance on the legal issues that surround information and records management in the U.S. and abroad. Mr. Montaña is the author of the ARMA- and AIIM-sponsored research *Legal Obstacles to e-Mail Message Destruction* and a recent white paper titled *Access Rights to Business Data on Personal Computers,* sponsored by the ARMA Educational Foundation, as well as many other publications.

Both Mr. Cunningham and Mr. Montaña are frequent speakers at annual professional association conferences, regional seminars, and local meetings. They have contributed to membership activities, technology and systems initiatives, and the publications board for ARMA International, the records management professional association. Mr. Cunningham is a member of ARMA, of AIIM (the Association for Information and Image Management), and an associate member of both the American Bar Association and the D.C. Bar Association. He can be reached at gccunningham@pelligroup.com. Mr. Montaña is a member of ARMA and the American Bar Association and can be reached at jcmontana@pelligroup.com.

Introduction

The Lawyer's World

Lawyers live on information. The easier it is for lawyers to get the right information, the easier it is for them to do their jobs well, to provide high-quality client service, and to contribute to their office's performance. This truth applies in large law firms and small law firms, in the offices of solo practitioners, and in the offices of those who serve in an organization's office of the general counsel. It applies as well to those lawyers who serve in government at federal, state, county, and municipal levels.

Most lawyers know intuitively how important timely access to the right information is to their work. On the other hand, most lawyers have little or no knowledge or interest in filing systems and methods, indexing, database architecture, and other mundane issues that enable records management as a practice tool. Such issues are, so the conventional wisdom goes, the responsibility of others. Because of this, the lawyer's world has to some extent become governed by a paradox embedded in the practice of law: lawyers live and die with information, yet many lawyers all too often have little or nothing to do with the management of their most vital resource.

This lack of knowledge about records management practices and lack of involvement in daily operations makes the average lawyer in many firms a bit of a packrat. The lawyer knows the information in a case file is important—or at least some of it is—and she understands that she likely has some ethical duties concerning it. However, because she is not sure that the records and information are well organized and managed, and because she does not know what exactly her ethical duties might be, she tends to keep old files and records indefinitely to guard against a vague but clearly felt likelihood that she would be in deep trouble if anyone ever asks for a record that she cannot produce. Locating and retrieving what is needed from the unstructured and largely unresponsive system currently in place may be another matter, but until that need arises, the lawyer gets some peace of mind knowing that everything is probably out there someplace and if it was disposed of, it wasn't because of her.

Our Objectives

This book is intended to address these and other issues arising from the need to manage records and information in a law office. Our goals are to:

- Provide the lawyer with the skills and tools necessary to address the practical, ethical, and business concerns of both the individual practitioner and the firm concerning records and information;
- Provide answers, solutions, and strategies that will permit the effective management of necessary information and records; and
- Do so without imposing an undue burden on the lawyer and her time.

Among the issues we will discuss are

- The philosophy and ethics of records management—Why it is important and why a good records program is far more than just a filing system.
- Taxonomy and filing systems—How to group information so you can find it later, whether it is hard copy, word processing documents, or e-mail, so daily maintenance is less onerous.
- Records retention—How to determine what records a lawyer should keep and how long they should be kept, including resources for identifying legal requirements (for Administrative Records Retention Schedules) and Ethics Opinions (for Case File Retention Schedules).
- Technology—The selection and appropriate use of software and electronic records management tools.
- Procedures—The processes that hold everything together, including the standards for performance.

In this book, we will address records management within the practice of law. While our focus will be on law firms, we also will address records management as an element of practice in all types of law offices, and we will endeavor to be sensitive to the needs of both large and small offices, and of the techno-centric lawyer as well as the techno-phobic practitioner.

What Kinds of Records Are We Talking About?

It is no longer possible to say that the largest single collection of information, in terms of both sheer volume and value for the intelligence it contains, is in hard copy form. Different lawyers, often in the same office, and depending on their age and/or their comfort level with technology, may say that one or the other, hard copy or digital, is more important; the truth is that both must be addressed. In addition to the case files, valuable information is contained in research collections and "form files," and again, these may be in hard copy or digital/electronic format. Any lawyer who fails to address both types of records does so at his or her own peril.

This book deals with the management of legal/case files, research collections, and with what we will call "administrative records." How do we differentiate between case files and administrative records? The easiest way to define administrative records is to say that if it is not case files or legal research, and if it does not belong in the library and it does not relate to a personal matter, it is probably an administrative record. Administrative records include those relating to accounting, facilities management, firm management, human resources, marketing, recruiting, tax, and other areas; the *stuff* that is about the running of a business, but not about the practice of law.

Why Be Concerned About Records?

Common Practice Today

In the worldview of the average lawyer, records are not among the critical items on which great attention should be lavished. Lawyers would much rather practice law and use information than be involved in its daily management. Case files are of course important, and when a matter is active the file is of interest. There are also a few other records—billing records, for example—that are of interest, but even these, like the case files, are of real interest only when they are active or when we are trying to get the money that is owed us. Most records, aside from active case and billing files, are of almost no interest to the lawyer, either when active or later in their life cycle. Even during active representation, lawyers in modest-size offices have administrative staff and paralegals whose duties include management and handling of related records. This delegation, in the minds of many lawyers, presumably addresses all related client service, practice management, productivity, information integrity, and risk management needs. The lawyer thinks she has little reason to be concerned.

This personal desire to make records management someone else's responsibility is at serious odds with the long-term interests of the lawyer as an individual practitioner and of the law firm as an organization. As an individual practitioner, it is a pretty straightforward issue; if you cannot access your own files to find what you need when you need it, you cannot do your job.

Law Firms Are Different from Most Other Businesses

As an organization, a law firm is a business, and is therefore subject to all of the requirements and considerations—payables, receivables, human resources, and so on—that any business has, and in which records and information play a vital and often required role. In its role as a law firm, the firm has issues in which records play a central role, issues that transcend those of concern to other businesses.

Malpractice and Ethics Compliance

Records in both hard copy and digital form, and their effective management, play important roles in risk management and ethics compliance. As a result, malpractice insurers are interested in ensuring that functions such as conflict checking, calendar and docket management, and records management are responsive and reliable. Should there be a malpractice claim or disciplinary complaint, records will be vital to its resolution.

Work Product and Knowledge Management

Another way in which law firms differ from other businesses is in their extreme reliance on work product created for one client in the later service of another client. Every law firm should have a considerable interest in proper management of what is often valuable, expensive, and painfully built and acquired intellectual capital in the form of briefs, memoranda, legal boilerplate, and other documents created or acquired during the course of practice. Whether they are called research files, brief banks, or knowledge management systems, such collections represent a law office's second most valuable asset after its lawyers.

The Personal Viewpoint or "Why Should I Care?"

The wise lawyer will find that the firm's interest in managing information properly coincides with his or her own interests. From an objective perspective, proper knowledge management is an obvious tool for improving personal productivity, delivering better client service, and thereby furthering the lawyer's own career. On a more specific level, every lawyer has a clear stake in any process that serves to mitigate risk and avoid or successfully defend against malpractice or disciplinary actions. From the more mundane but equally important perspective of business operations, the perceptive lawyer knows that properly managed records and information contribute materially to the profitability of the firm both by containing costs and improving the use of time. Whether in a law firm or general counsel's office, whether the lawyer is a sole proprietor, partner, or shareholder, or whether the lawyer receives bonuses based on performance or the overall profitability of the firm, good records management should be a matter of intense personal interest.

Simply stated, if both hard-copy and electronic files are in good shape, records will be easier to find and use, client service will be better, we will be more productive, and all will thrive and prosper. If we cannot find what we need, when we need it, we are not going to do as well financially and we may be creating ethics problems in the process.

And If It Is Not Part of the Client File?

For other kinds of information—such as billing, conflicts checking, personnel, facilities, and so on—the benefits of good records management are very real if sometimes less immediately apparent.

♦ Accurate timekeeping and billing records and supporting procedures are obviously necessary to generate income for the firm.

♦ If new work is taken on, even for an existing client, absent a proper conflicts check, a real risk to the individual and to the firm is created and the appearance of shoddy practice is institutionalized. Conflicts checking and other records, including those that document client intake and due diligence, when properly created and maintained, serve a valuable defensive function in avoiding problems in the first place, and defending against complaints, malpractice actions, and disciplinary actions that might occur.

♦ Poorly maintained and administered human resource records create a vulnerability to unfounded claims.

♦ Renovations, build-outs, maintenance, relocation, and daily facilities management are far more costly when the right information is not available. This distracts from attention to client service, overall effectiveness, and profitability.

How Much of This Do *I* Really Have to Do?

We have mentioned a few examples of the many ways, large and small, profound and mundane, obvious and hidden, that proper records management can greatly help the lawyer and the firm. Some of the effort in building and managing the processes and controls that are part of good records management can and should come from support personnel such as paralegals, secretaries, IT staff, and records staff. Some, however, including overall direction, agreement on strategy, and the establishment of certain rules, can and should come from the lawyer.

The lawyer typically does not feel much incentive to invest time in records management, regardless of the relationship of the records in question to the matters at hand. Billing demands and other artifacts of law firm business and culture usually have the opposite effect—lawyers groan because they see time spent on administrative activities such as records management as taking time away from activities viewed by the firm and its other members as far more valuable. Effective records management therefore usually requires a cultural shift on the part of lawyers at all levels in the firm as well as changes that affect support staff. Lawyers at all levels and support staff must come to place greater value on the management of records and information, and the firm or the office must be willing to commit some lawyer time, staff time, firm money, and other resources if both lawyer and firm are to realize the benefits of proper records management.

The question then becomes "What are those benefits?" It should be remembered that while lawyers go to law school, the rest of the staff does not. So, in a situation where support staff have not been well trained, the lawyer who creates a brief or memorandum of law and holds on to it may well be the only person in the firm in a position to classify and manage that particular record since she created it and she still has it in her possession. Further, she is the party most effectively and authoritatively positioned to attach the metadata—indexing, keywords, and the like—that will permit its management and retain its subsequent value to both the lawyer and the firm. Since most lawyers really do not want to do this, it stands to reason that the firm needs a system with effective rules that everyone should be trained to use.

Records Management in Law Firms

Traditionally, hard-copy client files are initially grouped by matter, in a single folder or file pocket. As the volume of information grows, the pocket may be further divided into folders by document type or topic. In the best systems, these folders are indexed—on the front of the pocket, in a special index document at the front of the file, and today most often in a special records database. This expanding pocket also has been referred to as a Red Rope, Red Wallet, Red Weld, Bellows, and bucket. For the sake of consistency, and to avoid trampling on anyone else's intellectual property, we will refer to it as a *pocket*.

In matters that generate large volumes of documents, the pocket often contains one or more manila or pressboard folders, which we will refer to as *folders*. We will use the term *file* to refer to the complete collection of folders, subfolders, and documents, both digital and hard copy, for a single case or matter. In some cases, items other than folders find their way into pockets. We will refer to these other items as *inserts*.

What sort of documents end up in client or matter files? Documents created by the firm, documents received from the client, research documentation, court records, attorneys' notes, exhibits, and more. Today, a great deal of electronic data must properly be considered as part of the client file as well—even though it usually does not end up being physically stored with the traditional hard-copy case file—but for now, we will stick to the traditional paper file in order to discuss basic principles.

Lawyers use their files in two different ways.

Matter-Specific Needs

A lawyer's most frequent need is for one or more specific files or documents that are required to perform some matter-specific task. This task can be the review of a contract, the updating of a will, or the analysis of a deposition or some other document preparatory to a hearing. In this case, the lawyer knows the client, the matter, and, hopefully, the title of the file folder in which the document is located. Next, the lawyer requests that a secretary, paralegal, or a file clerk retrieve a specific folder or the entire file (a few lawyers actually perform the retrieval personally).

Issue-Specific Needs

In dealing with research issues, document retrieval is more complex. The lawyer wants information about how a specific issue was dealt with previously ("Did we ever negotiate a contract similar to this one?"), a particular individual ("Have we ever run into this particular expert witness?"), or a specific opinion ("Where is that great opinion we cited in 2003, and what case did it refer to?"). When these questions arise, if the lawyer has no system to enable retrieval, the lawyer must rely on memory to recall the specific client, matter, and file to which the documents are related. Absent a records management program, if memory fails or if the lawyer is trying to find out if someone else in the firm has crafted a useful opinion, the "holler-down-the-hall" approach is typically used. In small offices, where everyone is in close proximity, the "holler" approach may be effective if everyone knows what they have created, where it is, and if they are there when the hollering occurs. The hollering approach has proven much less effective as paper volume has grown, the number of lawyers has grown, and firms have expanded to multiple offices.

Other Historical Approaches

As the practice of law has changed, so has the practice of records management. Until as recently as the early 1980s, most law offices and practitioners viewed records management simply as a matter of filing documents in a few folders and keeping those folders in a file cabinet located in or near the lawyer's office or the secretary's desk. When a lawyer wanted a document or a file, he or she asked for the "Smith matter" and looked through two or three folders to find the specific document.

Prior to the 1960s, there were few or no dedicated support staff with primary responsibility for managing the files in most law offices; file maintenance was the job of the secretary, or in some cases, the lawyer took care of it personally. The 1960s saw the emergence of file clerks, with specific responsibility for keeping the files of one or more lawyers. The volume of paper increased along with the complexity of the legal work done on specific types of cases, so the need for more control and the search for more efficiencies and economies in the management of that paper emerged as a concern. Above all, however, the primary concern of each individual lawyer remained that of maintaining individual control over his or her own records.

With a limited amount of paper to manage, and a ratio of secretaries to lawyers closer to 1:1 than today's more common 1:3 (and in some cases as high as 1:4 for new associates), the combination of secretaries and lawyers was sufficient in most cases to handle the records management load. When the "super firms" started to emerge, back-office functions that had routinely been handled by the secretaries and lawyers grew their own staff, and central filing or records departments, along with other departments, were born.

In large firms, the number of specialized support staff increased while the number of secretaries decreased as the large firms sought economies of scale and efficiencies through the deployment of specialists. Paralegals appeared in large numbers to meet the demand for research and organization on specific cases. While lawyers continued to review and edit bills, in many firms, the majority of the bookkeeping tasks became the responsibility of a growing accounting function. The infrastructure grew to include today's list of support services:

- firm administration
- data processing
- records management
- conflict-of-interest checking
- calendar and docket
- libraries
- secretarial services

- mail
- messenger and courier
- copy and distribution
- purchasing and supplies
- facilities (space, janitorial, etc.)

Initially, these services came under the control of one or more lawyers who assumed responsibility for these administrative functions. Later, professional managers without practice or client relationship responsibilities became more common as the lawyers shifted their attention back to practicing law and started moving toward the use of professional managers to handle other aspects of firm operations.

Central Filing Operations

By the early 1970s, centralized filing operations had appeared in many of the larger firms based on the premise of economies of scale; consolidating the space and staff needed to manage records resulted (at least theoretically) in a smaller footprint with a lower total cost for floor space. When the central files department became a fact of life, so did the need for a person to run it. Known by titles ranging from lead clerk, to files supervisor, to today's fairly common records manager or director of records, these individuals were often secretaries or former clerks who (a) had a penchant for neatness and order, (b) had shown a certain level of organizational skill, and (c) were willing to take on a job that many considered thankless.

The hallmarks of these early, centralized operations were

- a central location housing banks of cabinets or open-shelf files;
- a staff of clerks and runners under the direction of a supervisor; and
- some form of indexing, most frequently large sets of 3 × 5 cards, less frequently lists written on the outside of the folders, or all too often, no index at all.

The services provided were basic, but since they presented an incremental improvement usually at a somewhat lower total cost, they were sufficient to meet emerging expectations. Files were housed centrally, but in many cases the filing of documents within the files remained the purview of the secretaries or in some cases paralegals. When someone wanted a file, they came to the file room to get it, or they called to arrange for retrieval and delivery. When the central space filled up, the supervisor negotiated with individual lawyers for removal of files to less expensive, off-site storage.

While individual practitioners, and the small to mid-sized firms, continued with far less infrastructure, and left the files with the secretaries and the lawyers, the larger firms started to see costs hit the bottom line that in some cases could not be passed along to clients. The most evident of these costs was the bill for off-site storage of inactive records. This was followed by the cost incurred for more frequent build-outs and interior renovations to house expanding central file rooms and to provide more file space in and around lawyer and secretary work areas. Large workrooms, with the paralegals to staff them, became repositories for large sets of active, inactive, or closed litigation files. Then things changed.

Client Records Management Today

Several influences have combined to drive a change in how client files are managed in law offices, but the greatest influences have been the emergence of data processing as a powerful tool in the practice and management of law firms, and the move from centralized to distributed access to large databases.

Technology and Technology-Friendly Lawyers

Most law offices now routinely provide lawyers desktop access to a series of technology tools and expect them to use those tools with a certain level of proficiency. Recent law school graduates are much more computer literate than their predecessors. Associates and some partners routinely draft their own documents using word processing software, and many firms have mandatory online timekeeping systems. Many firms provide partners with direct access to practice and financial management tools and data, and giving lawyers access to computerized brief banks and work product retrieval systems is now commonplace.

Records Management Software Applications

The number of vendors offering true, law firm–specific records management software has grown dramatically. Increasingly, this software is integrated with other applications (more on this later), and in many cases records management software shares a large "parent" database or set of tables with one or more of the other applications with which it is integrated.

Resource Sharing

In addition, lawyers from different offices in the same firm are sharing responsibility for work on the same matter. Providing these lawyers with access to files and documents that relate to the same matter eliminates guesswork and enhances responsiveness.

Mergers

Mergers among law firms and acquisition by large firms of smaller firms, or practices from other firms, requires combining file management systems if the acquiring firm is to avoid the high overhead cost of maintaining separate records management systems.

Increased Lateral Hiring

Most practitioners agree that the concept of a lawyer having a lifetime relationship with a single law firm is no longer realistic. Partners and associates coming from other firms often bring with them expectations about services and levels of support from their old firm that they want the new firm to match.

Increasing Space Costs

Many firms that entered into long-term leases during periods when office space was less expensive have found it necessary to maximize the use of this expensive space. In such circumstances, the cost of providing space to maintain all records on-site, without any limitations, has proven to be a severe financial drain. These firms are looking for ways to reduce costs without adversely affecting service.

Off-Site Storage Costs

Large, well-established firms are seeing the costs of off-site storage mount each year. For some firms, these costs may exceed $400,000 per year. Even small firms are becoming concerned about the inexorable growth of and seemingly unending fee increases for this increasingly visible budget line item.

Cost Control Initiatives

The desire for greater profitability, at times spurred by periodic economic contractions, has prompted a greater focus on controlling expenses. Firms are restructuring themselves to be more competitive and have started implementing firm-wide cost control measures. One of the first places they look for cost-cutting opportunities is in the back office. A records management department in a large firm with a million-dollar budget, or one in a small office with a $100,000 budget, becomes a tempting target.

Records Management Tomorrow

Planning

To get the most from this book, and to make your records and information management efforts as responsive and cost-effective as possible, remember that when planning for a program that is workable today, you must plan for the future as well. Like any good system, your records management program should conform to the changing strategic requirements of your firm, and to the changing environment and technologies around it. The program should be designed and implemented knowing that the law and technology that surrounds the practice of law will continue to evolve, just as the people who deal with them evolve in their understanding and utilization of that technology. Finally, the program must be developed with the understanding that the way your firm practices law, and where it practices law, may change as well.

Technology

The progression of technologies successfully applied to records management is impressive. We have seen bar coding become routine and radio frequency identification (RFID) emerge as a productive tool for file tracking. We are seeing improvements in document management software that provide quick access to internally created documents maintained online in full text. Leading-edge firms have pushed vendors of records management software to establish full integration with document management software and its document-level indexing so users can move directly from the records management software into the body of an indexed document.

Imaging and other electronic information technologies are routinely used in litigation support and are being explored as a cost-efficient alternative to large, paper-based records management systems. The databases that drive paper-based systems have much in common with the databases that drive imaging systems. A well-planned progression should allow efforts aimed at improving paper-based records management systems to be a direct investment in an eventual move to systems that manage paper, images, microforms, and online information.

Shared Databases

As we mentioned earlier, large firms are implementing records management systems that integrate with one or more other applications. Given the time and cost involved with assuring data integrity, firms increasingly are following the model of shared databases or tables within databases that manage information for multiple applications:

- accounting and financial services
- records management
- conflicts checking
- marketing and business development
- human resources

◆ calendar and docket
◆ workflow

Administrative Records

Before we move on to a more in-depth discussion of how to design and implement a records management system, we should take a quick look at administrative records and their management.

Administrative records are part of every organization. In the law office, these records support management of the firm rather than directly supporting the practice of law. Although administrative records usually make up less than 20 percent of a law office's total records, they are critical to effective firm management. Among the many interesting issues that an office must deal with when addressing administrative records is that of legal retention requirements. Thousands of statutes and regulations concerning retention of administrative records exist at the federal, state, and local levels of government. Researching and analyzing these laws to develop a solid policy for management of administrative records can be a bit of a challenge, particularly for multi-jurisdictional firms. Law firms and law offices are subject to these legal requirements as are other organizations. The fact that a law firm is a law firm affords it no special protection. Fortunately there are resources available to firms seeking to improve management of administrative records. Like client files, administrative records can become costly to maintain if left to accumulate. And, if not included in a firm's records retention schedule, administrative records may expose the firm to unnecessary risk. Among the issues of growing interest to law offices are regulations stating that failure to properly manage accounting records may result in the IRS holding the firm's chief financial officer personally responsible.

A firm is therefore well advised not to ignore the issues surrounding administrative records, regardless of how mundane they may seem. As with any of the firm's other assets, they should be organized in a way that furthers the firm's goals and advancement, and helps it maintain profitability.

Rationale and Benefits 2

In the first chapter, we talked about records management generally—what it is, where it came from, and from a fairly high level, why it is important. Now we are going to drill down and address some very specific reasons for developing, implementing, and managing records in all media in ways that measure up to today's best practices. Later chapters will deal with the *how* portion of records management. This chapter deals largely with the *why,* the important factors aside from ethics and risk management that justify the time, money, and effort that are required to implement and maintain a responsive information and records management program.

In this chapter we are going to address staffing issues and how some of those play out. We will take a look at productivity and direct costs, particularly those that apply to off-site storage. We will take our first look at processes from a high level and start considering electronic records and look at the range of solutions that are available. In the next chapter we will move on to a different set of reasons for embracing records management, those that have to do with ethics compliance and risk management.

That good records and information management should be a part of every law office may seem obvious to most observers. To others, however, including many lawyers, the idea of devoting staff and financial resources to records management and making it any kind of priority is rejected as being an unjustified distraction from lawyering.

For many reasons, this is not so. Sound information and records management practices are a significant asset to any law office, while conversely, poor information and records management practices get in the way of doing things right, serving the client, collecting your fees, and staying out of trouble. They are a drag on the practice. Even beyond the issues of basic client service and productivity, sound information and records management priorities are in many ways not an option. Rules and guidelines exist, and failure to adhere to some of the most basic records management precepts may be punishable in a variety of ways, by a variety of authorities.

How lawyers react to the obvious and most-recognized reasons for improving records management, some of which we mentioned in the first chapter, varies depending on the perspective of the individual law office or lawyer, and the relative importance of these reasons is often shaped by the specific problems with which they are most concerned. The full range of benefits derived from a sound records management program, however, are of value to almost every lawyer, whether in a general counsel's office or in a large firm, small firm, or solo practitioner's office. All lawyers seek to serve their clients, and to do that well, they need to manage risk for themselves and their clients.

Benefits fall into two major categories, those that are measurable and tangible, and those that may not be quantifiable but make good sense for the lawyer and for her clients. The measurable and tangible benefits range from space and equipment savings to faster access to specific records and the resulting ability to spend more time practicing law and less time trying to find information. The intangible benefits, those more difficult to measure, include improved client service, risk avoidance and management, ethics compliance, information integrity, and improved response to discovery requests.

Many of the reasons for managing records correctly ultimately boil down to real money—sound information and records management practices can put money on the bottom line by reducing costs and increasing profitability while poor practices can be a significant drain on revenues. This is especially true when considering the effects of a malpractice judgment where penalties may include lost revenues, increased insurance premiums, and even the loss of the ability to practice law. If you cannot work at your craft, you can not make a living as a lawyer.

Beyond pure money costs and the whip of enforcement are issues of client service, efficiency, and duty. Most lawyers take their duties to clients seriously, and many embrace tools that make for better client service. And, as we will see in the next chapter, lawyers' ethical duties to clients have a significant records management component. Good records management implies good client service, so investing in records management is a good use of the resources of any law office.

Many of the productivity and efficiency gains to be had from sound records management are small when viewed alone: a few minutes here, a few dollars there, or a few dollars a year to store a box somewhere. It is easy to dismiss modest incremental savings, but to do so is a mistake. The particular nature of many of the accrued records management costs and inefficiencies is they do truly increase and multiply over time to the point that all of a sudden you (a) see a huge cost that brings no value to the practice or (b) have to deal with ever-increasing drags on performance and productivity—just finding what you want gets to be more and more time consuming. There is no good reason to delay in dealing with records management issues.

Staff

As with virtually everything in a law firm, records management begins with people, and good records management begins with educated people who are well trained in a good system. The lawyers, paralegals, and secretaries of a law office may or may not want to be records managers, and they may be good or bad at the work that it involves, but in the absence of dedicated records management staff, they will have the job. So, as any examination of records management in a law firm environment begins with people, let us look at the roles of the various players.

The Needs of Lawyers

One of Murphy's Laws that comes into play in law offices is, *"The one file or record you need to answer a caller's question is the one file that has gone into hiding."* This law is the genesis of one of the most aggravating things a lawyer has to do: tell the client *"Wait just a minute while I find the file."* (And, of course, the only thing that is even more aggravating is when the lawyer hears the same thing from a member of the support staff while the client is on the line.) Not only does this create a delay, it makes the lawyer look confused and disorganized. And, of course, we know that client is thinking "Hey—just a minute here—what do you mean? Why can't my high-priced help find my file?" All too often, the problem is one that the lawyer created in the first place. Leaving aside the possibilities that the file in question actually grew legs and walked away on its own to hide in the car or at home, or was misfiled by some spirit in the wrong directory on our hard drive, it will usually be found after some (nonbillable) effort in one of several places depending on the size of the practice and the habits of the lawyer. Quite commonly, it is actually hiding right on the lawyer's desk, again either physically or digitally, subject to a records control and location system known as "Pile Management."

The only filing system that provides instant lawyer access to all records at all times without relying on anyone else is the one that puts everything the lawyer might ever need in the same (or in a nearby locked) room with his desk, telephone, and computer. As the practice and workload increases, so does the volume of paper and so do the problems associated with controlling the pile. The truth is that few offices provide sufficient space to house all of the records all of the lawyers have ever created, and few lawyers are willing to personally provide the maintenance that such a situation requires. The question therefore arises, "What do we do with the pile when it gets bigger than the office where we are trying to keep it?" Or put another way, "Should we have centralized or decentralized filing operations?"

Almost every lawyer needs some files within reach. These are usually the files relating to the matters on which the lawyer is working, or plans to work on, today. In some cases, it also makes sense to keep within reach the most critical documents or records of a key client who is known to call with questions that must be answered immediately. The trouble usually starts when the lawyer tries to extend the concept of fingertip access to all records, or when the lawyer decides to tell those responsible for filing how to do their jobs, and, absent a good system, this is going to happen with amazing regularity. The lawyer then gets involved with the request and retrieval process and starts taking time away from client work.

Larger firms often have central filing operations, which can, depending on how they are run and staffed, be either the black hole of filing or the best way to assure the controlled availability of any record. Repeated experiences with bad file rooms do not engender confidence. The thought is *"Hey, you lost it last time and you are likely going to lose it this time. So thanks, but I'll just hang on to it myself."* This builds little confidence in even the concept of an efficient central file room. So the first thing we have to do is convince those wallowing in fear that it can be done, that a well-run central filing operation can indeed be a thing of beauty. So, let us take a look at what should happen, and what all too frequently can happen, when looking for files.

Theoretically, the process *should* go like this:

1. Highly focused lawyer extends hand and asks for file;
2. Devoted and efficient staff put file in lawyer's outstretched hand;
3. Lawyer opens properly sequenced file to correct version of the correct document;
4. Lawyer finishes with file and tosses it in the outbox along with new document(s); and
5. File ends up back in the right place on the shelf and new documents are immediately and accurately filed in the right sequence, in the right folder, in the right pocket.

What really happens, particularly if there is no good system in place, is often more like this:

1. Highly focused lawyer extends hand and asks for file;
2. Nothing happens since she temporarily forgets there is no file room or records program in this firm;
3. Lawyer tells staff to find the file and waits while much churning ensues;
4. Lawyer gives up on the staff and spends personal time locating *the file;*
5. Lawyer then spends time looking for the right *pocket;*
6. Lawyer spends more time identifying the correct *folder,* and then looking for the right *document* in that folder. (All of this assumes that the file and its components have some integrity. Consider the problem that comes with finding the folder and then realizing that it is empty!)
7. Lawyer finishes with file, squirrels it away, and swears never again to let any file on an open matter get more than 10 feet from her person.

Without some sort of rational and consistent approach to structuring the overall file, to titling, sequencing, and internally arranging the pockets and folders, and to maintaining the documents within the folders, different systems will emerge based on the perceived needs and the personality traits of the individuals who create them. (Think of a range driven by *obsessive-compulsive* at one end of the spectrum and by the *drop-anything-in-any-open-space type of slob* at the other end.) When one person starts looking for something in a system designed by another person, a system that she may not understand, the possibility of frequent misfiles (from her perspective) and lost records is very high. As long as people are involved in the process, and the process is not documented or audited, errors will be made and they will compound. And without a solid, well-documented, and well-managed system, lawyers by default are either spending a lot of time just looking for information, or they turn into file clerks—not a good use of their skills or time.

The process of retrieving a file may include the lawyer initiating the request through a secretary or a paralegal or (if a central records room does actually exist) by making a call directly to the file room. If there is a problem in finding the record, then the lawyer invests additional time in explaining the urgency of the situation or perhaps even gets personally involved in the search. If the lawyer does decide that it is necessary to get involved, things will become uncomfortable for support staff.

Considering the number of people who might be involved in retrieving files, and the number of transmutations the request might go through before it reaches the person who goes to the shelf, it stands to reason that errors will occur a certain percentage of the time since people are involved.

Each manual step or person involved in the request and retrieval process represents another opportunity for an error to occur.

As a reminder, remember that in today's law office each time we refer to a file or record it is just as likely to mean a digital file or record as it does a physical file or record.

Lawyers as File Clerks

The solo practitioner and lawyers in many small firms generally operate without benefit of a central filing operation. This usually means no rules and no staff with responsibility for filing according to those rules. In such cases, the result is that the lawyer may be tasked, by default, with retrieving records kept in his or her own office or in the secretary's work area, or from a closet down the hall or somewhere else. While it is easy to make a case for keeping the files in close proximity, space and workflow permitting, it is difficult to make a conclusive case for lawyers maintaining and retrieving all of their own files in any but the very smallest of offices. The value of a lawyer's time argues against an investment in serving as a file clerk.

The major problems arising when the lawyer is the sole source for finding things (which occasionally will be misplaced, or not-so-occasionally will never get filed in the first place) are that errors in process and execution never get corrected and systems never improve. Each lawyer generally knows where he or she thinks things should be, but that doesn't mean that they file the same thing in the same place each time. Because a document should be "right there in that folder" does not mean the lawyer put it in that folder. This is commonly expressed as "Who moved that document?" There is no one in the hierarchy who is going to counsel the lawyer to *"Improve your filing . . . and make sure all these documents get filed promptly from now on."* Lawyers simply are not evaluated on their records management skills. Support staff are, more often than not, evaluated at least to some degree on their records management skills, assuming their job descriptions reflect their records management duties and they have been told what to do and how to do it.

Classic Pile Management

Another unfortunate side effect of lawyer-operated and maintained filing systems is that of effectiveness. Again, history and experience tell us that, for the most part, the law gets practiced before the filing gets done. In fact, a lot of law usually gets practiced before any filing gets done. This usually leads to another familiar saying among lawyer/filer types, "Don't touch those piles of paper! That is my filing system and I know what pile to look in when I need something." This is classic pile management. Added to this is the fact that most lawyers simply are not as good at filing as a well-trained secretary or records clerk. To this add the burden of the lawyer being interrupted at work while someone else comes in to look for the file if it is kept in the office, and conflicts arise. And, even for those lawyers who are sure that they are just as good as any file clerk or secretary who ever filed a folder, and who may really be that good, it makes far more sense for the lawyer to spend her time using the information on behalf of the client, or generating new business, than on finding and filing the documents. What kind of lawyer has the amount of free time needed to keep a well-oiled filing system running? Finally, there is the question of evaluation and career advancement—lawyers are judged on many qualities, and possession of those qualities is critical to career advancement. Serving the client, billable time, rainmaking, winning big cases, and many other factors fall into this mix; records management does not. Given this mix of incentives, only unenlightened lawyers will opt to spend any real time as a records clerk working in context of their own personal system. In situations where lawyers must do so, the mix of incentives must be altered so as to encourage them to spend the necessary time on it, and the system they use should be well thought out.

The Role of Paralegals in Records Management

The limits within which paralegals can be effective in executing records duties are directly related to their willingness to do the work, their familiarity with the matter at hand, and the records management procedures governing the creation and maintenance of the files. Generally speaking, the role of paralegals in maintaining records varies depending on the size of the firm and the scope of their other duties. In larger firms, paralegals often support specific practice areas. When their area is litigation, paralegals must be productively employed in maintaining records, particularly in large cases. In offices with *centralized* records operations, paralegals frequently are devoted to the management of records relating to the active cases with which they are involved. Large firms with *decentralized* filing operations often rely heavily on paralegals to perform many of the routine file creation and maintenance tasks, or to share these tasks with secretarial or clerical staff. In smaller firms, where paralegals are required to support a number of different practice areas, or a large number of cases, their skills may best be utilized providing technical support and research rather than in clerical roles. But in all cases, in large and small firms, the need is to move records through the system as rapidly as possible, eliminating backlogs of records waiting indexing and transfer and keeping the paralegals focused on productive (and hopefully billable) client work.

Staff Conflict

Many paralegals see nonbillable records management—filing, retrieval, and related activities—as being more suited to the skills, abilities, and station of the secretarial staff. Records management work—particularly post-closing clean-up work—is far less challenging and interesting to them than getting immersed in a new case, and they feel the pressure to move on to active work and let the inactive stuff go. So paralegals will tend to find other things to do that are far more interesting to them—and often more highly valued by the lawyer with whom they work—than cleaning up low activity matters, indexing, and transferring inactive records to less expensive maintenance areas, or categorizing and shipping files off-site. Space and equipment devoted to these inactive records therefore increases as the files sit waiting for paralegals to make time to do the clean-up. This means that, wherever possible, paralegals try to push records-related work onto the secretaries.

Secretaries

Secretaries, in turn, have their own issues. In some firms, secretaries have continued in their roles as the general, all-around assistant performing a wide range of support tasks, including those relating to records management. In many firms, however, the role of secretaries is changing as they are increasingly called on to support a larger number of lawyers, and the type of work they are expected to perform changes. What used to be taking dictation and typing briefs for one lawyer has changed to include travel coordination, calendar management, document preparation, and personal errands for multiple lawyers whose schedules do not always allow time for keeping up with the minutiae of everyday life. This evolution in the role of secretaries pushes routine filing to a lower priority. When filing work is pushed onto secretaries by paralegals, they in turn may resent the paralegals not carrying what the secretaries see as the paralegals' fair share of the work. If this conflict arises, it will require resolution within the office by directive or guidance, or the firm will bear the results—a lack of integrity in file titling and document sequencing, if anything gets filed at all—of having a filing system run by two sets of unmotivated employees who do not communicate, and who are likely not even using the same rules and conventions in filing.

Client Resistance to Overhead

Law offices are encountering increasing resistance on the part of clients to pay for what they consider to be routine overhead such as filing and clerical duties. When this is the case, paralegals who have been assigned to large cases that have gone inactive are pushed to move on to other billable work and the clean-up of the records on the inactive case is postponed. The consequences of these delays, when they become institutionalized, are to create an ever-increasing backlog in war/case rooms and offices that are full to overflowing with both active and inactive files. All too often, the people charged with doing file clean-up see it as such a low priority, and so hopeless, that they abandon the task altogether. Stern admonitions by lawyers to *"Clean it up!"* result in records being shoved out of the way or boxed and transferred off-site without indexing. A far better approach for most offices is to devise a system where paralegals and secretaries are tasked to maintain the most active files on open matters and records staff are used to maintain the less active folders on open matters and to index, close out, and transfer records off-site when a case is closed.

The Role of Records Management Staff

In firms where the available resources permit it, and proper design will permit it, the solution to many of these issues is the deployment of dedicated records management staff. Alternatively, where this will not work, a well-designed and properly set up records system makes everyone's job easier, especially when records and filing duties must by default be shared among lawyers, paralegals, secretaries, and the occasional part-timer.

Lawyers should concentrate on client matters and billable activities. Paralegals in large firms are more productively employed in managing the hard-copy and digital records collections related to large cases, rather than the smaller tasks of creating folders and closing out records on inactive cases. In small firms, paralegals may effectively support a firm's records management needs but only if the procedures are sound and they understand they are going to be rated, at least in part, on how well they fulfill their obligations. Secretaries in both large and small firms have a tendency to put off filing tasks under pressure to meet more immediate demands for other things by the growing number of lawyers they are assigned to support.

Records management staff relieve lawyers, paralegals, and secretaries of nonbillable work, generally at a lower unit cost and with much better results. Records-related tasks are their primary duty; when well trained, they do it better, faster, more economically, and more accurately. Dedicated records staff are by their nature specialists, in much the same manner as paralegals. Suitably qualified records staff will have the training and background in records management policy, procedures, and practice to effectively deliver records management services in the office. Their availability and expertise allows lawyers, paralegals, and secretaries to focus on the more demanding and profitable day-to-day elements of their work lives without sacrificing the integrity and accessibility of records.

When records staff are operating according to established procedures, turnaround time on new file creation is faster, files are created with consistent titling and indexing, retrieval is faster, and inactive files are moved out of active space quicker. The overall efficiency and cost-effectiveness of the firm is substantially enhanced, resulting in improved client service and more effective and happier lawyers.

Cost Avoidance

Anyone who has spent any time at all around a law office realizes that it can be a very expensive business to operate: office space is costly, as are attorney and staff salaries (for example, in a large firm, a first-year associate often starts at a base salary well in excess of $125,000 per year, as of this (2006) writing) and the myriad other items of overhead that go into making a functioning law office. Anyone who has spent time in a law office also realizes that the practice of law is about deadlines. The ability to efficiently and effectively meet the constant deadlines of law practice is highly prized.

Quick access to the right information factors heavily into this equation. Records management, whether it is a discernable line item or is buried in the unnecessary use of lawyer and staff time, can be a substantial overhead item. Consider: one of the enduring images of the law office is the filing cabinet. In any law office, there are likely to be large numbers of them in proportion to the number of lawyers and staff in the office. Large offices may have hundreds, even thousands of such cabinets. In law offices without a records program, and particularly those without a retention schedule, inactive or low-activity records accumulate in expensive active office space, creating management and retrieval problems while exposing the firm, and the client, to unnecessary risk. When the paper glut becomes unbearable, the first reaction is to purchase additional file equipment.

File Equipment, Supplies, and Space

A study on the cost of maintaining these cabinets done over a decade ago, in the early 1990s, confirms how expensive they can be: the total cost of maintaining a standard five-drawer file cabinet in active office space in Texas in 1989 was over $1,200 per year.[1] Factor in total inflation since then and an appropriate factor for the relative cost of office space in the relevant location, and you will have an accurate number for today. Multiplying this by the number of filing cabinets in any law office will yield a fairly substantial number proportional to the size of the office. Divide this by the number of billing staff, and it will yield the amount of revenue each must produce to keep those cabinets there. Then consider the following facts.

In most law offices, a high percentage of the hard-copy documents in those cabinets can be destroyed immediately. A similarly high percentage could be stored much more cheaply—sometimes at one quarter of the cost—in off-site box storage facilities.[2] If the rest of the records were converted to electronic format or filed in open-shelf systems instead of filing cabinets, the floor space needed to house records in traditional vertical or lateral files in active office space would drop by over half. The gains are even more astounding when the necessary files are maintained in high-density filing equipment. Add the simple and cheap use of letter sized, side-tabbed, color-coded filing to the mix and you have a substantially better filing system that is easier to use, with much faster retrievals and significantly fewer misfiles and that costs substantially less to operate.

If a law office has plentiful and inexpensive premises, and space is not a problem, and everyone intuitively knows where everything is filed, none of the above (with the possible exception of more efficient filing) may matter. Alas, this is not the case. Law firms and lawyers tend to rent or own expensive space, and a growing firm tends to run out of it rapidly, requiring the acquisition of still more space. If the office in question is in downtown Manhattan, and if, as is often the case, it is crowded with filing cabinets, then the above proposition is an expensive one indeed. Substantial savings can be had in space, equipment, and staff time. If a law office is considering a move primarily to deal with the problem of paper crowding out people, it is worthwhile to look at the records, and even incur some one-time costs in the process, to see if enough space can be reclaimed to delay the move and the attendant costs. If the costs cannot be avoided or delayed, relocation and build-out costs may well be reduced by moving some of the records off-site. The resulting savings and improvement in operations can be substantial.

Off-Site Storage

Consider next the question of off-site hard-copy storage. Law firms that run out of space commonly and quite logically resort to commercial off-site storage facilities. The first and most obvious rule is, *"It costs less to keep old stuff there than it does to keep it here, and besides, we need the space."* Records are boxed and sent to the facility, and stored there for a monthly fee. When needed, they are recalled to the office, and then (hopefully) sent back to storage again when they are no longer needed. Fees attach to every step in the process: a fee to pick up the box; a fee to in-process and put the box on the shelf the first time; a monthly fee to store it; a fee to retrieve it from the shelves; a fee to deliver it; a fee to pick it back up; and a fee to reshelve it. In almost every case you continue to pay for storage even if you have retrieved the box and held it in the office. If you wish to destroy it, there is still another fee, maybe two, one for the destruction itself, one for the "permanent removal" of the box from the vendor's inventory (also known as the hostage fee). If rush deliveries or other services are needed, additional fees apply.

On a per-box basis, these fees may not seem substantial: As of 2005, monthly storage fees for a single box, depending on total volume, ranged from $0.12 to about $0.36 per month, or as much as $4.30 per year. Retrieval and refilling (separate charges) cost from $1.50 to $3.00 per item, delivery and pickup $1.00 to $3.00 each, plus an additional charge of several dollars for the entire pickup or delivery. The in-processing charge (on top of pickup and delivery) for each new box ranges from $1.50 to $4.00, and destruction starts at about $4.00 per box and goes up. The lower price generally applies to records the vendor is going to resell to a recycler. Secure disposition can cost substantially more.

In aggregate, as small as they seem individually, these charges can add up rapidly. In law firms with no records retention program, boxes sent to storage remain there permanently. The size of the collection grows, fees go up every year or so, stuff gets pulled from storage and not all of it is returned, and costs increase rapidly. Even though it costs less to store old or inactive files in off-site warehouses than it does in active office space, those savings are limited, or can evaporate, if the relationship and process is poorly managed, if controls are not in place to track the files, if money is spent storing records that need not be retained at all, or by storing files for excessive periods of time. Analysis of box storage costs in law firms and large companies typically yields the conclusion that a large percentage—as much as 40 percent of the total set of boxes—could be destroyed during the initial implementation of a retention schedule. Commonly, a high percentage of that disposable volume is duplicate information or other short-term material that should not have been sent to storage in the first place. Limiting what is sent to off-site storage to that material which has ongoing value and must be maintained (and disposing of the rest outright), and establishing a finite retention period for the remainder adds to the savings derived from limiting maintenance of inactive records in high-cost active office space. Thereafter, even modest reductions in the retention period of the remaining material yields even greater savings.[3] Apply this concept to digital files and the result is the same.

The problems and costs encountered by excessive retention of value-less records is exacerbated by other aspects of poor inactive records management: boxes sent to storage are frequently indexed, packed, and labeled so poorly that retrieving a single document may require recalling dozens or hundreds of boxes—at a cost of several dollars each—to find that one particular item. On top of the direct costs of large-volume retrievals are the attendant costs of staff (think paralegals or new associates at substantial hourly rates) culling through the boxes. All of this adds significantly and unnecessarily to firm overhead if the cost is absorbed or to client costs if it is charged back.

Finally, consider these facts in the context of a single office of one major law firm in a major city. In 2004, this office had 250,000 boxes in storage, and was adding to that total at the rate of 4,000 boxes per month. The storage and handling bill alone was in excess of $2 million per year for this single office. The potential total cost just for moving the records to another commercial storage vendor was estimated at between $2 million and $4 million because they had signed a contract with unfavorable terms. This is not a hypothetical case, and for large firms, these are not uncommon numbers. Even if you are not in a large firm, at some level and on some scale, these numbers are relevant to every law office. Absent a good records management program and a properly implemented records retention schedule, honest investigation will lead to the conclusion that your firm has way too many old records that are costing way too much money every year. In every case, to the extent that these costs can be avoided or eliminated, they directly impact the profitability of the firm. This in turn takes money out of everyone's pocket. The total savings that can be achieved by these and other simple methods should not be underestimated.

How Much Is Enough?

An informal 2003 survey among mid- to large-sized law offices shows a wide range in the amount of office and secretarial area file space allocated to each lawyer, from a low of 12 linear feet to a high of 50 linear feet each. If the survey is extended to closets, workrooms, conference rooms, and on-site file storage areas, it is not unusual to find total on-site file storage that approaches 150 linear feet per lawyer. The firm at the higher end of the range is incurring a substantial and unnecessary annual cost, considering space and equipment that probably is not necessary. In law offices that have never dealt with the issue of records retention, it is not unusual to achieve 30 to 40 percent reductions in the space devoted to on-site records after developing and implementing a records retention schedule. Every square foot of space devoted to records that can be eliminated represents an ongoing annual savings to the firm. If the firm is willing to consider a centralized filing operation, the savings can be even more dramatic: The space required to house records in scattered locations is often twice that required to house the same volume in a centralized facility, and the cost of filing equipment, on a per-inch basis, can be substantially less with central filing. If all of the above are addressed in the context of a move to new premises, or a redesign of existing premises, still more savings can be factored into the equation. Through enforcement of records retention schedules and prompt review and transfer of inactive records, a well-conceived and managed records program can reduce the associated construction costs for such facilities as workrooms during the build-out, and the ongoing annual costs, by substantially reducing space requirements for them.

Productivity and Efficiency

Productivity can be measured in many ways. For the lawyer or support staff looking for files or specific documents, productivity as it relates to records management is most often measured by how long it takes to find the file containing the information or the document that is needed to answer a question or deal with an issue. We have touched on the costs of inefficient records management including searching for lost folders, looking through poorly described and labeled folders, researching someone else's file directories, and sorting through poorly indexed boxes to find a document.

When considering change, those who are unfamiliar with the tools at hand sometimes give up and say, *"Well, the cost to fix it is probably more than the cost of keeping it and besides, I don't have the time."* Actually, in most cases, implementation, particularly on a going-forward basis, may be both simple and inexpensive to achieve.

Some Quick Fixes

First, if you have not already stopped using legal-size paper and folders, stop today. Most courts that still accept paper require that it be letter size. If you look at the documents in really active cases, 99.99 percent of them are letter size. If you convert from legal to letter size, you can use the same 10 inch × 12 inch × 15 inch records box and increase the linear file capacity by one-third. If this is the only change you make, your office will be sending fewer boxes off-site and spending less money.

When you send boxes off-site, use a basic standard index, coupled with a short set of standard box packing and labeling procedures to (a) significantly reduce the time and effort required to retrieve documents from storage, (b) substantially improve the accuracy, integrity, and completeness of retrievals, and (c) greatly reduce delays in searching through multiple boxes and the attendant lawyer frustration. Faster, more accurate, and more complete customer service in-house ultimately means better client service.

In the case of open-shelf, color-coded hard copy filing, initial filing and retrieval is much faster, and misfiles are substantially reduced, thereby again achieving better customer service. In this case, as with box indexing and packing, the investment is comparatively small—the consumables required are quite inexpensive (and replace other consumables of essentially equivalent but sometimes higher cost), and the shelving is far less expensive—by as much as two-thirds less—on a per-file basis than are filing cabinets, while consuming less floor space. In both cases, a well-designed records management solution is a win-win situation.

These are just a few of the hard copy inefficiencies that can be alleviated by proper records management practices.

Electronic Records

Electronic Document Management Systems (EDMS)

An EDMS is a potentially powerful software tool used, not surprisingly, for the management of electronic documents, most commonly word processing documents, spreadsheets, presentations, and other material created in normal day-to-day operations. In a law firm, such software is used for creating and versioning pleadings, contracts, memoranda of law, and the many other types of documents created, modified, received, and managed by lawyers and other staff. Such software commonly has a search feature permitting retrieval of documents based on a number of parameters, including a categorization assigned by the creator. The software is capable of supporting an extensive and complex indexing hierarchy and facilitating rapid and accurate retrieval of electronic documents. This occurs, however, if, and only if, the organization using the document management software takes the time to create the requisite indexing hierarchy that makes the whole thing work. Most law offices do a poor job of realizing the potential of their document management system.

An analysis of the document management software at a major law firm revealed that the two most common profiling categorizations for documents on the system were "other" and "miscellaneous." These were closely followed by "general," "legal," and "documents." What might be in those categories? Very likely, anything. This approach pretty much eliminates any value the categorization function brings. So, how would someone find a document in one of these categories? Probably by using the full text search function, or perhaps by going through and opening every likely suspect in any possible category until the desired version of the desired document is found. In a large document set, both approaches take time, often a great deal of time, most of which is wasted. The cost of that waste is borne by either the firm or the client.

Do we then abandon the tool as unworkable and the investment as wasted? No. Again, the solution is conceptually simple: a structured index and assignment of the appropriate terms from it to each document, will, in combination with other suitably chosen metadata, allow the search features of the software (either the document management software itself, or records management software used in conjunction with it) to be fully utilized, and will result in much faster and more accurate search results.

E-mail

Next, consider the problem of finding e-mail related to a particular topic. What started as a wonderful tool has turned into a monster that eats up our day, consumes our system resources, and harbors nasty surprises. Most readers have experienced the annoyance of having to wade through dozens or hundreds or even thousands of e-mails looking for something in particular. This can be an extraordinarily time-consuming activity if, as is often the case, e-mail is stored in a single unstructured in-box or grouped simply by date (auto-archiving anyone?).

When e-mail headers are uninformative or absent, the user is forced to tediously scroll through and scan e-mail titles until, hopefully, the needed one is found. If e-mail is used for the transaction of substantive business, the problem may extend beyond mere annoyance: there may be significant business or ethical reasons why that e-mail must be located and preserved. The stresses of ethics and compliance are thus added to the mix. For anyone who has not figured it out yet, e-mail is on a par with hard copy and with other electronic records. Its value is in its content, not in its medium, and it needs to be managed consistent with its legal and business status, as simply another format for documents.

Solutions to the problem of e-mail management and the management of other digital objects range from the simple to the complex, depending on the resources and money available. If the organization is large and the resources are there, software is available to facilitate accurate categorization and management of e-mail, word processing, and other electronic material. If the organization is small and resources are limited, substantial improvements can be achieved by creating and enforcing the use of good indexing structures. Sound management solutions exist for all organizations, even when their resources are limited. It is amazing to see the impact that good design, effective training, and decent housekeeping can have on even the smallest organizations.

Simply using a standard format for capturing information on folder titles, in document profiles, and in e-mail subject headers, such as client-matter number and topic or document type makes a huge difference. Thus: "54312-038, Motion in Limine," in the context of a standard description structure or taxonomy for managing all records (hard copy, EDMS content, and e-mail folders) for each matter/client/issue (or whatever other subdivision makes sense in the circumstances), makes sorting, search, and retrieval of all records in all media far faster and more efficient.

Conclusion

The examples cited above are just a start. They by no means exhaust the possibilities. It is worth bearing in mind that the savings in cost and efficiency to be gained from records management are not an all-or-nothing proposition. Tools and solutions range from automated workflow (the automated routing of documents through predefined paths and with attendant rules and actions within the firm), to changing supplies and file equipment, to creation and consistent use of standard filing taxonomies. Benefits can be derived during the merger of firms and records systems or during a move to new space. In virtually every office, regardless of its budget or other circumstance, improvement opportunities exist. In some cases, for some offices, large investments in technology or equipment are justified to correct an undesirable records management situation. In other cases, more modest resources or strategies may be more appropriate. Whether a high-end solution is or is not practicable, there are many other pieces of the puzzle available to anyone wishing to use them. For many such pieces, the cost is modest—some new equipment and procedures. For others, there is virtually no cost at all, beyond the willpower to change bad habits, and learn and apply a few simple concepts. If nothing else is available, these are.

Notes

1. Eugenia K. Brumm, *A Cost/Benefit Analysis of the Records Management Program in the State of Texas,* RECORDS MANAGEMENT QUARTERLY, April 1993, Vol. 27, Issue 2.

2. *Id.*

3. *Id.*

Ethics, Compliance, and Risk Management

3

Introduction

In this chapter we address the pressing question, *"As a lawyer, do I really have to pay attention to this records management stuff?"* The answer is *"Yes,"* and we will tell you why.

The genesis of any lawyer's entry into records and information management should be an inquiry into its legal and ethical aspects. *Any* law office or solo professional is governed by a considerable array of legal constraints and ethical precepts. The lawyer, given her position as a fiduciary to her client, and her role as an officer of the court, is subject to more than most, and to a higher standard of care than most in respect of compliance with them.

To most lawyers, this will come as no surprise; there are rules and they must be followed. The issue here revolves around how to avoid breaking the rules when dealing with records and files. Regardless of practice area, or jurisdiction of practice, every lawyer is governed by the Rules of Professional Conduct (or as applicable, the Disciplinary Rules), court rules, specialized statutory enactments, and a variety of other authorities that affect her practice. The outcomes mandated by those authorities, and violations of them, may have powerful consequences for the lawyer, including the potential for loss of the lawyer's most prized possession, the license to practice law. The effect is that most lawyers are aware of at least those rules, the violation of which may result in severe penalties. We are not here to train lawyers in basic expectations. Those few lawyers who are not aware of and sensitive to such mandates as those governing attorney-client privilege or conflicts of interest need more help than we can give them here.

Ethics and Records Management

Many lawyers do not, however, have a good grasp of how their legal and ethical responsibilities extend to the management of records and information. What happens over time, what the lawyer's obligations are with respect to a client's file or other records and information associated with a representation is something with which most lawyers are unfamiliar. Some believe, mistakenly, that they have no responsibility and that records management is an issue to be dealt with by others, while the lawyer goes on to more productive work. Many lawyers who do think about an old or inactive file frequently do so in an ill-conceived manner. Since they do not know what to do, but realize that ethics is the backbone of the lawyer-client relationship, and that records, particularly the matter file, are the evidence of that relationship, they respond by keeping virtually everything associated with a representation—at least those things which have been reduced to paper—more or less forever.

Neither making it someone else's job nor keeping the paper forever is satisfactory, for several reasons:

♦ As we will see later, the concept of "matter file" as a physical file folder containing paper documents is outdated and inaccurate;

♦ The lawyer has ongoing obligations to the client, including obligations respecting the matter file that must be dealt with;

♦ Neither firm, nor lawyer, nor client is well-served by accumulating massive volumes of old records retained without plan or reason, or with no eye on cost, convenience, or risk management, more particularly since the firm must ultimately pay whatever costs are involved in satisfying ethical obligations to the client or to others.

Because the question of records and information management is so intimately tied to ethical considerations, a discussion of those ethics, and of how they impact a lawyer's records and information, is a worthwhile starting point when developing sound records and information practices. Let us take a look at the relevant ethics authorities, and consider their relationship to the lawyer's records.

Risk Management

Law firms have historically believed there were few risk management considerations surrounding their handling of records. The two primary rationales for this belief are straightforward—and flawed.

1. Many have viewed client-related "records management" as addressable by simply keeping matter files forever, or at least for a long period of time; and
2. They have tended to think that since they are lawyers, no one can get to their records, that they are essentially immune to discovery by other parties.

Neither assumption is true.

The fact that most of the authorities cited in the next section are ethics authorities of one sort or another should yield an obvious conclusion: failure to deal with records management in a manner that is compliant with the dictates of these authorities may be interpreted as an ethics violation, and in turn be deemed malpractice. Further, the notion that a law firm's files are immune to discovery by others is based at most upon a professional courtesy no longer applicable in the real world. The privilege that attaches to a lawyer's records is actually quite limited—it attaches generally only to attorney work product and attorney-client communications (leaving aside matter-specific items such as trade secrets)—and thus a wide range of material, including many client-owned documents, are available to others by means of legal process.

In recent years, what many lawyers considered only a possibility has become a reality. The hard truth is that the Enron bankruptcy case resulted in the subpoenaing of records from nearly fifty law firms by the special master. With increasing frequency, firms find themselves in the awkward position of having to turn over to third parties copies of documents in client files that formed part of the discovery in past representations. If the client actually has and implements a records retention schedule and has appropriately destroyed their copies of records, a law firm creates risk for those clients if they have no retention and disposition policy in place and documents are not disposed of—an awkward and embarrassing situation of the firm's own making. At least one ethics authority considers a records retention policy ethically mandatory for all law firms:

> Disclosure of a confidence or secret because of a nonexistent, inadequate, or unobserved retention policy would be a violation of The Rules of Professional Conduct.

* * * * *

A law firm, including a solo practice, is obligated to have a record reten-tion policy or plan in order to meet ethical obligations . . . [E]ach firm is obligated to establish and administer a record retention policy or plan, to educate all lawyers and non-lawyers in the firm as to its operation, and to monitor compliance.[1]

Thus, beyond any ethical or client service considerations, sound records management is a risk management activity. That this is true is well-known in the corporate/business world, where records retention scheduling and its many related activities have long been viewed as an exercise in risk man-agement as well as a vehicle for controlling costs. It is equally true in the business and practice of law. While most obviously true in the area of client-related records, it is equally true for those records not subject to ethics con-siderations. Substantial fines and other penalties associated with poor records management await the ill-informed.

Risk management as it concerns records management deals with three high-level issues:

1. *Poor organization.* To have a record and not be able to find it is, for most compliance purposes, the same as not having it at all. A good records management program, properly deployed, has many tools for accurately and efficiently finding hard copy and electronic/digital information when it is needed.

2. *Failing to maintain records long enough.* Dealing with this issue is one of the basic functions of a records retention schedule. The business needs and ethical and regulatory environment of the organization should be analyzed in sufficient detail to ensure that records of all types are maintained for legally and ethically sufficient periods of time. Guessing at the rules and making wrong assumptions about the need to manage e-mail and other electronic records are among the major causes of judgments resulting in sanctions.

3. *Maintaining records too long.* At some point, any record loses all via-bility. In the case of a matter file, the deal is closed, all appeals have been exhausted, and all applicable statutes of limitation have run. In the case of a business record, all applicable retention periods have been met and all business utility is gone. When this day arrives, beyond curiosity value, the record is at best valueless, at worst a liability. Its disposition becomes both a risk and cost issue. Destruction saves at least whatever cost in floor space or off-site storage is associated with its continued maintenance, and poten-tially a great deal more if its disposition short-circuits a subsequent attempt by a third party to obtain it. This is not to say that matter

files or any other records ought to be destroyed to keep evidence out of the hands of any party entitled to obtain it. One can and should, however, limit the period of time in which records are available to third parties to a reasonable one based upon business need, legal requirements, and ethics analysis. A well-designed and implemented retention schedule as a part of a sound records management program deals with these specific issues.

Within these high-level issues are subsumed the answers to common questions:

1. Should I notify the client prior to destroying an old file?
2. What retention period for a matter file is "reasonable"?
3. Shouldn't I really keep it all forever just in case the client calls with a question?

. . . and so on?

The basic principle is simple, however:

Some combination of administrative management in the form of indexing, physical storage arrangements and the like; combined with suitably chosen retention periods, creates a situation in which the firm and its clients are at lowest risk of any adverse consequence arising from poor management of records and information.

The trick is to determine that optimal amount of management, and its details. Since the ethics opinions surrounding the topic are imprecise, and sometimes contradictory, and case law and interpretation is inconsistent, it is likely that the optimal point will never be achieved. Practical and theoretical problems abound with attempts to create a perfect system. Understanding that 100 percent compliance with sometimes contradictory guidelines is likely impossible to achieve, even with an enormous investment and extreme granularity of oversight, and realizing that creating a totally risk-free environment is impossible, practitioners are searching for reasonable and balanced solutions.

In the most perfect system, each document would be purged/destroyed on the specific date that it becomes eligible. But, one would never go into files to retrieve individual pages for purging and destruction pursuant to a retention schedule. In the real world, hard copy purging and destruction take place on the file, matter, or box level, regardless of shorter periods that might apply to individual documents within these containers. By the same token, most time-based purges are executed annually to achieve economies of scale. In a similar manner, indices have a finite number of levels, and electronic records have a finite number of metadata points that can be attached to them.

Each of these limitations (and there are many others) serves to make the overall program suboptimal, but is necessary to make the program practical. From a risk management perspective then, the goal is to find the set of compromises that serves the overall goals of the records management program at reasonable cost and effort, and with the greatest likelihood of accurate and consistent application in practice.

Basic Ethical Considerations Related to Records and Information Management

The starting point for consideration of a lawyer's ethical responsibilities is, of course, the Code of Professional Responsibility or, as applicable, its newer sibling, the Rules of Professional Conduct. As a historical note, the Rules of Professional Conduct have gradually been supplanting the earlier Code since the 1980s, and at this point, at least 47 states have converted to the newer Rules or some variant of them. However, the Code is still in effect in some places at least for the time being, and both Code and Rules are cited in both case and ethics opinions. In addition, the Code and its requirements offer a historical context within which to view a lawyer's duties surrounding records. We will therefore use both in this discussion, with the caveat that local rules, opinions, and cases may affect specifics for any lawyer considering a records management program. Note also that over time, many states have modified the language and numbering of both Code and Rules, and the examples cited below may not conform exactly to those in effect in the reader's jurisdiction.

Either explicitly or inferentially, several of these rules impose ethical requirements and constraints on a lawyer's handling of records and information. Equally importantly, they serve as the foundation for the outcomes of ethics opinions, case decisions, and other authority attempting to deal with real-world situations concerning lawyers and their records. Let us start by considering some of the issues and the rules responsive to those issues. In later chapters, we will discuss the strategies, tools, and technologies needed to respond to these issues. For now, we will limit ourselves to the issue of ethics themselves.

The Disciplinary Rules

Conceptually, a lawyer's ethical duties regarding records management are simple, at least insofar as they are addressed by high-level ethical precepts. Virtually all authorities discussing the subject begin by citing the same authorities (note that the precise wording may vary by state).

[A] lawyer shall not withdraw from employment until the lawyer has taken steps to the extent reasonably practicable to avoid foreseeable prejudice to the rights of the client, including giving due notice to the client, allowing time for employment of other counsel, delivering to the client all papers and property to which the client is entitled. . . . [2]

Canon 4. A Lawyer Should Preserve the Confidences and Secrets of a Client.

Canon 5. A Lawyer Should Exercise Independent Professional Judgment on Behalf of a Client.

The Rules of Professional Conduct:

Rule 1.6. Confidentiality of Information. (a) A lawyer shall not reveal information relating to the representation of a client unless the client gives informed consent, the disclosure is impliedly authorized in order to carry out the representation or the disclosure is permitted by paragraph (b) [authorizing disclosure under very limited circumstances].

Although these Rules and Canons do not directly address records, they nonetheless set the tone for the lawyer's responsibilities concerning records, and may be summarized succinctly: A lawyer's management of her records must protect the client's interests, both during and after the representation, must protect the client's confidences and secrets, and must be governed by the lawyer's professional judgment in situations where handling of the records is not governed by rule or statute.

As always, however, the devil is in the details. The handling of a lawyer's records and information has many aspects, and the details of those aspects are not adequately addressed by a brief cautionary admonition to the lawyer to protect the client's interests. Fortunately, some of these aspects can be broken down into discrete topics for which there is at least some guidance, which, when combined with the "independent professional judgment" demanded of every lawyer, will yield sound records management principles, which can in turn be used as a basis for policies and procedures for the management of records and information.

Maintaining Confidentiality

One of the core ethical duties of a lawyer is to preserve the confidences and secrets of her client. Regardless of the applicability of records retention, client file ownership, and other more complex matters, every lawyer's records management must extend at least as far is as necessary to accomplish this.

The duty to preserve a client's confidences manifests itself as a records management matter in several ways. During the *active* life of a file, there may be duties of confidentiality arising from particular documents in the file, completely apart from any requirements imposed uniquely upon lawyers. One such example is personally identifiable medical information, which is subject to stringent privacy requirements under the Health Insurance Portability and Accountability Act (HIPAA). Regulations promulgated at 45 CFR Part 164 impose very stringent privacy requirements on personally identifiable medical information for any party who obtains that information in an insurance-related transaction. These requirements include allowing personnel to see the information only on a need-to-know basis, and provide for heavy penalties for violations, particularly if the violator is a sophisticated party such as a lawyer. Other information such as financial information may also be subject to independent privacy requirements.

The duty to maintain confidentiality does not go away when the file becomes inactive. A lawyer cannot just throw out the file when her work is done since the trash will contain a considerable amount of sensitive information. In a law office, such trash will include drafts of letters, pleadings, memoranda, and other items related to the firm's representation of its clients. To the extent that those discarded drafts contain information confidential to the firm's clients, simply throwing them into a dumpster or trash receptacle might well be an ethical violation, or at least give rise to the possibility of one. A long line of case decisions holds that there is no expectation of privacy in discarded trash, and any client-related material it contains is thus subject to recovery and perusal by anyone caring to do so. Nor is this just theory: "Dumpster-diving" as an intelligence gathering activity by journalists, law enforcement officials, and industrial spies is a well-known phenomenon, as are occasional scandals involving carelessly discarded confidential records being found in alleys and on sidewalks. Ethics authorities admonish that the duty of confidentiality continues even during the purge and destruction processes.[3]

This means that confidentiality comes into play in the management and disposition of closed matters as well. Closed matter files are commonly boxed up and sent to off-site storage facilities, which vary widely in terms of quality and security. A few ethics authorities have rendered opinions on the subject of storage of old files, and have concluded that matter files ought to be stored in a secure facility with controls over access and other safeguards.

These opinions are in conformance with general reasonable commercial practice—high-quality commercial records storage facilities will have access controls and other safeguards in place, as well as fire protection and climate control to prevent deterioration of the records. But not all vendors are high-quality. Lawyers contemplating use of a commercial records storage facility should vet candidates to ensure that the facility they select measures up. The lawyer should read the contract offered by the storage vendor carefully. Such contracts commonly contain risk and cost-laden language permitting the vendor to place a lien on records stored with them in the event of nonpayment (whether or not there is a valid dispute), and may also permit a sheriff's sale or discarding of them in this event. Finding oneself without access to matter files because of an unpaid bill, or worse, having one's matter files up for sale at a sheriff's auction would be a fiasco to say the least, and while it is not common, it has happened.

Finally, when disposing of old matter files, confidentiality must be considered. Discarded confidential records blowing around a landfill is another commonly encountered situation that can create a scandal, but one that is easily avoided. Secure destruction by a specialist vendor (often the same vendor used for storage, or one contracted by them), ensures that the records cannot be recovered and client secrets are not compromised.

Plainly stated, the duty of confidentiality with respect to old matter files boils down to this:

1. Use shredders in the office;
2. Make sure the place you store your old files is secure; and
3. Use a secure, bonded destruction vendor if you have a large volume of files to destroy.

Beyond these basics, the lawyer would do well to consider her basic strategy when using computers. A lawyer's computer will likely contain large amounts of information of a confidential nature. Is that computer password protected to prevent unauthorized access? Is the data on it encrypted? These may not be issues if the computer is located in reasonably secure premises such as an office accessible only by employees of the firm, but if the computer in question is a laptop, they may be issues of considerable importance. Laptops are frequently lost or stolen, and bad though this might be in and of itself, it is far worse when the loss results in compromising of client confidences and secrets.

E-mail is another area where consideration of issues of confidentiality is worthwhile. While no authority as yet requires the encryption of e-mail by lawyers,[4] and e-mail is itself relatively secure, a caveat is in order: e-mail transmissions over unsecured wireless networks such as those found in Internet cafés and airports are very easy to intercept. Lawyers using wireless networks to discuss and transact client matters should consider using one of the many available technologies to secure their transmissions. These include virtual private networks (VPN), secure socket layers (SSL), and the e-mail encryption functions found on many e-mail programs.

Metadata security may be equally problematic. Word processing and other Microsoft Office software files contain large amounts of metadata, often including language that has been deleted from the original, and that can easily be restored and discovered. If the metadata contains information prejudicial to the client, the lawyer may inadvertently compromise the client's interests by not stripping it out prior to transmission of the document to others.[5]

Ownership and Possession of the Matter File

The most obvious artifact left at the end of a representation is the collection of information in its many forms that was created during the course of the representation. This collection includes documents and objects that the lawyer frequently does not recall or consider as part of the official case file but that nonetheless exists. In view of our increasing dependence upon computers, we must consider all the varieties of this information in all of its digitally recorded formats.

The lawyer traditionally keeps the matter file after the matter closes, not because of any conscious decision on the part of either lawyer or client, but rather by default. There is nothing particularly wrong with this arrangement, and much that is right: the lawyer is much more likely than most clients to keep a fairly complete file that has some level of integrity; and if the client has another matter, the lawyer in possession of the last matter file can more easily get up to speed on it, particularly if it is related to the previous matter. Finally, should the client ever need the matter file for any reason, its possession by the lawyer in the interim permits the client to easily obtain it from her.

If the lawyer and client agree on this arrangement, and concur about who is responsible for keeping what, the continued possession of the matter file by the lawyer poses no issue. There are, however, times when the clients' view that they are entitled to "on-demand" possession of the file while putting the full burden on counsel for maintenance creates a burden for the lawyer. The clients may feel that, having paid for the representation, they are entitled to possession of the file without further payment, regardless of any costs the lawyer may incur in the course of its long-term storage and eventual production to the client. Or, the client and lawyer may disagree as to exactly what parts of the matter file are the client's—and thereby subject to their demand for possession—and which are the lawyer's, and so immune from such a demand. Or, the lawyer may wish to dispose of the file, or charge the client for its continued maintenance. In other cases, the client may not have fully paid for the representation, and the lawyer may wish to withhold the file as collateral against the unpaid fees. In still other cases, the client may want copies of materials not formally associated with the matter file, such as billing records or electronic data objects stored in the lawyer's computer system and perhaps never even committed to paper.

The conflict potentially arising from these divergent views may be exacerbated by other factors. At some point, the lawyer may have run out of either room or money for storing old files, and would like to dispose of them. If the client assumes that the lawyer is retaining them indefinitely (and in the absence of some agreement to the contrary, this is likely to be the case), the lawyer may be assuming some risk in disposing of them without notification to or permission from the client, particularly if any of them are likely to contain anything potentially important or useful to the client. If the lawyer has lost touch with the client, or if a corporate client has dissolved, merged, or otherwise changed identities, contacting the client to determine what their wishes are with respect to the file may be difficult or impossible.

In each of these cases, the lawyer's ownership (if ownership it is) of the file, and the client's assertion of some right, creates a conflict. Although this may pose a problem for the lawyer, it makes an excellent starting point for consideration of the lawyer's ethical responsibilities regarding case files in particular, and records and information management in general.

That the client has some sort or ownership or possessory right in all or part of the file arising from a representation is not a new idea. Consider the last version of the old Virginia version of Disciplinary Rule DR 2-108 (D), in effect in one form or another from at least the early 1970s:

> Upon termination of representation, a lawyer shall take reasonable steps for the continued protection of a client's interests, including giving reasonable notice to the client, allowing time for employment of other counsel, delivering all papers and property to which the client is entitled. . . .

This rule is grounded in the proposition that the lawyer owes a continuing duty to the client not to harm the client's interests, and that delivering up the records and information associated with the representation is part of that duty. DR 2-108 (D) contemplates that the client may have need for at least parts of the file, and clearly implies that the client has a possessory interest in at least some parts of the file. Other rules also either imply or state a possessory interest by the client in at least some of the material related to the representation:

> A lawyer shall: . . . (4) Promptly pay or deliver to the client as requested by a client the funds, securities, or other properties in the possession of the lawyer which the client is entitled to receive. . . .[6]

The standard formulation for client ownership of matter-related material is found in Rule 1.16 (d) of the Model Rules of Professional Conduct:

> Upon termination of representation, a lawyer shall take steps to the extent reasonably practicable to protect a client's interests, such as giving reasonable notice to the client, allowing time for employment of other counsel, surrendering papers and property to which the client is entitled and refunding any advance payment of fee or expense that has not been earned or incurred. The lawyer may retain papers relating to the client to the extent permitted by other law.

Similar language is found in DR 2-110 of the Disciplinary Rules. In one form or another, this is the rule in most states: after termination of the representation, the lawyer must continue to take reasonable steps to protect the client's interests, and among those interests is an interest in the papers associated with the representation.

Of course, these rules fail to address exactly what it is that the client might own, or even what a paper is in today's world. Presumably, the client might own, or have a right to, only some of the material in the file, and the lawyer might thereby be entitled to withhold other material from the client, but the rule never quite specifies exactly who owns what.

In the course of issuing advisory opinions, ethics committees considering the matter have generally avoided enumerating a laundry list of materials owned by the client. They have instead focused on the issue of the lawyer's continuing duties to the client after the close of a representation. As is the case during active representation, a lawyer has an ongoing duty to avoid prejudice to the client's interests upon the termination of representation, including, as necessary, turning over the file or other material to the client.[7] As with rules, for years ethics opinions often did not specify exactly what material might be owned by the client and what by the lawyer, and often concluded whatever advice they offered with the predictable if unhelpful admonition for the lawyer to exercise "sound professional judgment."

Fortunately, states have begun to address this question in more detail in recent versions of the Rules of Professional Conduct. Virginia's rule is:

> All original, client-furnished documents and any originals of legal instruments or official documents which are in the lawyer's possession (wills, corporate minutes, etc.) are the property of the client and, therefore, upon termination of the representation, those items shall be returned within a reasonable time to the client or the client's new counsel upon request, whether or not the client has paid the fees and costs owed the lawyer. . . .[8]

California has adopted much more sweeping language:

> A member whose employment has terminated shall:
>
> > (1) Subject to any protective order or non-disclosure agreement, promptly release to the client, at the request of the client, all the client papers and property. "Client papers and property" includes correspondence, pleadings, deposition transcripts, exhibits, physi-

cal evidence, expert's reports, and other items reasonably necessary to the client's representation, whether the client has paid for them or not. . . .[9]

As has Louisiana:

Upon termination of representation, a lawyer shall take steps to the extent reasonably practicable to protect a client's interests, such as giving reasonable notice to the client, allowing time for employment of other counsel, surrendering papers and property to which the client is entitled and refunding any advance payment of fee or expense that has not been earned or incurred. Upon written request by the client, the lawyer shall promptly release to the client or the client's new lawyer the entire file relating to the matter. The lawyer may retain a copy of the file but shall not condition release over issues relating to the expense of copying the file or for any other reason. The responsibility for the cost of copying shall be determined in an appropriate proceeding.[10]

Massachusetts:

(e) A lawyer must make available to a former client, within a reasonable time following the client's request for his or her file, the following:

(1) all papers, documents, and other materials the client supplied to the lawyer. The lawyer may at his or her own expense retain copies of any such materials.

(2) all pleadings and other papers filed with or by the court or served by or upon any party. The client may be required to pay any copying charge consistent with the lawyer's actual cost for these materials, unless the client has already paid for such materials.

(3) all investigatory or discovery documents for which the client has paid the lawyer's out-of-pocket costs, including but not limited to medical records, photographs, tapes, disks, investigative reports, expert reports, depositions, and demonstrative evidence. The lawyer may at his or her own expense retain copies of any such materials.

(4) if the lawyer and the client have not entered into a contingent fee agreement, the client is entitled only to that portion of the lawyer's work product (as defined in subparagraph (6) below) for which the client has paid.

(5) if the lawyer and the client have entered into a contingent fee agreement, the lawyer must provide copies of the lawyer's work product (as defined in subparagraph (6) below). The client may be required to pay any copying charge consistent with the lawyer's actual cost for the copying of these materials.

(6) for purposes of this paragraph (e), work product shall consist of documents and tangible things prepared in the course of the representation of the client by the lawyer or at the lawyer's direction by

his or her employee, agent, or consultant, and not described in paragraphs (2) or (3) above. Examples of work product include without limitation legal research, records of witness interviews, reports of negotiations, and correspondence.

(7) notwithstanding anything in this paragraph (e) to the contrary, a lawyer may not refuse, on grounds of nonpayment, to make available materials in the client's file when retention would prejudice the client unfairly.[11]

Minnesota:

Client files, papers, and property, whether printed or electronically stored, shall include:

1. All papers and property provided by the client to the lawyer.

2. All pleadings, motions, discovery, memorandums, and other litigation materials which have been executed and served or filed regardless of whether the client has paid the lawyer for drafting and serving and/or filing the document(s).

3. All correspondence regardless of whether the client has paid the lawyer for drafting or sending the correspondence.

4. All items for which the lawyer has advanced costs and expenses regardless of whether the client has reimbursed the lawyer for the costs and expenses including depositions, expert opinions and statements, business records, witness statements, and other materials which may have evidentiary value.[12]

Nebraska:

[A] client is entitled to:

All documents provided to the attorney;

All documents or responses acquired by counsel through the discovery process;

All correspondence in pursuit of the client's interest;

All notes, memoranda, briefs, memos and other matters generated by counsel bearing on the client's business and resulting from the employment of counsel.[13]

and Tennessee:

Upon termination of the representation of a client, a lawyer shall take steps to the extent reasonably practicable to protect a client's interests, including:

* * * * *

(2) promptly surrendering papers and property of the client and any work product prepared by the lawyer for the client and for which the lawyer has been compensated;

(3) promptly surrendering any other work product prepared by the lawyer for the client, provided, however, that the lawyer may retain such work product to the extent permitted by other law but only if the retention of the work product will not have a materially adverse affect on the client with respect to the subject matter of the representation.[14]

* * * * *

So far, we have been describing the prevailing view on documents to which the client is entitled. The minority view distinguishes between *end products* of the representation, including such items as pleadings actually filed in an action; correspondence with a client, opposing counsel, and witnesses; and other papers used publicly or formally during a representation; and *work product* including internal legal memoranda and preliminary drafts of pleadings and legal instruments, and used by the lawyer during the course of the representation to develop the end product. Under this view, the end product must be provided to the client, but the work product need not be, unless the client can demonstrate a need for them in order to understand the end product documents, with the burden of justification on the client.

> Upon termination of representation, a lawyer shall take steps to the extent reasonably practicable to protect a client's interests, such as giving reasonable notice to the client, allowing time for employment of other counsel, surrendering papers and property to which the client is entitled and refunding any advance payment of fee or expense that has not been earned or incurred. A lawyer is entitled to retain and is not obliged to deliver to a client or former client papers or materials personal to the lawyer or created or intended for internal use by the lawyer except as required by the limitations on the retaining lien in Rule 1.8(i). Except for those client papers which a lawyer may properly retain under the preceding sentence, a lawyer shall deliver either the originals or copies of papers or materials requested or required by a client or former client and bear the copying costs involved.[15]

Other recent authorities take essentially the same tack for both the client's right of possession and the exceptions to it.[16] The clear trend in the U.S. is toward a very expansive right of possession given to the client or ex-client.

Recent case decisions have ratified the majority position and expanded in considerable detail not only upon what is owed the client, but upon the rationale as well: In *Sage Realty Corp. v. Proskauer Rose*,[17] the New York Court of Appeals examined the then-current state of law in this area, attempting to determine, not only the boundary of the client's ownership or possessory interests in records and information associated with a representation, but also the current doctrines and rationales in use. After a falling out between them, Sage Realty, an ex-client of the Proskauer Rose law firm, sought to obtain a wide variety of information related to its representation. Proskauer Rose turned over a great deal of the requested material, but refused to turn over some material, including internal legal memoranda, drafts of instruments, mark-ups, notes on contracts and transactions, and ownership structure charts.

In requiring Proskauer Rose to turn over the additional material, the court concluded that the majority view, which it adopted, requires that virtually *all* material related to an ongoing matter must be surrendered to the client in order to avoid the potential of prejudice to them, unless the attorney can "demonstrate that a particular document would furnish no useful purpose in serving the client's present needs for legal advice":[18]

> [A] former client is to be accorded access to inspect and copy any documents possessed by the lawyer relating to the representation unless substantial grounds exist to refuse.[19]

and

> We can discern no principled basis upon which exclusive property rights to an attorney's work product in a client's file spring into being in favor of the attorney at the conclusion of a represented matter.[20]

The court also observed that:

> [T]he minority position adopted by the courts below [requiring the client to specify the precise material needed from the lawyer] unrealistically and, in our view, unfairly places the burden on the client to demonstrate a need for specific work product documents in the attorney's file on the represented matter. Again, this case is illustrative that in a complex transaction where the file may be voluminous (commensurably increasing the likely usefulness of work product materials to advise the client concerning ongoing rights and obligations), the client's need for access to a particular paper cannot be demonstrated except in the most general terms, in the absence of prior disclosure of the content of the very document to which access is sought.[21] (bracketed text not in original)

A similar view of both the duty and the exceptions was taken by the court in *Swift, Currie, McGhee & Hiers v. Henry*,[22] which concluded that:

> An attorney's fiduciary relationship with a client depends, in large measure, upon full, candid disclosure. That relationship would be impaired if attorneys withheld any and all documents from their clients without good cause, especially where the documents were created at the client's behest.[23]

In disapproving a theory that material created during a representation was the property of the attorney and so immune from client access, the *Swift* court observed that:

> [T]he work product doctrine does not apply to the situation in which a client seeks access to documents or other tangible things created or amassed by his attorney during the course of the representation.[24]

The *Sage* court did, however, carve out exceptions to their requirement of general surrender of records and information to the client:

> [The lawyer] should not be required to disclose documents which might violate a duty of nondisclosure owed to a third party, or otherwise imposed by law. Additionally, nonaccess would be permissible as to firm documents intended for internal law office review and use. . . . This might include, for example, documents containing a firm attorney's general or other assessment of the client, or tentative preliminary impressions of the legal or factual issues presented in the representation, recorded primarily for the purpose of giving internal direction to facilitate performance of the legal services entailed in that representation.[25]

A similar exception was carved out by Arizona in an advisory opinion:

> [The attorney's obligation to turn over documents to his client] does not, however, extend to such things as the attorney's own notes and memos to himself; nor to his myriad scratching on note sheets; nor to records of passing thoughts dictated to a machine or a secretary and placed in the file; nor to ideas, plans or outlines as to the course the attorney's representation is to take. Those recorded thoughts remain the property of the attorney and, in our opinion, he need not release those even though his bill has been paid in full.[26]

In considering the above landscape, the lawyer should consider also its applicability to electronic records and data. Analytically, there is no meaningful difference between say, a formal written letter to a client and an e-mail to them.[27] Therefore, *any* data object created during the course of the representation may be viewed by a court or other authority as presumptively belonging to the client, thus requiring an affirmative demonstration by the lawyer that it does not in order to withhold it.

For the lawyer, this trend, and its extension to electronic data objects, poses a substantial records and information management issue. Aside from the pure question of ownership, DR 2-108 and the many authorities that have followed it imply sound management of records and information associated with a representation: part and parcel of the duty of delivering records to the client is the obligation to maintain the records and information in a manner that will facilitate their delivery to the client. If the records are poorly maintained or lost, the lawyer may well be unable to comply with the client's reasonable demand to deliver them, thereby subjecting the lawyer to potential disciplinary action.

For the basic hard-copy matter file in a centralized operation, this may pose no issues beyond cost and annoyance: generally, the matter file, even if not particularly well-organized, is at least all in one place and labeled as a single file. For other data objects, and, in particular electronic data objects associated with a representation, the situation is likely to be considerably more challenging. Most computer users create and maintain their electronic data in a manner inconsistent with sound records and data management principles. Structured electronic file systems and directories are the exception rather than the norm, and formal taxonomies and naming conventions for electronic files are generally nonexistent.

The problem is exacerbated in larger organizations, where every individual has his or her own (and frequently bad) system for naming and saving files, often in reality no system at all. Law firms pose particular challenges, since most firms have a culture of independence, with little or no central control over the way a lawyer handles her electronic records. Even if the firm has purchased and implemented tools such as document management software, they are of little help if indices, taxonomies, and other data management structures have not been implemented and enforced. In such circumstances, responding to a client's demand for all data objects relating to a representation poses a formidable and expensive challenge.

In cases where a firm uses e-mail to transact significant matter-related business, these challenges multiply. Most e-mail systems are badly disorganized, and may be subject to policies that create the possibility of conflicts with ethical requirements. E-mail policies that call for the deletion of all e-mail after 30 or 60 days are an example of this: if, as is usually the case these days, e-mail is being used extensively to conduct client- and matter-related business, such a policy may result in deletion of significant amounts of relevant material including client communications that are not being maintained elsewhere, or that might require inconvenient and costly restoration from sources such as backup tapes. Managing data objects such as voice mail or instant messaging logs, which are notoriously disorganized, or data from unified messaging data systems[28] may prove even more burdensome if the installation parameters and ongoing management of the system is not carefully thought out and implemented.

So, from an ethical standpoint, client- and matter-related data, regardless of source, repository, or medium should be considered as a unified whole, and indexed and managed as such. That management should include such attributes and use such tools as will permit its retrieval in its entirety at reasonable cost and effort.

What About Liens?

The question of matter file ownership may be clouded by the matter of liens. In the case of a fee dispute or unpaid fees, the lawyer can, at least in theory, place a lien on the file and refuse to turn a copy of it over to the client.

There are two species of lien that a lawyer may assert against a matter file to assure payment of fees: the charging lien, a lien against the proceeds of a judgment or settlement, and the retaining lien, a lien on the matter file. Of the two, the retaining lien concerns us most in this discussion.

Although some states still permit the assertion of a retaining lien against a file, the practice is generally out of favor.[29] Even states allowing liens often strongly discourage their use, for example Texas,[30] Montana,[31] and South Carolina.[32] Some jurisdictions that were formerly receptive to liens have reassessed their position and switched sides on the question.[33] In some jurisdictions, the practice is flatly banned by either rule or ethics opinion.

> [A lawyer shall] promptly release to the client, at the request of the client, all the client papers and property . . . whether the client has paid for them or not . . . .[34]

> A lawyer shall not condition the return of client papers and property on payment of the lawyer's fee or the cost of copying the files or papers.[35]

Jurisdictions that do permit imposition of liens may place severe restrictions upon the right of a lawyer to assert a lien on a file. Thus:

> An attorney's right to assert a lien may be limited, however, by the ethical obligation to avoid foreseeable prejudice to the client's interests.[36]

> [A] lawyer may not refuse, on grounds of nonpayment, to make available materials in the client's file when retention would prejudice the client unfairly.[37]

> A lawyer may withhold documents *not constituting client files, papers and property* until the outstanding fee is paid unless the client's interests will be substantially prejudiced without the documents. [italics added][38]

> [A lawyer may withhold records and documents] only if the retention of the work product will not have a materially adverse affect on the client with respect to the subject matter of the representation.[39]

> The lawyer may retain papers relating to the client to the extent permitted by other law only if such retention will not prejudice the client in the subject matter of the representation.[40]

West Virginia requires giving the client:

> . . . all material provided by the client; all correspondence; all pleadings, motions, other material filed and discovery, including depositions; all documents which have evidentiary value and are discoverable under the Rules of Civil Procedure, such as depositions and business records.[41]

. . . regardless of outstanding fees, but permits a lien against "work product as defined by the civil discovery rules," thus appearing to limit severely the scope of any lien that might be permitted to those items least likely to be actually needed by the client. Other states disapproving of liens include Mississippi, South Carolina, and South Dakota.[42]

Among the states, Florida is unusually protective of an attorney's right to the client file. Past Florida decisions have concluded that the file is the property of the attorney.[43] Recent cases have continued to uphold the right of an attorney to assert a lien. Thus, in *Foreman v. Behr*,[44] the court of appeals upheld a retaining lien for payment of fees on a client file, even though the former client had instituted a malpractice claim against the attorney. In summarizing Florida law, the court stated that:

> Only in rare cases will the files be released without payment or the furnishing of adequate security, such as when the lawyer's misconduct caused his withdrawal or when the client has an urgent need for the file to defend a criminal prosecution and lacks the means to pay the fee or post a bond. . . . Courts have also found an exception where the attorney has filed a counterclaim or an independent action seeking to collect the fee.

In summary, a lawyer should in most instances be prepared to deliver the matter file to the client upon demand. Although some states limit the scope of material that the lawyer must turn over, and some permit the use of liens to ensure payment of outstanding fees, the lawyer contemplating either course of action should weigh them carefully before declining to turn over any significant material. The national trend is toward requiring more complete production to the client, and toward discouraging the use of liens to ensure payment. This, combined with studies that indicate that two-thirds of all malpractice actions arise as fee disputes,[45] may make it inadvisable to pursue such a course, even if it is permissible in the jurisdiction in question.

Disposition of Closed Matter Files and Other Client-Related Records

At some point, most lawyers and law firms discover that either they are running out of space to store closed matter files, or they are paying excessive amounts of money to maintain them, whether in active office space or in off-site storage at a commercial storage facility. The questions then arise, "Can we dispose of these old files? If so, how?" The short answer is "Yes, provided you follow certain safeguards." Again, we turn to certain ethics opinions for guidance.

Traditionally, the justification given for a law firm records retention program was cost savings. Perpetual storage of old files eventually leads to overcrowding and massive storage bills, which the records retention program seeks to mitigate. Thus, early authority on the subject recognizes both the cost issue and the need to respond to it. ABA Informal Opinion 1384 (1977), an oft-quoted authority on the topic, observes that:

> All lawyers are aware of the continuing economic burden of storing
> retired and inactive files. How to deal with the burden is primarily a ques-
> tion of business management, and not primarily a question of ethics or
> professional responsibility.

Even at this early juncture, however, the potential for ethical issues was
clearly recognized. Thus, ABA 1384 also observes:

> [C]lients (and former clients) reasonably expect from their lawyers that
> valuable and useful information in the lawyers' files, and not otherwise
> readily available to the clients, will not be prematurely and carelessly
> destroyed, to the clients' detriment.

Both statements form the basis for most subsequent discussion of the
topic, and ABA 1384 is cited as prior authority in ethics opinions from many
jurisdictions.[46] There is no rule of law in any U.S. jurisdiction requiring
indefinite retention of files from closed matters. Those jurisdictions that
have addressed the matter are universally of the opinion that closed client
files may be destroyed after a reasonable period of retention. See, e.g.,
American Bar Association Informal Opinion 1384;[47] Virginia LEO 1690.[48]

More recently, attention has shifted to the ethics and risk management
aspect of file disposition. Many documents in a client file, including such
things as records obtained from the client and from third parties, are not
privileged. Thus, their retention in the matter file past the period during
which they are retained by the client may put the client, and thereby the
lawyer, at risk.

In subsequent chapters, we will discuss the specifics of developing a
retention schedule. For now, bear in mind the general principles and rules
that govern the disposition of matter-related records. Ethics authorities and
courts universally state that the client's interests must be protected when
contemplating any action regarding the client file or related records. This
forms the basis for the various procedural safeguards that have been suggested or mandated by authorities commenting on the topic. The most general rule to bear in mind is stated in California Ethics Opinion 2001-157:

> The basic principle is that the attorney may destroy a particular item
> from a former client's file if he or she has no reason to believe that the
> item will be reasonably necessary to the client's representation, i.e., that
> the item is or will be reasonably necessary to the former client to estab-
> lish a right or a defense to a claim.

Beyond that, a series of specific requirements can be distilled. They may be
summarized as follows:

- ◆ Original client-owned documents should be returned to the client
  promptly at the end of representation;

- The remainder of the file may be given to the client at this time, or in the alternative, may be retained by the lawyer for a reasonable period of time;
- At some time prior to destruction, the file must be reviewed to ensure that any documents that could be needed by the client in the future are provided to them;
- While the file is in the possession of the lawyer, it should be reviewed to determine if it contains work product of ongoing value to the lawyer and, if so, it should be copied into another repository and indexed in a way that makes it retrievable;
- Prior to destruction of the file, the client should be contacted, preferably in writing, and given the opportunity to take possession of the file or give the lawyer further directions with respect to it;
- If the client cannot be contacted after more than one attempt, or if the client says it has no further interest in the file, the file may then be destroyed;
- Destruction must be carried out in a fashion that protects the client's and the lawyer's interests; and
- If any documents are subject to independent legal requirements, these must be retained for the term set forth in that requirement.[49]

With respect to retention periods for closed matter files, suffice it to say at this point that the periods suggested by ethics authorities are quite reasonable.[50] The longest period opined is 10 years.[51]

Matter files are not the only client-related records subject to ethical requirements. Every state has a statutory or rule-based retention period for client trust fund accounting records. This is usually, but not always, six years, and ranges from five to seven years. Other documents may also be subject to specific requirements. Retainer and compensation agreements, as well as a variety of other compensation or client-fund related correspondence, which may or may not be maintained in the client file are, for example, subject to a mandatory retention period of seven years by New York Disciplinary Rule 9-102. Other states have document-specific requirements as well.

Other Laws and Other Records

Beyond the ethics requirements of the legal profession, a law firm is subject to a variety of other requirements. As a business, it is subject to tax laws; as an employer, it is subject to employment laws, including a wide variety of payroll-related and benefits laws. Managing records in compliance with these laws implies many of the things also implied by ethics compliance—

they must be managed in such a way and for such a period of time as to satisfy any substantive requirements, and to permit those parties with authority to view them—auditors, labor inspectors, and others—to do so with a minimum of difficulty and delay. As with matter-related records, the solution requires a combination of process and procedure, and judicious use of technology. The lawyer thus need not fight two battles—a sound solution in either area, matter-related or business-related, will have applicability for the other.

Conclusion

If nothing else, this chapter should have demonstrated that the management of client-related records is a cradle-to-grave proposition. The very first document created during a representation, the retainer agreement, may be subject to an explicit retention requirement, and the very last act involving an old file, throwing it out, is subject to a hodgepodge of requirements. In between, an array of rules, opinions, and considerations govern the records and the lawyer's responsibilities at every stage of the game. Fortunately, meeting this array of responsibilities is manageable. Implementation of sound records and information management principles, combined with standard conceptual tools such as indices, workflow design, and proper implementation and use of technology aids, can turn what may appear to be a quagmire of frustration and competing requirements into a well-run and ethically compliant records system. There are, of course, many details to be worked out. It should, however, be apparent that the governing principles are simple, and in basic harmony with the lawyer's duties to client, court, and society. And as we will see, many of those details do not pose unmanageable obstacles if approached with knowledge, logic, and a basic understanding of records management.

Notes

1. Michigan Ethics Opinion R-5 (1989).
2. DR 2-110 (A)(2), New York.
3. *See, e.g.,* New York Ethics Opinion 641 (lawyers must comply with paper recycling laws, but must use shredders or other destructive disposal techniques to maintain client confidentiality); North Carolina Ethics Opinion RPC 133; Vermont Ethics Opinion 97-8.
4. *See., e.g.,* New York City Bar Assn. Ethic Opinion 1998-2, concluding that law firms need not encrypt all e-mail, but should advise clients that e-mail may not be a secure as other forms of communication.

5. *See* New York Ethics Opinion 782.

6. DR 9-102(B) (4), Ohio.

7. *See, e.g.,* Arizona Bar Association Ethics Opinion 98-07 (1998); California Formal Opinion 2001-157 (2001); Florida Bar Association Opinion 81-8 (1981); New York Bar Association Opinion 460 (1977); Virginia Bar Association LEO 1690 (1997); Pennsylvania Ethics Opinion 90-25.

8. Rule 1.16 (e), Virginia Rules of Professional Conduct.

9. Rule 3-700 (D), California Rules of Professional Conduct.

10. Rule 1.16 (d), Louisiana Rules of Professional Conduct.

11. Rule 1.16 (e), Massachusetts Rules of Professional Conduct.

12. Minnesota Ethics Opinion 13 (1989).

13. Nebraska Advisory Opinion 2001.3 (2001).

14. Rule 1.16 (d), Tennessee Rules of Professional Conduct.

15. Rule 1.16 (d), Montana Rules of Professional Conduct. *See also* Arizona Ethics Opinion 92-01; Illinois Bar Ethics Opinion 94-13; North Carolina RPC 178 (1994); Rhode Island Ethics Opinion 92-88 (1993).

16. *See, e.g.,* Alaska Ethics Opinion 2004-1, *supra,* Montana Ethics Opinion 950221; South Dakota Ethics Opinion 96-7.

17. Sage Realty Corp. v. Proskauer Rose LLP, 689 N.E.2d 879 (1997).

18. *Id.,* 91 N.Y.2d 30 at 37.

19. *Id.,* 91 N.Y.2d 30 at 35, *quoting* Restatement [Third] of the Law Governing Lawyers § 58.

20. *Id.,* 91 N.Y.2d 30 at 36.

21. *Id.*

22. Swift, Currie, McGhee & Hiers v. Henry, 276 Ga. 571 (2003).

23. *Id.,* 276 Ga. 571 at 573.

24. *Id.*

25. Sage Realty Corp. v. Proskauer Rose LLP, 91 N.Y.2d 30 at 37.

26. Arizona Ethics Opinion 82-30.

27. *See, e.g.,* Armstrong v. Executive Office of the President, 1 F.3d 1274 (D.C. Cir. 1993).

28. Systems that capture voice mail, e-mail, and sometimes instant messaging in a single electronic data system.

29. *See, e.g.,* Florida Ethics Opinion 88-11; Utah Ethics Opinion 91 (1989); Maryland Ethics Opinion 85-40; Montana Ethics Opinion 860115; Oklahoma Ethics Opinion 295 (1979).

30. Texas Ethics Opinion 411 (1984), *"[A]n attorney refusing to relinquish possession of a client's file on the basis of a common-law retaining lien does so at personal risk."*

31. Montana Ethics Opinion 880218, "[I]t is prudent to refrain from this course of action. . . . Retention of client files when they have been requested is seldom justified."

32. South Carolina Ethics Opinion *93-30.*

33. *See e.g.,* District of Columbia Ethics Opinion 250, "It seems clear to us that retaining liens on client files are now strongly disfavored in the District of Columbia, that the work product exception permitting such liens should be construed narrowly, and that a lawyer should assert a retaining lien on work product relating to a former client only where the exception is clearly applicable and where the lawyer's financial interests 'clearly outweigh the adversely affected interests of his former client.'"

34. California Rule 3-700 (D).

35. Minnesota Rule 1.16 (g). See also, Louisiana Rule 1.16 (d), Virginia Rule 1.16 (e).

36. Florida Ethics Opinion 88-11 (Reconsideration 1993).

37. Rule 1.16 (e) (7), Massachusetts Rules of Professional Conduct.

38. Minnesota Ethics Opinion 13 (1989).

39. Rule 1.16 (d) (3), Tennessee Rules of Professional Conduct.

40. Rule 1.15 (d), Texas Rules of Professional Conduct.

41. West Virginia Ethics Opinion 92-02.

42. *See* Mississippi Ethics Opinion 144 (1988); South Carolina Ethics Opinion 02-11; South Dakota Ethics Opinion 95-16, all disapproving of attorney liens.

43. *See, e.g.,* Dowda and Fields, P.A. v. Cobb, 452 So.2d 1140 (Fla. App. 1984).

44. Foreman v. Behr, 866 So. 2d 705 (Fla. App. 2003).

45. *See* Jill Schachner Chanen, *Fending Off Fee Disputes,* ABA JOURNAL, May 2004, 44.

46. *See, e.g.,* Mississippi Ethics Opinion 98 (1984); New Hampshire Ethics Committee Advisory Opinion 1986-87/3(1986); South Carolina Ethics Opinion 86-23 (1986).

47. "[A] lawyer does not have a general duty to preserve all his files permanently."

48. "A lawyer is not a permanent storage facility for clients' closed or retired files, of course." *See also* Alaska Ethics Opinion 95-6 (1995); Maine Ethics Opinion 74 (1986); Michigan Ethics Opinion R-5 (1989); Nebraska Ethics Opinion 88-3 (1988); New York Ethics Opinion 623; Nevada Formal Opinion 28 (2002); New Hampshire Ethics Committee Advisory Opinion 1986-87/3 (1986).

49. *See,* Arizona Ethics Opinion 98-07 (1998); California Formal Opinion 2001-157 (2001); Florida Bar Staff Opinion TEO 82507 (1982); Michigan Ethics Opinion R-5 (1989); Nebraska Ethics Opinion 88-3 (1988); New York Ethics Opinion 623 (1991); Nevada Formal Opinion 28 (2992); New Hampshire Ethics Opinion 1986-87-3 (1986); South Carolina Ethics Opinion 86-23 (1986); Utah Ethics Opinion 96-2 (1996).

50. *See e.g.,* Arizona Ethics Opinion 91-01, five years; South Carolina Ethics Opinion 92-19, six years; Michigan Ethics Opinion R-12 (1991), five years; Iowa Ethics Opinion 91-20, five years; Illinois Ethics Opinion 94-19, five years; Florida Bar Staff Opinion TEO 82507 (1982), six years.

51. *See* West Virginia L.E.I. 2002-1 (2002).

Records Retention Schedules

4

Introduction

The purpose of the records retention portion of a records management program is to assure the maintenance of those records that the lawyer must keep to meet either operational or regulatory requirements, while ensuring the timely and efficient disposal of those records the lawyer, firm, or office does not need or should not maintain. As we have already pointed out, lawyers and law offices are subject to a variety of ethics-based, risk-based, and productivity and cost-based reasons for having a retention schedule. A records retention program outlines the life cycle of records, and provides for the orderly disposition of those records once a firm no longer needs them to meet either operating or legal requirements.

Definitions

- *Active* means the record or the file is still being used on a regular basis.
- *Inactive* refers to records that are only being referred to once in a great while.
- *Open* in law firms generally refers to a client file the lawyer is working on.
- *Closed* generally refers to that point in the maintenance of a client file when no more work is being done and sometimes when all pending opportunities for continuing work have come and gone. Every law office should have a specific definition of closed as the term refers to client files.

- *Retention* refers to that specific time period a record is maintained when in the active (on-site) and inactive (stored) parts of its life cycle, until final disposition.
- *On-site* means in the office. Look around your office and you see that on-site does not necessarily mean *open* or *active*.
- *Off-site* means in storage of some sort. It can mean lots of different places, such as in the basement, in mezzanine storage, in a u-store-it facility, in a professionally run commercial records storage operation, in a not-so-professionally run commercial records storage operation, or in a warehouse that is administered by your firm or office.
- *Disposition* is the final action taken regarding a particular record. While disposition often means destruction, it may also mean return to client, transfer to other parties (another law firm, library, etc.), or retention for the life of the organization. (Notice we did not say permanent.) Each law office must decide for each type of record which method of disposition best meets its requirements.

Basically, records management is pretty simple: The program documentation consists of three core items, none of which is very complex:

1. A formal policy statement;
2. A records retention schedule, which documents the time frames for maintenance of all the records in the firm; and
3. Procedures for executing and enforcing the policies and guidelines.

These documents themselves are not conceptually complex either. A policy statement deals with issues of ownership of the records, staff and employee duties in context of the records program, guidance over authorized copies and maintenance locales, and responsibility for program maintenance. A records retention schedule is, fundamentally, only a list of record types or categories, along with retention periods for those records. Similarly, the procedures are simply instructions for managing the retention and disposition processes. Write a legally compliant policy, choose an appropriate retention period, write some commonsense procedures, and you are in business.

As always, however, the devil is in the details: the considerations that go into developing retention periods may be complex, and in some cases the answers are not obvious. Political and cultural considerations in the firm may require negotiation of time periods and adjustments to policies and procedures, and actually implementing the schedule against large collections of paper and electronic documents may prove challenging. And, all of this must occur within the context of client service and ethics compliance, which are central to the practice of law.

The Need for a Records Retention Schedule

Traditionally, the justification given for a law firm records retention program was cost savings. Perpetual storage of old files eventually leads to overcrowding and massive storage bills, which the records retention program seeks to mitigate. Thus, early authority on the subject recognizes both the cost issue and the need to respond to it. *ABA Informal Opinion 1384* (1977), an oft-quoted authority on the topic, observes that:

> All lawyers are aware of the continuing economic burden of storing retired and inactive files. How to deal with the burden is primarily a question of business management, and not primarily a question of ethics or professional responsibility.

Even at this early juncture, however, the potential for ethical issues was clearly recognized. Thus, ABA 1384 also observes:

> [C]lients (and former clients) reasonably expect from their lawyers that valuable and useful information in the lawyers' files, and not otherwise readily available to the clients, will not be prematurely and carelessly destroyed, to the clients' detriment.

Both statements form the basis for most subsequent discussion of the topic, and ABA 1384 is cited as prior authority in ethics opinions from many jurisdictions.[1] Subsequent authorities have, however, examined the topic in considerably more detail than ABA 1384. In the course of that subsequent discussion, the short and rather general pronouncements of ABA 1384 have been expanded upon in considerable detail, and the concepts behind the general ethics pronouncements of it have been expanded upon. In particular, ethics authorities have begun to recognize that other ethics issues are also present:

> Disclosure of a confidence or secret because of a nonexistent, inadequate, or unobserved retention policy would be a violation of [The Code of Professional Responsibility].[2]

In view of this and other considerations, the same authority states that:

> A law firm, including a solo practice, is obligated to have a record retention policy or plan in order to meet ethical obligations. . . . [E]ach firm is obligated to establish and administer a record retention policy or plan, to educate all lawyers and nonlawyers in the firm as to its operation, and to monitor compliance.

In the view of this ethics committee, the only way that the firm can ensure that all duties to the client regarding the matter file are fulfilled is the establishment of a formal records management program. Most authorities have not gone so far as to require a formal program. Further, many ethics authorities have articulated views that are consistent with having a formal program and have contributed to processes that are part of that formal program. Thus, such tasks as notification to clients prior to destroying a file, offering the file to the client, consultation of applicable substantive law in developing a retention schedule, and review of the file for client-owned documents have been mandated by ethics authorities.[3]

The Myth of Permanence

A common myth that gets in the way of developing and implementing a records retention program is that of the "permanent record." In its usual form, this myth takes the form of an objection that the proposed retention period for some record set is grossly inadequate because the records have (1) permanent enduring value, and/or (2) some law requires them to be kept forever.

Permanent is a long time, and although many people, lawyers and non-lawyers alike, would like to think that their records have permanent value, this is almost never the case. In the case of general business records, the vast majority of legally mandated retention periods are well under 10 years, as are the limitations periods for the theories under which legal action involving them might be pursued. The few exceptions tend to involve narrowly defined record sets dealing with very specific situations such as toxic substance spills and the like. Nor is business need likely to require permanent retention since the actual business utility of most records diminishes rapidly after their creation and initial usage, and commonly drops to near zero within a few years.

In the case of law firm matter files, for almost all types of matters, a specific closing date can be defined: the case or deal is closed, the appeals period runs, the statutes of limitation and repose all expire and so on, and at some point, the matter is beyond recourse by any party. As with general business records, there are exceptions: Such things as matters involving minor children or trusts and estates matters may remain open for many years, pending some specific trigger event required to close the matter, even if inactive. Even in these cases, however, there is an end of things: the minor reaches majority, and sooner or later, the life now in being plus 21 years (a theoretical maximum of 140 years) has elapsed. Only in a very small minority of situations involving such things as perpetual trusts will a matter of real permanence exist, and even in these cases, if the representation goes to another firm, an end date for the originating firm can be calculated.

For most people and most matters then, the reality is that, though the matter may be of supreme importance while active, at some point it is resolved, and once resolved, the related records are no longer useful. People think differently for one of two reasons. First, people usually view their own work, and the records it generates as important, and they equate importance with extended retention of those records. Second, most people simply do not know what an appropriate retention period might be and are concerned about the consequences and penalties of disposing of records prematurely. These two factors coalesce into an attitude that keeping records for a very long or "permanent" period constitutes a sufficient solution (read this as *the safest thing to do*) on the issue of retention. Over time, this default attitude and subsequent inaction have coalesced into a belief in the mythical law or rule that requires permanent retention.

The Cost of Permanence

As noted elsewhere in this book, and for a variety of reasons, permanent retention can create problems. Permanence is not free, or even cheap, and it is certainly not easy or free of ongoing housekeeping burdens. When a collection of retired files reaches the point that it fills hundreds or thousands of boxes in a storage facility, the total dollar cost of maintaining those boxes is substantial, it continues to grow and is, by its very definition, never ending. For a smaller firm, the total box count may not be as large, but the proportionate cost is. Further, to the extent that anything in the files—briefs, memoranda, or the like—actually *is* of value, keeping everything on the off chance that something someday may be of some use is an expensive proposition. And wading through a vast collection of old files to find it is a poor use of staff time. If something has work product value, it should be maintained where it is identifiable and accessible and in a format that does not create risk for the client—not in some huge unstructured physical or virtual pile.

The Risk of Permanence

Remember, both client and firm will likely be at risk when files are kept too long. If the client has a retention schedule, client staff may be busily disposing of their own copies of these records, and making decisions or offering answers to other parties based upon their own schedule. Neither client nor counsel are well-served if the law firm is defeating the client's actions by retaining copies of the client's records after the client has destroyed them.

Any claim that some record set requires very long or permanent retention should be viewed with caution. Analysis of risk, utility, and other matters will usually reveal that such retention is unwarranted. When it is, it will typically be confined to a narrow subset of the records in question. The questioning may initially require a *reductio ad absurdum* approach: "Who will care about these records, and why, in a thousand years?" However, once the basic proposition has been established, it is generally much easier for all parties to agree no one is likely to care much about most records in twenty-five or even ten years.

Historical Records

It is wise to beware also of the argument that many records have "historical" value, and should be kept permanently. This may well be true for a very few items, but the reality is that most transactions and matters, and the records generated by them, are routine, and from a historical perspective, not particularly interesting, regardless of what their creator may think. If preservation of records for historical purposes is contemplated, a professional archivist or historian should be consulted to separate the wheat from the chaff.

What Does a Records Retention Program Do?

It Controls Costs

Fundamentally, the records retention portion of a records management program simply formalizes movement through the "records life cycle," from active to inactive status and from the office to storage to ultimate disposition. In so doing, the schedule reduces the total volume of both hard-copy and electronic records, and places them in the most economical maintenance environment situation based upon the firm's anticipated need.

It Tells You About Your Information

Good schedules also record other points of value, such as the person or department designated as responsible for reviewing a file, for sending records to inactive storage, and for authorizing their ultimate disposition. In the course of so doing, the schedule and its supporting procedures documents the following important items:

1. The length of time during which records generally have practical, legal, or economic value;
2. How to know when a record should be transferred from active to inactive or closed status;
3. When a hard-copy file should be transferred off-site to either firm-managed or commercial storage;
4. Which legal, ethical, and operational retention requirements affect the organization's records;
5. How the process of notifying clients that the records are due for disposition is to be handled;
6. How records should be destroyed once destruction is approved;
7. How records are to be transferred to another entity if such a transfer is approved;
8. How the schedules are to be updated;

9. How to conduct compliance audits.
10. Provisions for identifying and managing exceptions to retention periods;
11. The application of the retention program to all forms of records: originals and duplicates, paper, microform, and electronically stored records; and
12. Under which circumstances specific records might be considered of historical value.

Vital Records

One of the things that a records retention schedule does not do well is deal with vital records. By definition, a records retention schedule deals with series or categories. And, again by definition, vital records protection deals with specific documents. To indicate that a given category in the schedule may contain some vital records has minimal value at best. That they exist says nothing about where they are, who is responsible for them, how they are to be treated, where they are to be maintained, the frequency with which they are to be updated, who is responsible for the updating, the type of updating, or the medium in which they exist. Such things are appropriately the topic of a different set of guidelines and procedures.

It Documents Applicable Laws and Ethics Influences

A firm's records retention program must be legally adequate in order to protect the organization in the event of claims, litigation, audits, investigation, and client disputes. This requires compliance with a wide variety of statutes and administrative regulations, as well as ethics rules and decisional doctrine, and a rule of reasonableness. These authorities quite often address retention periods specifically, but also address other matters of considerable importance, such as clients' rights and client notification, acceptable methods of disposition, and other matters.

For purposes of records retention, the United States is divided into more than 50 federal, state, and territorial jurisdictions. The laws within and across all of these jurisdictions may or may not be uniform or compatible, but all must be considered in those jurisdictions applicable to the firm. An unfortunate side effect of this lack of uniformity and compatibility is that the creator of the schedule must take into account that several authorities may rule on the retention of a single record type and come up with different retention periods. Thus, a payroll record may, within a single state, be subject to multiple retention requirements from federal and state (and occasionally even county or municipal) wage and hour agencies, workers' compensation agencies, unemployment compensation agencies, retirement and benefits agencies, and so on. In the case of a matter file, there may be statutes, court rules, ethics opinions, and even administrative regulations that bear on its retention and disposition.

Policy, procedures, and schedule must be vetted to ensure that all of these relevant authorities are considered. This may require a substantial investment in legal research and analysis.

The Concept of Grouping

At a law firm, as with any other organization, there may be several hundred to well over a thousand individual file categories or record series. And it is not at all unusual for a mid- to large-sized firm to have several million individual records. Listing each record as it is created and assigning a retention period to it at that point just does not work. This takes us to the issue of grouping, the creation of records series. Accounts payable, for example, will have vouchers, receipts, expense reports, vendor packets, invoices, and so on, to the tune of a dozen or more individual types of documents that are created or collected during the process of recording and processing accounts payable. And, while we do not recommend it, it is possible to construct a retention schedule by simply listing all of the record types in each department and then attaching a retention period to each. This is often the first approach someone tasked with creating a retention schedule takes.

While the process of listing document types or categories for a department sounds good at first, it proves cumbersome over time, and problems arise from its use. First, the schedule is excessively long: if the number of individual record categories gets to be more than a few hundred, a schedule that is just a list rapidly becomes unusable. In practice, retention schedules constructed in this manner have been known to reach hundreds of pages in length, rendering them completely useless. Second, since actual record descriptions or titles (for the same items) may vary by department or location, the result is that the same types of records are called different things depending upon where they are held and who is referring to them. The truth is that the same records are seldom identified in the same way across the organization, and users tend to define them differently depending on their particular perspective on their use and value. Certainly, records are seldom identified in a way that makes it easy to relate them to laws or other authorities. This leads to confusion, and confusion leads to inconsistent application, one of the biggest single problems with poorly constructed schedules. Third, even within a department or business function, similar records may have very dissimilar titles among individual users, causing them to once again refer to the same records by different names. Each of these results in multiple categories for the same records sprinkled throughout the schedule.

A look at the nature of the laws and doctrines surrounding records retention, and at the records themselves and the purposes of records retention, reveals a way around these issues:

- ◆ Laws and legal doctrine governing records retention do not generally specify particular records; rather, they specify fairly general classes of information such as the generic Internal Revenue Service requirement to maintain all records needed to substantiate a position taken on a tax return for so long as they are relevant for enforcement of the tax laws.
- ◆ From a business perspective, recreating or analyzing a particular circumstance or transaction often requires reference to several or many related records.

With these things in mind, it is clear that retention requirements for both legal and business purposes should be based upon a need to retain *categories* of information, rather than particular information objects such as "form 1234." So, for purposes of records retention, a large number of records in, say, the accounts payable category can be grouped under a single heading "accounts payable documentation" or the like, and a single retention period attached to this category. This category is called a "record series" and is a fundamental part of an effective records retention schedule. Most records within any organization, including a law firm, are susceptible to this concept of grouping into record series. Use of record series as a basis for retention rather than individual record titles will dramatically simplify use of the retention schedule, first by shortening it, and second, by ensuring that records of like function are treated in like fashion. The truth is that the easier a schedule is to interpret, the more likely people are to actually use it.

Laws and other authority can be grouped in like manner. If the firm does business in ten states, there will be ten states' worth of payroll laws, tax audit limitations periods, and so on. Since retention periods will in most cases be made upon the collective requirements of this set of laws, it makes more sense to group it for analysis up front, rather than dealing with the inevitable de facto grouping that will arise anyway, should a one-to-one match-up of authority and records be attempted.

It is useful to remember that records management deals with categories or series, document management deals with individual documents, and while the two need to be integrated, they are not the same thing.

In general then, the records retention program and schedule should attempt to deal with categories of things rather than individual items. How broad or narrow the categories will be depends upon a variety of factors, which we will discuss in more detail later. Well-defined categories make the process of developing a records retention schedule much easier.

Documentation

The core documents of a records management program are its policies, procedures, and records retention schedules. Other information, largely transactional in nature, should exist as well, things like lists of users, logs recording the transfer of records to inactive storage, audit trails documenting the movement of active records, and records review and disposition details attesting to the ultimate fate of retired records. Most of this supporting detail is captured in either manual or automated logs and is ancillary to the core document set. Development and maintenance of this ancillary information is important to the program: it is evidence of program execution, of the decisions made with respect to records retention and other matters, the instructions for carrying out the philosophy and decisions, and the activities ultimately carried out. Operationally, program documentation serves a practical, day-to-day purpose, that of informing personnel about what to do and what has already been done. Strategically, it serves as the firm's proof that its program is what it is claimed to be, and that actions taken pursuant to it comply with both the program requirements themselves and with whatever law or other authority may govern the firm's records retention activities.

We will go into more detail later about program documentation. For now, let us just say that developing core program documentation is a key step in program development overall, and that documenting decisions and activities in the program is an important part of the overall administrative risk mitigation value of the program.

Consistency

In devising and implementing a records retention schedule, consistency is a key concept with two faces. First, consistency refers to the way records are treated on the schedule, and second, consistency refers to the application of the schedule across all records. Conceptually, the ideal goal is to have in hand the entire record of a given transaction for the desired period of time, and then to have that entire record eliminated (and by eliminated, we mean here completely and unrecoverably obliterated) as a unified whole at the same point in time, a point identified by policy and schedule well in advance of the purge itself, so that the only remaining record of the transaction is the record of the purging itself: its date, the nature of the records destroyed, and sufficient proof that the records were purged as part of an ongoing, routine business process. The only exceptions would be material retained as reference, and materials returned to clients or intentionally maintained on their behalf beyond the firm's policy-based records retention schedule.

In practice, perfect consistency is difficult to attain; some compromises are usually necessary to make a program workable, and absolute consistency of implementation is unlikely in all but the smallest or most tightly managed and administered record systems. However, the records retention schedule, and all supporting documentation—policies, procedures, workflows, and so on—should be developed with the goal of achieving as much consistency as possible. Similarly, actual implementation, retrospective and day-forward, should pursue the greatest possible consistency through the following:

◆ *Predictability.* One of the great annoyances of poor records management (and one that often rises far above mere annoyance) is being uncertain as to whether some set of records even exists or what it is really called. This uncertainty wastes considerable staff and lawyer time when, as usually happens, a compelling need arises to either find the record or establish its absence. The ability to quickly and easily confirm the presence or absence of a record set by reference to a schedule and its associated destruction certificates will save time and minimize stress.

◆ *Legal Sufficiency and Reasonableness.* When detected by adversarial parties, erratic or inconsistent retention and destruction of records quite commonly gives rise to a suspicion that the program is negligent, or worse, that some records are being destroyed to hide evidence. Those adversarial parties, and with their help, courts, have become adept at detecting this behavior, and in asserting spoliation claims against the alleged perpetrators. In recent years, the imposition of heavy sanctions upon parties found guilty of such practices has become common.[4] A program designed and implemented with consistency in mind minimizes the likelihood of such allegations, and if they arise, it helps to defuse them.

◆ *Exception Management.* There is another area in which consistency is key—exception management. Just as the retention portion of a records management program should consistently identify and deal with records due for disposition, so too it must consistently identify those records that must be temporarily excluded from the disposition process. Although almost every document, record, or communication, regardless of type, begins as a candidate for ultimate destruction under a records retention schedule, any of them could become a candidate for exclusion under the right circumstances. In general, these circumstances include:

1. Reasonable notice that the records may be germane to a lawsuit, regulatory investigation, or similar legal inquiry;
2. Reasonable notice or other reason to believe that the records may be needed to preserve or advance the rights of a client or ex-client; and
3. Reasonable notice that records may be needed to support an authorized audit.

Failure to segregate and maintain records when on notice of any of the above circumstances may have very serious consequences for the organization, and possibly for individual employees, shareholders, or others. Therefore, the program must include a very robust mechanism for:

1. Identifying circumstances that may require the preservation of records otherwise scheduled for destruction;
2. Identifying the records that are responsive to the need identified;
3. Quickly and accurately informing the appropriate personnel of the identity of the records involved and of the need to preserve them; and
4. Securing, segregating,and preserving those records until such time as the circumstances requiring their retention have ceased.

This issue should not be used as an excuse not to have a records retention program, and no rule of law or case decision has ever so suggested. Properly developed and implemented, an exception process need not interfere with the overall program, and indeed, should facilitate it: accurate identification of records subject to a hold permits disposition of other records to continue.

Setting Up a Records Retention Program

Creation and deployment of the records retention portion of a records management program can be broken into three major phases:

1. *Preparation and Permission.* First things first. Your preliminary work should be devoted to raising awareness, educating end-users and management, gaining authorization to proceed and buy-in from key players, and establishing and obtaining budgets. In a law firm, this translates to going through all of the steps required to obtain the blessing of and authorization to proceed from the executive committee and their commitment to funding.
2. *Development of Key Components.* This phase breaks down into a number of tasks that roughly come under the headings of data collection,

analysis, modeling, research, process creation, and testing. Data is collected from personnel, preexisting documents, and other sources and is assessed for value and utility. Key users are interviewed and their issues are addressed as conditions to proceeding with schedule development. An enterprise records policy statement is created and approved. Workflow is designed and translated into working procedures to manage all aspects of the life cycle of hard copy and electronic records. Research into legal and ethical issues is completed and linked to records series in a model retention schedule. The policy, procedures, and schedule are vetted and tested, and the components are assembled and prepared for rollout.

3. *Implementation and Deployment.* After development and testing of the major components of the program (or at least its first iteration) are completed, the time comes to actually provide the tools to the users and to apply the retention schedule to the information assets of the firm—*all* of the information assets. If the firm has multiple file rooms, one or more collections of poorly sorted boxes, large quantities of poorly structured electronic data, e-mail repositories, and client portals, then this will likely prove to be the most challenging aspect of the entire endeavor.

Let's consider each of these phases in turn in some detail.

Preparation and Permission

What we want first is agreement among the powers within the firm that it should indeed consider this project. Since records management initiatives do not always take shape at the highest levels of the organization, authorization from those levels is always required before any substantive progress can be made. Even in a small or consensus-driven firm, the need is there to obtain approval or buy-in from management in the form of the managing partner, executive committee, or key shareholders. The decision to proceed involves many parties, and those parties must support and actively bless the process. Even if some of them do not have the ability to give the go-ahead, they may have the ability to shut things down through obstructive passive-aggressive behavior. Failure to get buy-in from everyone who is in a position to affect the project's progress can have a disastrous effect on the project. In larger or command-and-control organizations, this is even more true.

Whatever the size of the firm, success in getting support for a records initiative, just as in a courtroom, will favor the well prepared. Be prepared with your rationale (continue to sell both the concept and the benefits) and a full series of planning documents: timelines, budgets, deliverables, cost justifications, and so on.

Remember the political and human components of what you are proposing. Obtaining buy-in for development of a records retention program may require some political maneuvering to get what you need. There may be competing initiatives seeking funds from the same pool, in which case either some accommodation between the competing initiatives must be reached, or the records retention initiative must be demonstrated as the superior value to decision makers. Some of the resistance may be organizational ("Get off of my turf!") or it may result from a very human aversion to change in any form, sometimes voiced as, "I am too busy to deal with this!"

Management folks seldom become management folks if they are adverse to all change in any form. When pitching to management, the key is to learn from the past and to identify the reason for any resistance. Lay out all of the reasons for building a records management program but emphasize different aspects to different decision makers.

One of the great things about records management is that there are so many reasons for investing in it. Focus your presentations on individual sensitivities and perspectives. Some will react more strongly to the risk management issues while others may react more strongly to the ethical compliance, client service, cost containment, or attorney productivity aspects of the justification equation. Get help from the people in accounting to find and document soft or hidden costs if necessary, and then give them credit for helping. If someone will be looking for benefits in the form of risk avoidance and mitigation, which can be a tough sell in a firm that sees itself as not having significant issues in these areas, sell separately to that person without boring the rest of the management team.

Remember that not all managers are receptive to the idea of spending hard dollars to avoid soft costs. Management resistance may also take the form of simply not being comfortable with the idea of destroying records, particularly client-related records. Many lawyers and law firms have never destroyed any client-related records, and are unsure about if or how this might be properly done. Lawyers grounded in traditional culture and practice—and this may include many of the decision makers within a firm—are either simply uncomfortable with the idea of doing so, or persuaded that either law or sound practice mitigate against doing so. These folks will likely react well to a presentation about best practices and a list of firms where compliance with an established records management program and records retention schedule is the norm.

Once we have agreement that, for many reasons, records management and records retention are good ideas, our next step is to get permission to move ahead. Since we are dealing with decision makers (people authorized to spend the firm's money); we are well advised to thoroughly understand and effectively distill for management review the cumulative economic costs of not having a records retention program, and the return on invest-ment of implementing the program, including risk management returns. This requires a budget.

Before approving budgets and timelines, the decision makers in the firm will need to know in some detail where investments will be necessary, what approximate expenditures will be required, and why they are neces-sary. Before making a decision, they will want to know the precise scope of the initiative (*What are we doing and why?* Remember, repetition may be necessary.), the current state of affairs (*How do we stack up against other firms?*), the extent to which remedial measures will be needed (*How much do we really need to spend?*), and the capabilities and availability of in-house talent (*Why can't we just do it with internal staff?*).

Once these issues have been addressed, you are ready for your next big task, creation of a project work plan. If you do not know how to do this, get help. Just because management agrees that it is a good idea and they are willing to spend some money, they are not going to open the gates and give you a blank check. They are going to want to know exactly how their money is going to be spent and how they can be sure that they are getting their money's worth.

A good project plan contains a lot of detail and answers the following questions:

- What is to be done and in what sequence? (tasks and subtasks)
- What preceding task does this one rely on? (predecessor events)
- What following task does this one affect? (successor events)
- Who is involved? (responsible parties)
- What is each participant supposed to do? (measurement points)
- How do I know when it is complete? (deliverables)
- How long is it supposed to take? (time)
- How much will it cost? (budget)

The work plan and related timeline should enable at least a preliminary identification of necessary resources and related costs in the areas of pro-fessional services, technology acquisition and deployment, and other costs.

Mistakes to Avoid

There are many reasons why records management initiatives fail. Some of them apply to the preparation and permission phase and some to the devel-opment and deployment phases, but all bear stating, repeating, and studying.

1. *Overestimating internal resources*—Avoid overestimating the expert-ise and availability of internal staff resources, particularly if the firm has no dedicated and trained records management staff and it is the

firm's first real foray into records management. Also beware of overly optimistic estimates of how much work in the form of records or box inventories or the like can be accomplished in an hour or day by one staff member. Estimates made by persons without substantial experience in these matters tend to be wildly optimistic, and even dedicated service providers get burned regularly by overestimating productivity in some labor-intensive tasks.

2. *Lack of clear management support*—Avoid this by getting management buy-in upfront and maintaining frequent communication with the project stakeholders and the end-user population.

3. *Insufficient end-user involvement*—Avoid this by ongoing end-user involvement in the data gathering phases of the project.

4. *Poor education*—Avoid this by providing continual targeted educational bulletins on the *what and why* of the project to users along with an opportunity for them to provide feedback. Schedule frequent but brief personal meetings with key stakeholders to deal with issues and sell the concept. Consider creating a project portal on the firm's intranet to provide access to key project documents.

5. *Inadequate training*—Avoid this problem through development of sound procedures and a variety of training tools and approaches for dealing with both hard-copy and electronic records management tailored to the needs of specific user groups. Since some of this will involve culture and change management, work closely with in-house training resources to leverage existing processes and strategies.

Development of Key Components

Developing a record retention schedule involves several broad steps:

- *Data gathering and analysis*, to determine the kinds, location, usage, and other attributes of the information objects owned and controlled by the organization. The primary end product here is a taxonomy that describes all of the records in the firm by type. You should end up knowing what you have. Gather information on best practices as well: What is happening in those firms considered leaders in applying records management principles? The challenge here is constructing and following an approach that yields all of the information you need.

- *Policy and strategy discussions*, to determine the goals, risk tolerance, and other factors that will determine the specifics of retention policies and procedures. In this step you determine what the primary influences are to be when determining the retention times in the schedule.

- ◆ *Legal research and analysis*, to determine legal requirements and considerations, and ensure that policies, procedures, and schedules are legally compliant. This is self-explanatory. Here you are collecting all of the legal requirements and influences, including laws, regulations, and case law.

- ◆ *Document drafting*, turning the analysis from the above steps into a concrete set of policy documents. At this point you are linking the citations to the records series that make up the taxonomy and coming up with time frames based on legal, ethical, and firm-specific operating requirements as well as best practices.

- ◆ *Vetting and revision*, involving an iterative review, correction, and re-review of draft documents. Now that we have the schedule in a draft form, we need to create a review process that gives prime users the opportunity to review and comment on it. This is a good time to make sure that all of the heretofore unspoken fears that accompany the concept of destroying records are addressed.

- ◆ *Adoption and sign-off*, the final approval of the policies and procedures as set forth in the policy documents. Now it is time to go back to the folks who authorized the program. Put your new, well-researched records retention schedule in the hands of the executive committee and tell them what you did, how you did it, who was involved, and what your next steps are.

Each of these phases involves a variety of tasks. Again, let us look at some of the details.

Data Gathering

When you start developing a records retention program, you need to find out certain things about your firm's records. Specifically, you will want to find out:

- ◆ *What you have*—Types or kind of records used in each practice and business function, including record titles and functional descriptions of their use;

- ◆ *Its medium*—Whether the records exist in hard copy, microform (fiche, roll, aperture card, etc.), or electronic format;

- ◆ *Where it is*—The locations of records repositories such as hard-copy file rooms, work rooms, and staging areas, including electronic repositories;

- ◆ *Operational life*—The period of time a record has some sort of real business utility to the firm; how long a given record is needed to satisfy real business purposes;

- *Compliance life*—How long you need to keep records to satisfy both legal and ethics requirements; and
- *Risk management life*—How long a given record might be needed to satisfy the demands of dispute resolution, litigation, audit, or investigation and at what point its continued retention might start creating risk for your client.

And in order to create useful and productive processes and controls, you will want to find out other information, such as:

- When and how information is created or received;
- How it is distributed and managed within the firm during its active life;
- How and why duplicates come into being—and where they can, and should, end up;
- How information is circulated and whether this happens according to any particular processes (aka workflow); and
- How much hard-copy and electronic volume we need to address during implementation (number of filing cabinets and boxes, linear feet of open-shelf filing, digital repository size, etc.).

. . . and so on. Capturing all of this information will require different approaches to data gathering—from personal interviews and surveys to creation and generation of system-generated reports and including everyone's favorite task, inventorying old records.

No single approach to data gathering is best. An assessment of the situation in each firm—a look at its age, the current state of affairs in records management, the sophistication of its architecture, and other factors—will help determine the appropriate mix of data gathering approaches that will yield best results. Suffice it to say that more is better than less, and relying solely on surveys seldom gets you where you want to go.

Let us briefly consider the virtues of two approaches to collecting some of the data needed to develop your taxonomy, the first step in creating a retention schedule: (1) a combination of interviews, surveys, and questionnaires; and (2) the physical inventory. Some practitioners prefer one method over the other, but in truth, both bring value and have their places in the development process. A survey alone can be executed more quickly and easily than a physical inventory, but it is not as thorough and complete. Even if a physical inventory is conducted, interviews will be needed to supplement it—the interviews are the vehicle for obtaining information on usage and practice, risk management and litigation issues, and other information beyond the bare question of what records are in use.

Which of these, or which mix of them, is best depends upon several factors:

◆ *Actual need:* If preliminary surveys indicate that records are rea-sonably well ordered and reasonably well identified, and staff have a good understanding of their locations and other management attributes, a physical inventory may not be necessary, or it may be possible to defer inventory until the implementation phase when inventory is needed for actual processing of the records prior to disposition. If, on the other hand, records are not clearly labeled, or if labeled they are out of order or files are missing, or if there are significant repositories of unknown records (as in that bank of file cabinets or pile of boxes in the basement that has been there as long as anyone can remember, and whose contents are unknown), an inventory will be required for at least some records to ensure that the retention schedule accommodates all types of records actually being maintained.

◆ *Budget:* There are inventories and there are inventories. A complete and very detailed physical inventory of all of the organization's records is a labor-intensive and expensive process. Unless the firm is in a position to make a substantial commitment of staff time and/ or money, a complete physical inventory may not be possible. More economical sampling of collections may yield almost as much useful information and may be far less expensive. The key is in knowing how to determine what should be sampled and what needs detailed inventorying.

◆ *Time and schedule:* A complete physical inventory of all of a firm's records can take a considerable period of time—weeks, months, or more, depending upon the size and age of the firm, the actual vol-ume of records involved, how ordered or disordered they are, and the actual labor and expertise available to do the work. If other fac-tors permit it, and the firm is on a short timeline for adoption of the program, sampling, deferring a physical inventory to the implemen-tation phase, or some other approach may be the only way to meet key project timelines.

Regardless of the method chosen, it should be borne in mind that, prior to implementation of the retention schedule, the firm must know how the schedule is to be applied to every data object (file, binder, document, data-base, e-mail and attachment, etc.) in its collection.

◆ For administrative records, the record series into which the data object will likely fall;

◆ The creation date (or some later substitute such as the date the object went to inactive storage) of the data object, for purposes of calculating the retention period and destruction date; and

◆   For client files, the client name, matter number, or other precise identifier for the data object, for purposes of ethics compliance.

The only real option available if this information cannot be obtained at reasonable cost is to default to a very conservative (meaning long) retention period, bearing in mind that it may be necessary at some future point to inventory them anyway, for example, in response to a dispute or investigation.

In most cases, at least a partial inventory will be required at some point, although it can often be deferred: Interviews and surveys may well be more than adequate to develop retention schedules, with actual inventory work needed only when it comes time to implement the schedule against say, the boxes in inactive storage.

Use of a Preexisting Records Listing

Another common starting place for developing a taxonomy is the analysis of existing records listings from storage or elsewhere. This approach offers the potential of being a tremendous timesaver that will jump-start the project, but it is seldom complete enough to replace the combination of surveys, interviews, and inventories. Limitations of using listings include:

◆   *The age of the listing:* The older the listing, the less likely it is to be accurate today, particularly if the organization has undergone any substantial changes in the interim.

◆   *The comprehensiveness of the listing:* Unless it was done under the auspices of trained records personnel, it is likely to be incomplete. A listing entry that reads, *"Closed files—1996"* has no value.

◆   *The detail in the listing:* Quality of detail usually depends on whether or not specific guidelines and formats were used. Just telling someone to inventory the files without giving them the forms to do it and training in use of a specific data capture structure usually results in a rapid deterioration of quality as the inventory goes on. People get bored and tired and then they start taking shortcuts.

The problems that result from relying solely on old records listings should not be underestimated. Most listings are created by nonrecords personnel who did not understand or use records management terminology, and who put little time or effort into creating them, with the result that record titles may be meaningless. When the inventory is a low-priority task for untrained personnel with little motivation and no resources with which to do the job properly, the results are predictably bad. If listings are old, these problems are compounded by changes in the organization and its records.

The lesson is that any preexisting records listing must be viewed with some caution. Going through long lists containing hundreds of nearly useless record titles can be a maddening experience. Before relying on them, sample any available listings to see if they contain the required level of detail, if they are consistent in what they show, and if they are comprehensive enough to add value to the data gathering process.

The Inventory Process

A physical inventory is just what it sounds like—a physical examination of records to gather and record information about them. In the case of paper records, this consists of methodically going through the contents of files cabinets, boxes, workrooms, staging facilities, closets, unoccupied offices, and other temporary storage locations. In the case of electronic repositories, it consists of using indexes, directory structures, and other listings for the same purpose. The details of conducting an inventory are beyond the scope of this book, and several publications covering the topic in depth are available; nonetheless, it is worth examining the merits and problems of this approach.

Conducting a Physical Inventory

Again, first things first. Our first task is to answer the question, *"How many collections do we have and where are they?"* When conducting a physical inventory of the files, the first step is to identify all of the repositories. It sounds simple, but we consistently see collections that everyone assumed belonged to someone else. *"I thought that was yours!"* As we indicated above, every file cabinet, workroom, staging facility, closet, unoccupied office, off-site storage facility, or other location where files are being maintained should be listed along with whatever is known—or assumed—about the information and records housed there. Get a good set of floor plans and do a complete walk-through of all of the offices. Know what is behind every door and do not take someone else's word for it. No set of files or records should be exempt, and no individual is so important that his or her files are too special to be included.

If files are segregated and secured under a court directive, that is fine— we just need to know what the collection includes and to make sure that the records behind that locked door are actually supposed to be there.

By the time it has completed its job, the inventory team will have examined every repository of the organization or department in question and methodically listed and described their contents. In so doing, they will have dealt with the issue of comprehensiveness. Properly done by well-trained personnel, a properly structured inventory will yield very accurate and very comprehensive results—far more accurate than an old or partial listing obtained by any other method. Properly captured, the inventory will also provide a well-ordered dataset that can be captured in a records management database and easily managed with regard to location and activities appropriate to its point in the records life cycle. To get the results we want, we need to pay attention to our staff and our process:

- *Training and commitment:* Find smart and capable staff to do the work and train them well. Tell them what they are doing, why they are doing it, and emphasize the need for consistency and accuracy. Give them processes and controls that allow them to set aside problems and concentrate on volume first—you can address problem items later on without bringing the entire process to a halt. If possible, compensation should be based on volume and quality, not time spent doing the job.

- *Resource consumption:* Physical inventories are resource intensive. Depending upon file thickness, clarity of labeling, complexity of contents, and other factors, it may take fifteen minutes to an hour or more to inventory a single file cabinet. The hours required to complete an inventory can add up very rapidly when resources are multiplied by hundreds (or even thousands!) of file cabinets, desk drawers, boxes, piles on table tops, and other physical repositories in what may be very distributed locations, and dozens to thousands of computer servers, each with multiple repositories and the same issues as paper with respect to labeling and clarity.

- *Segregate tasks and crosstrain:* Assign data capture, indexing, data entry, and other tasks to different people and then rotate the staff through the different jobs. There is nothing like personally doing a job to understand how a poorly executed task affects the next step in the process.

- *Time and task:* A complete inventory of a sizable organization may take months to complete. Even a single, small department with a couple of dozen file cabinets may take several people a week or more to properly inventory. Do not wait until all of the data capture and indexing is done before starting the data entry, and remember to use the data entry portion of the job as a quality check on the initial indexing.

- *Cost:* Inventories are not cheap. Understand that the combination of the above factors can make a physical inventory a relatively expensive proposition—but not nearly as expensive as losing your best client because you did not manage his records well.

As we mentioned earlier, the strong likelihood that the firm at some point will implement a comprehensive records management software package makes the inventory even more valuable. Among the attributes of this type of software is that it allows for tracking the location of every physical file and electronic data object in the firm. Because of this, even more information can be gathered, including the location of each item inventoried.

Neither of these approaches provides a complete solution. The trade-offs involved in using just one or the other reduces the decision down to speed versus thoroughness.

Issues That May Hinder a Physical Inventory

If you do not have the available intelligent bodies, in-house expertise, and the stomach to be in it for the long haul, it is not a wise idea to attempt a physical inventory using purely internal resources. Failure to complete a physical inventory is one of the most common reasons why organizations fail in attempts to develop a records retention schedule. Other reasons for failure are

- ◆ *Attempting an inventory using scrap time.* Organizations needing an inventory but lacking in committed resources often assign the inventory to a group of personnel on a time-available basis. This approach is usually doomed to failure, because competent personnel rarely if ever have the large blocks of time needed available, and projects assigned time-available status are by definition low priority. This combination of factors guarantees that the inventory will die on the vine in virtually every case.
- ◆ *Attempting an inventory using personnel who lack records management experience.* Although inexperienced personnel may be used successfully, their successful deployment requires that the inventory be supervised by persons with records management expertise. The absence of meaningful oversight and feedback results in the issues already discussed—incomplete inventories, inventories that are useless, and so on. Experienced supervisors will also typically facilitate a much more efficient work process, resulting in a faster and cheaper inventory.
- ◆ *Making the inventory the responsibility of individual departments or locations.* This approach has all of the undesirable qualities of both of the above approaches, and virtually guarantees that a high percentage of the resulting inventory will be useless or nearly so. Pre-existing records listings often come from this process, so any departmental inventory will have the same undesirable characteristics as have been described for preexisting listings.

Constructing the Schedules

Mixing administrative records and client files is seldom a good idea. And although certain types of records may seem to be a natural fit for inclusion in the client or matter file, they should be segregated. The matter file schedules should include only those records that are truly part of the work done for the client. If records that apply to the internal management of the case are included in the actual file, then if the file has to be given to the client or transferred to another firm or lawyer, then it must be scrutinized, document-by-document, to make sure that no inappropriate documents make the trip. These include such things as:

- Billing information. (*Correspondence concerning billing disputes should not be intermingled with other correspondence on a matter.*)
- Internal staffing and scheduling information. (*Who would benefit the most from training on this type of work?*)
- Records pertaining to the acquisition of the client. (*Do we really want to take on this client? If we take them on will it preclude us from doing more desirable work later on?*) and
- Internal discussion and matter due diligence information. (*We do not really need a waiver on this one, do we?*)

So, once we have drafted taxonomies, creating structures with categories for all types of information within the firm, our next steps involve turning those taxonomies into a retention schedule and establishing the rules for how long the firm will be keeping things and why. The first step in this process is considering the types of information the taxonomy describes.

All organizations share certain types of information—accounting, human resources, administrative and governance records, and so on. The primary differences between the appropriate retention periods for like records in different organizations' records retention schedules usually comes down to the laws affecting them because of the types of business they are in and where they conduct that business.

Records Appraisal and Analysis

All records have a primary value. This value is based on the purpose for which they were created. Most records also have a secondary value (i.e., a value other than the original value for which the document was created). Each record will have one or more of the following values: (1) administrative or operational value; (2) research value; (3) historical value; and (4) legal value. Any or all of these values may bear on retention of a record; therefore they must all be considered during the evaluation and analysis process.

The goals of the appraisal are to assess our taxonomies and refine them as necessary to develop records series, to determine the business value of the records, to resolve related issues such as how long a record should remain in active filing before being moved to box storage or other low-cost storage, to identify vital records, and similar issues.

While a records retention and destruction schedule states how long a record must be kept, it may also track where it should be kept, as well as other information of value. Records should usually be maintained at or near the point of use while they possess primary value, but they may be transferred to remote storage for the duration of their secondary value.[5] On the schedule, this usually translates into values for "active" versus "inactive" retention or the like for each series. Analysis based on information gathered during the survey/inventory process will form the basis for these two values.

A great deal of other interesting information may surface during the analysis process. However, for purposes of records retention, the analysis should at least result in data permitting the development of sound record series and resulting in a good understanding of business requirements and other factors essential to developing valid retention periods.

The appraisal of records requires a working knowledge of the law firm's goals and objectives and its hierarchial structure, as well as an understanding of general records management principles. This being the case, it is a process best undertaken by or with the assistance of someone with records management experience.

Records Classifications: The Record Series

After the records inventory and other data gathering, and the creation of our taxonomy, records must be analyzed and classified according to the function they perform. This analysis is the basis for the development of record series. Record series are simply categories of records: On a high level, these can be quite obvious—accounting records, human resource records, matter files, and so on. Within these high-level categories, subcategories and sub-subcategories can be developed to gain as much detail as needed. How much detail is needed depends on the complexity of the records system itself, and the need to track detailed subsets of records. Several trade-offs are involved:

- ◆ *Retention period.* The retention period for any item within a record series always defaults to the longest retention period of any single item within the series. Greater granularity in the record series permits the separate management of items with differing retention requirements, thereby permitting earlier disposition of some items. Broader record series means a smaller schedule with fewer categories and fewer decisions, but longer retention periods for many types of records. This type of schedule is easier to administer. Our trade-off then is greater control and complexity versus ease of administration, longer retention periods, and the possibility of increased risk.
- ◆ *Targeted management.* The record series on the retention schedule will in many cases double as a file plan, or at least serve as the basic structure for one. Purely for the purposes of records retention, a high-level series such as, say, "accounting records" might work

perfectly well in some organizations. For other purposes such as identification and retrieval for tax audit, such a classification would be totally inadequate. Even for pure retention purposes, very high-level series may be inadequate. One could, for example, create a "human resources" record series and leave it at that. Within this high-level category, however, are a wide variety of records, used for a wide variety of purposes: vetting and hiring, benefits administration, disciplinary actions, and so on. Some are required by law, others not; some are routinely subject to audit or litigation, others not; and they will have a mix of retention periods ranging from very short to very long, some with required triggering events and others not. Managing such a mixed bag as a single series is problematic.

◆ *Ease of use.* The more detailed and complex a schedule is, the less likely it is that staff will use it accurately, or at all, unless it is a targeted, Web-based application that brings an individual user's rules and categories to his or her desktop in a very responsive and intuitive fashion. Expecting staff to leaf through a printed retention schedule of hundreds or even a thousand or more pages and accurately make choices from among thousands of entries on a routine basis is unrealistic.

How Complex Should It Be?

There is no hard-and-fast rule as to how much complexity is needed. Sound judgment on the part of development personnel will be required, and the result will likely be a mixture of high-level and granular series. That said, it is worth noting that even large and complex organizations rarely have more than a few hundred *meaningful* record series, and many smaller organizations get by nicely on 200 or so.

If you complete development of your record series and discover you have over a thousand of them, or see that you have gone more than three or four layers deep into subseries, you have probably overdone it. Or, what you developed is really a *file plan*, which is an organizational scheme similar to a retention schedule, but used for the classification of records for active management and retrieval purposes. In complex record sets where very accurate retrieval from large record volumes is required, the overall file plan may be very detailed indeed. If you find yourself in this situation, you may wish to retain the detail for other purposes, but it will be necessary to nest up the sublayers into a more manageable and usable tool.

In most cases, extreme complexity results from listing every document type as a separate record series or listing all document types that exist in each department as separate records series on the schedule. For example, all accounts payable records usually can be retained for a single defined time period, assuming controls are in place to manage exceptions for claims or audits. In an extreme case, however, accounts payable can go three levels deep and include twenty or more records series on a retention schedule. With a well-crafted and designed schedule, such a highly complex approach is not necessary.

Beyond limiting the record series to a reasonable number, the other goals of record series development are clarity and utility. The record series will have names, and normally some sort of description. Both names and descriptions should be meaningful and intuitive, so that staff are easily guided to the correct choice. The series must also correlate to data objects susceptible to retention management. Series that would require, say, pulling individual items out of files or boxes for disposition will prove useless—in the real world, no one will ever actually do this on any consistent basis.

In some cases, the choices for record series will be obvious—"accounting," and within it, "accounts payable," "accounts receivable," and so on; or "matter files" and within it, by practice type, categories such as "pleadings," "legal research," and so on. In some cases, additional analytical work will be required to develop series that are both meaningful and practical, particularly in highly regulated industries.

Never, Ever

Under no circumstances should a records retention schedule include categories for "general" or "miscellaneous" records. There is no such thing as a "general" record, nor is it possible to develop a meaningful retention period for any data object placed in such a category. When used, they commonly end up as dumping grounds for staff who are uninterested in spending the time to properly categorize their records, and as such contain a hodge-podge of records whose identities can only be determined by careful examination. They are thus an impediment rather than an aid to a records retention program.

Development of record series is not an area where shortcuts are desirable, particularly given the relatively small investment of time required to develop them and the long life of the resulting work. Good record series are an essential ingredient of a good records retention program, and the time spent developing them will be richly repaid for the duration of the program, which may be a very long time indeed.

Legal Research and Analysis

Once we are pretty well set on the categories, or records series, it is time to undertake the legal research and analysis and determine what law applies to the firm's records. Preliminary work can start almost immediately during the development process. As mentioned earlier, every organization has tax and accounting records, human resources records, and so on, and every law firm has matter files. Knowing this, and knowing the jurisdictions in which the firm operates, makes it possible to initiate the legal research.

If legal research is commenced prior to having a decent preliminary taxonomy and list of records series, it may be necessary to fine tune it some later, perhaps more than once, as other information is captured and analyzed. It is, for example, relatively easy to guess in advance that the human resources department will have applications, resumes, and personnel files. However, in the absence of either prior experience or good results from data collection, the later addition to the records series of COBRA notifications or OSHA 300 logs may come as a surprise, and require additional work to determine if legal retention requirements apply to them.

Records retention legal research can be one of the more time-consuming steps in the development of records retention and destruction schedules. There are several reasons for this:

◆ Records retention laws are often quite obscure. The recordkeeping requirement in a law is often buried deep within a provision governing some substantive requirement, and may not show up on any index or other finding aid. Electronic searches are hampered by the varied terminology used—"books," "files," "accounts," "data," and many other synonyms and near synonyms for "records" turn up in laws on recordkeeping.

◆ The Balkanized nature of U.S. law may mean multiple authorities from multiple sources in multiple jurisdictions governing a single record series. In extreme cases, this can result in several hundred laws being applicable to a single series.

◆ The data objects described in laws may be vague or general, or match the real-world data objects in actual use very poorly. (Does your firm still use the "time book" commonly set forth in payroll laws to track employee hours and pay?)

The time and resources needed to perform thorough legal research should not be underestimated. Notwithstanding its obscurity, a substantial volume of data collection and recordkeeping law exists and it usually requires some digging to find it.

Similarly, it is not a good idea to assume that federal requirements trump state requirements, or that requirements across the various jurisdictions and authorities within those jurisdictions are uniform. Federal and state authorities often exercise some form of concurrent jurisdiction, and within a jurisdiction agencies and other authorities may well promulgate requirements without regard to any other requirements affecting the same records that may already be in place.

When the research is complete, it must be organized. Notwithstanding its somewhat haphazard nature, the citations will fall into categories. There will be, for example, statutes and regulations governing payroll records, ethics opinions, and case decisions on matter file retention, statutes of limitation on various topics, and so on. An important point is to remember that retention schedules must be reviewed and updated every year. You do not want to be in the position of saying, *"Sorry, Your Honor, I know that as a law firm we should be sensitive to these issues, but we just didn't take the time to update our schedule to reflect new legal requirements and so we dumped those records when we shouldn't have."*

Rather than assign citations to record series individually, it is generally best to develop a structure for citations similar to that developed for record series. Such a structure will, at its simplest, put accounting laws into a group, human resources laws into a group, authorities on matter files into a group, and so on. In more complex schemes, it will subdivide these groups into more granular groups, potentially many of them. It may be tempting to skip a step, and assign citations to record series individually, but little will be gained by the attempt. Since multiple authorities will in many cases apply, the result will be *de facto* grouping of laws anyway, without the assurance of consistency that a formal grouping and analysis will permit.

As with record series, no hard-and-fast rule can be stated as to how much granularity is required. However, since each category or group of laws will necessarily account for the requirements of every law or other authority within it, larger groups will necessarily have a collective retention period reflecting the longest retention period contained in it, and will necessarily be applicable to more record series by virtue of its greater scope of authority. More granular groupings of laws will, on the other hand, permit more precise assignments of legal authorities to record series, and so permit shorter retention periods for those records for which this is legal.

The correspondence between the groups of laws and record series is not one-to-one or perfect. In the case of matter files, for example, although there will be a group of authorities specifically on retention of matter files, there will also be statutes of limitation that may be applicable to the analysis, for example, of malpractice or breach of contract. These, in turn, may also be applicable to other record series. Any assignment scheme must account for this multiple relevance.

Analysis of the Legal Research

The results of the legal research will be a hodge-podge of hard-coded explicit requirements, statutes of limitation, case law, and advisory authorities such as ethics opinions. The role of each must be considered:

- *Explicit requirements provide the minimum retention requirements.* If there are multiple explicit requirements applicable to a record series, the longest of these is the minimum retention period that can be assigned to a record series.
- *Statutes of limitation and repose describe the boundaries of a specific risk envelope.* After the running of applicable limitations, the risk of disposing of a record is essentially gone, or at least drastically less.
- *Advisory authorities describe a risk envelope, and give an indication of what may be viewed as "reasonable" conduct.* This is particularly important for records that do not have an explicit legal retention period.

Potential retention periods arising from this mix of authorities will range from the legal minimum permitted by the group to the longest possible period required by the worst-case situation postulated by the risk envelope described by limitations periods and advisory authorities. Where on this spectrum the retention period chosen will lie is a function of several factors surrounding organizational risk tolerance and the firm's actual experience and history. If, for example, the length of limitations periods applicable to some record series significantly exceeds the length of any explicit requirement applicable to it, it may be necessary to consider the likelihood and value of any litigation that might arise, as well as the delay in institution of litigation after close or termination of the matter. If analysis reveals little risk, or some finite, short window within which disputes and litigation arise, retention periods may well be near or at legal minimums. If, on the other hand, analysis yields a conclusion of high risk or strong potential of latent claims, it might well extend to the full period of the longest statute of limitation or repose.

The physical result of the grouping process will be some sort of tabular listing of legal authority that permits the assignment of indexing, summaries, or other metadata to each citation. This can happen in one of several ways:

- *Listing citations on the retention schedule alongside the record series they relate to.* This works well only if the number of citations is small. Otherwise the formatting rapidly becomes cumbersome, as does any look-up process for the individual citations. Unless the citations are also listed elsewhere, space limitations usually preclude the presentation of much metadata for each citation.
- *Listing the citations in a separate table and numbering them consecutively.* This again only works well if the number of citations is small, for the same reason; but metadata can be assigned.

◆ *Listing the citations by category in a separate table, and linking categories to record series by a code or other identifier.* This approach works best with large numbers of citations.

Whatever approach is chosen, citations should be clearly linked, either individually or in groups, to their assigned record series, for purposes of internal analysis during the development process, to answer questions that may arise later, and to facilitate the annual review and updating process. If you do not know which categories or records series a citation pertains to, it is difficult to accurately update the schedule if that citation changes.

Trigger Events

Many (perhaps even most) retention periods commence only upon the occurrence of some triggering event. A trigger event could be the termination of a matter, the completion of a contract, termination of an employee, or any of a number of other events. Although it is not common, multiple trigger events could apply to a single record series, either in series or in the alternative.

Trigger events are sometimes mandated by law. Other times, they arise out of business needs. In either event, they must be captured and reflected on the retention schedule in order to ensure that records retention periods are properly calculated. Once captured, they must be tracked to ensure that retention periods actually do commence running during implementation.

Assignment of Retention Periods on the Schedule

How do we come up with the actual time frame we put on the schedule next to a records series? As we have stated, several factors will go into the assignment of a retention period to a record series:

◆ *Business need*, including its subconsideration such as reference value;
◆ *Legal requirements*; and
◆ *Legal considerations*, such as statutes of limitation or advisory authority.

Which of these takes precedence varies. For some series, all three will apply and you will simply choose the longest. For others, there may be neither explicit requirements nor meaningful risk considerations. As between business need and legal requirements, the longer of the two usually applies. As between the first two and legal considerations, some analysis as discussed above is required to determine a suitable period. During initial development, it is helpful to list each of these considerations for each record series, along with any triggering events, in order to remind administrators of the schedule that more than one scenario is in play and, depending on circumstance, differing retention periods may apply. After adoption of a final schedule, it may be possible to conceal these optional periods from users, but they should remain up front for the personnel involved with program and schedule administration. Most employees are uninterested in the interpretation, wanting only to know that their records are being taken care of and that they have no personal exposure. Similarly, few end users need to see specific citations.

Review and Revision

Once you finish the process outlined above, you will have a draft schedule. Now it is time to streamline it. Generally, revision first occurs throughout the drafting of the schedule and the research and analysis process. For example, legal research may call attention to records overlooked during the capture process, or may require the reorganization of record series to accommodate conflicting legal requirements. If, when doing the legal research, you find reference to types of information in applicable citations that are not included on the schedule, but that should logically be there, it is time to go find them.

Upon completion of a first draft, with records series and recommended retention periods in place, the schedule should be distributed for review by selected personnel, or those who for political reasons should be involved in the process. Their review of nomenclature, definitions, structure, and retention periods may result in feedback that prompts revision. These requests may well result in a second draft which must in turn be submitted for review, additional suggestions and revisions, and so on. It is normal to go through at least two reviews and not uncommon for three or four to be required before a working schedule is ready. Once everyone is on board, the schedule and a high-level description of supporting procedures and workflow should be submitted for approval. If things are going well, each set of revisions should be smaller and easier than the last.

Approval and Distribution of the Schedule

The records retention and destruction schedule should be reviewed and approved by several key stakeholders in the firm prior to authorization and distribution. Key reviewers usually include one or more of the executive committee members speaking on behalf of the committee as a whole, the Executive Director or COO, the CFO, and the CIO. The records manager should be acting as a facilitator and explain the process and answer questions as necessary. The approval chain of command may vary depending on the composition of each organization. Approval may require some negotiation on retention periods or other matters, in order to satisfy each of these players that their requirements are being met. This is a normal aspect of the development process, and reasonable delays in obtaining approval from these normally very busy people should be planned for.

Once the powers that be have signed off—and do get signatures and dates—then the sparkling new records retention schedule can be formally issued and distributed to all departments, along with its associated policies and procedures, and implementation can proceed.

Policy and Procedures

Like the rest of the records management program, a records retention program requires policies and procedures. A substantial portion of the firm's general records management procedures is built around the management and retrieval of active records so users can find what they need, when they need it. Many of these active records procedures will impact the records retention portion of the program, but other procedures must be developed specifically to facilitate records retention and disposition. Among the more important are

- An enterprise records management policy statement;
- Procedures governing the creation, receipt, and management of active records;
- Guidelines for determining when records change from active to inactive or closed status;
- Procedures for moving records from one location to another, including transfer to storage;
- Procedures for periodically identifying records that are candidates for destruction;
- Guidelines for determining what must be offered to the client before disposition;
- Procedures for obtaining the necessary destruction approvals;
- Controls over transfer and actual destruction processes; and
- Required documentation of key steps in establishing a secure and workable audit trail.

It is not a good idea to dispense with any of these since each is part of an interrelated sequence or process. For most firms, a sound and complete set of policies and procedures is a necessary part of the records management program. They state the firm's position, provide guidance to personnel, and provide a structure for recording actions taken. In addition to supporting and enabling the records access and control processes, they provide proof and justification should they ever be required. Details of activities that must be formalized by procedures will be discussed later under "Program Implementation."

Consideration of policies and procedures should start early on. Policies and procedures must ensure smooth operation of all records life-cycle processes, addressing routine operations of the program as well as dealing with any issues and obstacles that are identified. This can only happen when the drafters have a full understanding of those issues and processes.

Duplicates, Reference Material, and Other "Extra" Records

Some programs deal only with the official files or the record copy, conceptually contemplating a records program managing the single "official" copy of each record. For many reasons, this is bad practice:

- ◆ For many, if not most record types, duplicates (lots of duplicates) may exist as copies within working files, personal files, and other repositories outside of the official file or repositories.
- ◆ It is common practice in most organizations for users to create their own working or project files, the contents of which may not correspond meaningfully to anything on a retention schedule that considers only one file or a single copy of a document.
- ◆ Records created or acquired as part of a business transaction or matter often turn out to have transcending value as reference material beyond the reason for their original creation or acquisition.
- ◆ Particularly in law firms, documents may go through many preliminary drafts prior to their finalization.
- ◆ Most users, absent guidance, consider documents other than originals in their possession their personal files and subject to whatever controls they think are appropriate.
- ◆ Even if the official record set or file has been disposed of, any copies that exist are still discoverable and may create a risk for the client if maintained past the point when the client might have disposed of them.

Each of these issues must be dealt with in the procedures. Consistency is key to effective records retention. It is of little value to dispose of official copies of records pursuant to a records retention schedule if significant numbers of duplicate copies are being retained in personal or project files, or if large volumes of official files and records are routinely held past the expiration of their retention period because some item within them might have reference value. Organizations that have failed to consider these issues have in the past paid a price for doing so.[6] On the other hand, organizations that have consistently, in the course of routine business practices, executed a records retention program have prevailed in court when challenged.[7]

It is not, however, workable merely to have a policy forbidding the creation of project, personal, and reference files. Staff need to create hard-copy and electronic duplicates to get their work done, and forbidding the creation of duplicates, assuming such a policy could be enforced, would make it difficult for them to do their jobs. Similarly, well-drafted boilerplate or well-researched memoranda are significant assets to the organization and useful tools for attorneys and staff. Forbidding their retention as work product or reference material would not only be poor policy but would invite development of work-arounds intended to defeat the policy. The best strategy is to design a system that allows creation and management of such materials and the management of work product and knowledge in a way that does not create either compliance or retention problems.

Duplicate Copies

Since duplicate copies (other than those created for other official records) are created for the personal use and convenience of some staff member, they are usually quite short-lived. Occasionally their useful life may be somewhat longer, but in almost all cases, matter file duplicates will cease to have value at the close of the matter. Rarely if ever will they have any ongoing utility past closing of the matter. If it is determined that they do, then it may be that the lifetime of the matter needs to be extended and its disposition delayed for some period. This being the case, it is possible to formulate a rule: *duplicates made for the convenience of staff* should be retained only so long as they are needed for their initial purpose, but no longer than the active life of the matter to which they relate. *Under no circumstances* should they be retained longer than the retention period of the official copy. As a procedural matter, convenience copies should not be sent to inactive storage— they contribute, often substantially, to all costs associated with that process, while adding no value at all for the organization.

Project Files

Project files normally start life as someone's preliminary investigation into some assignment or pending transaction: a merger, a capital purchase, a new lease, development of a new (records management?) system, and so on. Project files may contain anything and everything germane to an inquiry into the subject: copies of internal cost accounting records or contracts, product brochures, RFPs, bits of Internet research, correspondence, copies of newspaper and magazine articles, and so on.

There are two key aspects of project files whose analysis permits their retention to be dealt with; first, to the extent that they contain copies of the organization's own records, those records are almost invariably duplicates and filed elsewhere. Second, the project file is normally a preliminary investigation that either winds up with no action taken, or turns into a formal action, and either one generally happens within a defined time. Projects almost always have a defined lifetime. The merger is effected, the equipment is purchased, the clerk is hired, or is not. In either event, the task is completed and the file is closed, either because of events, or by the mere passage of time: last year's calculations on the relative value of the merger candidate, equipment brochures, and price lists have no ongoing value, regardless of the decision made.

These things being the case, project files can normally be designated as having a retention period of "keep only until resolution of the issue" or some similar formulation, or in the alternative, a short period of years related to a trigger event, such as closed plus two years (noted in the schedule as C+2). Like duplicates, they are poor candidates for off-site storage. If items from the file are germane to a formal initiative resulting from the initial inquiry, they should be rolled into the record set for that initiative. And if specific documents have real ongoing research or work product value, they should be removed and indexed in a different repository.

In some cases, there may be "project files" of a more substantive and longer term nature, such as those dealing with capital investments, investigations, regulatory inquiries, or the like. In such a case, it is important that the two kinds of project files be given different names and managed separately. To label them all as generic "project files" with identical handling and retention rules would result in either nonsubstantive files being kept too long, or substantive files being disposed of too early, neither of which is desirable. This illustrates an important records retention concept: record series should not be so broad or vaguely defined that data objects with widely disparate significance and retention periods end up in the same series. If this happens the efficiency of the schedule as a cost control or risk management tool is at best reduced. At worst, important information is destroyed prematurely, because the schedule (and thereby staff) fails to identify and segregate it.

Reference Material

Reference material can come from the pile of duplicates that make up a work file (*Hey, let's keep this great brief!*), project file (*I really like the format of this RFP.*), or from other sources. Generally, reference material can be thought of as falling into one of two categories:

- *Pure reference material*, created or acquired solely for reference purposes, and containing only reference information; and
- *Business records* that have acquired reference value.

Examples of pure reference material include publications, including excerpts from research publications such as photocopied cases, and reports from outside parties containing general information and analysis, but not referencing particular matters. Examples of business records include pleadings, memoranda, or other items relating to a particular case, which are found to have ongoing value because the language, analysis, or conclusions can be reused in other matters.

By definition, reference material has an indefinite and perhaps long-term value. It must therefore have a retention period somehow managed by a review process. (*If it is outdated, get rid of it.*) Disposition will occur only when a determination is made that the material is obsolete. For business records being retained for reference purposes, the situation is different: In addition to whatever information is deemed to have reference value, there will be information, often important information, about a particular matter or transaction. This information may also be confidential or privileged, if the item in question deals with a personal or client matter. This being the case, it may be prudent to consider redacting client identities or other identifiers from client-related documents maintained for reference purposes. And how do you know when it has outlived its usefulness? If it has not been looked at for several years, it should be considered a candidate for review and potential disposition.

Complete matter files should not be maintained past their regular retention periods merely because they may contain potentially useful reference documents, nor, if this is actually the case, should the only copy be sent off-site. *If it is not indexed and quickly available, it has no real value.* Retrieving a reference document from a case file, or worse, from a case file in off-site storage wastes time and money in the form of retrieval and refile fees, and both time and money in the form of staff time spent in box handling, all of which may be entirely wasted if the object in question cannot be located because it was not properly indexed in the first place.

A better approach is to identify, capture, and organize these documents in some sort of repository, traditionally known as a reference library or brief bank. Today, knowledge management applications are available for just this purpose, and if you do not feel like buying one (or can't afford it) you can create your own. Placed in a central repository with suitable indexing, keywords, and other finding aids, the contents of such a collection is a powerful tool, far more so than the uncontrolled and unindexed collection of individual items could ever be when spread throughout the organization.

Drafts

Defining an appropriate retention policy for drafts constitutes a vexing problem for many organizations, and none more so than law firms: many legal documents go through an extensive draft and revision process, and those drafts are the tangible evidence of the evolution of an analytical process that may be of considerable importance. On the other hand, many documents subject to multiple draft processes are commonly integrated documents such as contracts, and as such, the analytical process may have little legal significance. By the same token, drafts may manifest different strategies considered but not presented to the client since they may have been annotated with references to which the client, for confidentiality reasons, should not be privy and so should not be retained long term.

As a general rule, drafts are not subject to specific legal requirements as to their retention. However, there are possible exceptions to be aware of:

- A draft published to a client ceases to be a mere draft, and falls under the rubric of "client communication," which may have a specific requirement and which the client may have maintained anyway.
- Drafts created in the context of some heavily regulated areas such as securities may fall within the scope of a subject-specific regulatory scheme and may have value showing the evolution of a concept or piece of legislation.

Outside of exceptions of this sort, the key with drafts is to be consistent in how you handle them. Develop rules and follow them. Problems in this area do not typically come from having either a drafts or no drafts retention policy, but rather from having retained some drafts but not others, and having done so with no explanation of why. The best approach is to make a reasoned decision based upon business need as to whether retention of drafts after finalization of a document is necessary to serve the client and the firm. The decision need not be the same for every record series or every matter type, only rationally made based upon legitimate business considerations. Thereafter, this decision should be implemented as consistently as possible.

Chron Files

Chronological files are a response to systems that do not work and they generally have, at best, only a very short-term value. They generally contain a copy of everything that someone receives and sends in a pure chronological order, with the retrieval theory being, *"If I can remember about when it happened then maybe I can find the document."* The flaws here are numerous:

- Everything depends on memory;
- Nothing is grouped topically;
- Pulling together a collection by matter is nearly impossible; and
- No considerations are made for client documents.

Unless you deal only with one matter or issue—make that one *small* matter or issue—a chron file is a recipe for a mistake. And filing old chron files off-site, identified only by the name of the creator and the date range they cover, creates risk for the firm and the client and imposes a huge administrative burden should they ever have to be accessed as the only copy of a record.

Implementation and Deployment

We talked earlier about problems with inventories and how they should—or should not—be approached. Some of the same considerations apply to implementation and deployment of records retention schedules.

Implementation must be designed to accommodate two different sets of information, the current collections (this is your legacy collection) and those that include records that have yet to reach the inactive or closed stages (this is your day-forward collection). Some of the procedures you develop for handling the legacy collection will be easily converted to use in managing the day-forward collection.

Implementation against both legacy and day-forward collections occurs in two media worlds, the hard copy and the electronic. Neither one is a walk in the park, but the physical mess involved with getting the hard-copy records into shape sometimes presents more of a challenge. The goal of our hard copy implementation is a clear and simple one: get rid of old stuff that the firm no longer needs, and install a process for having this happen on an ongoing and regular basis. To make the task manageable, the implementation process should be broken down into all of the detailed tasks that must be accomplished. Among the issues to be considered are:

- If inactive and boxed records are poorly sorted, labeled, and indexed, part of the process will be to put them in some reasonable order so as to be able to identify candidates for destruction. In worst-case scenarios, this could mean pulling the box, opening the top, and identifying the contents. The firm will also need to develop procedures to prevent a recurrence of this situation in the future.
- If active filing systems are poor or nonexistent, it may be necessary to develop and implement a filing system, both to identify current candidates for destruction and to ensure future viability and efficiency of the program. There are no magic boxes to put your records through that will cure the ills of a really bad program. However, any order at all to the files and supporting information will be a help in determining what needs to be done.

- ◆ If the firm possesses significant repositories of substantive electronic data, and it likely will in today's world, it may be necessary to acquire and install software or other technology tools to track and manage electronic data and purge it when appropriate. Most commonly this is records management (RM) software that facilitates automatic retention and disposition of documents according to your retention schedule. Good RM software integrates nicely with electronic document management (EDM) software.
- ◆ Trying to implement retention schedules against legacy collections using the spare time of existing staff is a doomed concept, so budget accordingly using appropriate resources.
- ◆ Staff may require significant training in policies and procedures, technology usage, and other matters, or the program will fail for want of consistent implementation by them.

These and other tasks that go into designing the implementation process, and the order in which they should be addressed, depend on many things, including budget, availability of internal staff resources, political considerations within the firm, and other factors. Within the overall plan, however, some items will necessarily be priorities, and others will be necessary prerequisites to key tasks.

For example, one of the key tasks that must be completed prior to notifying a client that records on closed matters are due for disposition, it is necessary to have a profile that shows matter type, matter number, or other case identifiers along with the firm-assigned date of final closure of the matter. If these data are not in hand, you are well advised to delay further action until you do have them.

Once the records retention program is sufficiently developed to permit actual implementation, and the firm is ready to begin the process of reviewing and preparing for the destruction of physical files and the purging of electronic data, a plan and processes supporting all of these issues must be drafted. Portions of this process are conceptually, like much of the rest of a records management program, quite simple: for every type of record, an expiration date has been established. Bearing in mind a few caveats, all that is necessary is to throw out or delete everything that has passed its expiration date. The question is how to move forward with the process.

Making this happen requires the application of sound principles in an orderly fashion to our implementation process.

- ◆ *Process and procedure.* Like the rest of the records management program, implementation of the retention schedule requires rules of the road for proceeding in an orderly, consistent, and ethics-compliant manner. Document your processes thoroughly, and then test and validate each step. Many of the actual procedures for handling hard copy and electronic collections, both legacy and day-forward, will be different, but similarities will abound.

◆ *Actual disposition.* When all else is said and done, records and information will actually be destroyed or otherwise dealt with. Make sure your rules and processes are clear about which destruction processes apply to which types of records.

◆ *Education and training.* Good rules are useless if the people charged with carrying them out do not know that they exist or have never been trained in their use.

Operating Procedures

The need for sound process and procedural documentation first manifested itself when we were in the drafting stage of creating our records retention schedule. Although some claim that it is possible to have an orderly and consistent process without written procedures, try explaining to the judge why you never documented your procedures for disposing of sensitive documents. Other reasons argue as well for writing it down—staff turnover and differing personal interpretations of how to handle a specific process are just two reasons. Think of trying to train someone in an important task without any written procedures.

Procedures cover a wide variety of topics. Generally, they address (a) the process of immediate implementation and (b) the structure of ongoing day-to-day operations. Since the goal of records management procedures is to ensure orderly cradle-to-grave life cycle management for records and information, procedures dealing with the records retention and disposition portion of the records management program facilitate the process by ensuring that records and other data objects are

◆ *Identified* in a manner that permits their accurate identification as candidates for destruction or other disposition as identified on the record retention schedule;

◆ *Dated* with sufficient accuracy to permit the disposition of records that have reached the expiration of their retention period;

◆ *Segregated,* physically in the case of paper records and discrete electronic media objects, and logically in the case of pure electronic data objects, to ensure that objects due for destruction can be separated and disposed of without undue effort or cost; and

◆ *Disposed of* in a legally compliant and ethical manner.

Good controls and processes will have implications throughout the entire records management life cycle, not just at the disposition stage. For example, although identification of records by record series is a necessary part of a records retention program, at least the same level of detail will be required for the organization of records within a file plan and filing scheme. In a similar manner, techniques such as file naming conventions or standard directory structures for electronic data are necessary elements of both the active-file management process and the records retention and disposition processes. In both examples, a well-thought-out scheme for identifying and describing hard copy and digital records will serve the firm's needs—it provides double value for the creative effort expended. The following are basics for implementation of any records retention program:

- *File plans, indices, and other finding tools.* If you cannot find it—or identify it—you are not going to know what to do with it. Records that are not organized and indexed cannot be managed properly, which in turn means that a viable records retention program is not possible. An organization-wide file plan that is imbedded in, or is keyed to, the structure for the records retention schedule is a must for all records—paper, electronic, or microform.
- *Box packing and labeling procedures.* Most paper records go to inactive storage prior to ultimate disposition at the end of their life cycle. One of the great impediments to a properly functioning hardcopy records retention program—and one of the easiest to avoid— is boxes of records so poorly labeled as to make the identification of their contents possible only through opening the boxes and examining their contents. When this happens (and it happens *very* frequently), disposition is more difficult, time-consuming, and costly, frequently grinding to a halt. The solution is critical yet simple, and so is the procedure: whenever possible, a box must contain only a single type of record, or case, keyed to the records retention schedule. If the records are administrative in nature, they should be from a single, discrete date range, and must be labeled with this information in standard terminology at a standard location on the exterior of the box. And, whatever tool is used to track boxes—logbook, spreadsheet, database, or the most highly functional contemporary RM software available to law offices today—it must contain and present this box and file-level indexing information clearly.
- *Media labeling conventions.* Most organizations of any size find themselves in possession of a good many mystery computer tapes, discs, or even servers with little or no usable information available about their contents and perhaps no software available with which to read them. Because the contents cannot be identified, and the

original database from which they were derived, the original application, and even the operating system on which the old software ran may remain unknown, this information may remain archived or in storage for years or even decades. This is the electronic version of the box packing and labeling issue (It is also known as the *"Let's just save the hard drive"* approach to electronic record retention.) While dealing with the backlog requires some special procedures, on a going-forward basis, the problem is as completely avoidable as is the mystery box problem. The solution is a segregation and labeling process much like the box packing procedure discussed previously: the same issues present themselves, and the same solutions are required. The only differences are the medium of the records and the shapes of the containers.

◆ *Destruction and disposition procedures.* For information in all media, having identified records that qualify as candidates for destruction, those records must then be dealt with. At a minimum, this means a procedure for ensuring that destruction occurs in a regular systematic fashion (on a regular time schedule, according to a defined process, and with suitable documentation). For records containing sensitive or confidential information, procedures will be required for ensuring confidential destruction.

◆ *Hold procedures.* If any member or employee of the firm becomes aware of an audit, claim, investigation, pending litigation, or other circumstance giving rise to a duty to preserve records and information, that awareness must be communicated to the appropriate parties—general counsel, risk managers, or others so designated—in the firm. Those parties must then notify records management personnel, and all must work to identify, segregate, and preserve the records and information identified as germane until either the issue is resolved or further investigation has narrowed the scope of the inquiry and eliminated the need for a hold on some or all of the records. Failure to properly execute what is generally called a "legal hold" can result in severe penalties,[8] so the procedures for accomplishing this must be clear and thorough, and must be effectively communicated to everyone in the firm.

◆ *Client notification procedures.* Matter files may require client notification prior to destruction. This will require procedures for notifying clients and ex-clients that matter files are due for disposition, recording responses and nonresponses, and dealing with any requests for preservation or special handling that may be received in response.

Notes

1. *See, e.g.,* Mississippi Ethics Opinion 98 (1984); New Hampshire Ethics Committee Advisory Opinion #1986-87/3(1987); South Carolina Ethics Opinion 86-23 (1986).

2. Michigan Ethics Opinion R-5 (1989).

3. *See, e.g.,* Michigan Ethics Opinion R-5 (1989); Mississippi Ethics Opinion 98 (1984); Nebraska Ethics Opinion 88-3 (1988); New York Ethics Opinion 623 (1991); Utah Ethics Opinion 96-02 (1996).

4. *See, e.g.,* Zubulake v. U.S.B. Warburg, 2 Civ. 1243 (S.D.N.Y., filed 2002).

5. Stephens, David, CRM. "Making Records Retention Decisions: Practical and Theoretical Considerations," Records Management Quarterly, Association of Records Managers and Administrators, January 1988.

6. *See, e.g.,* Carlucci v. Piper Aircraft, Corp. 102 F.R.D. 472 (S.D. Fla. 1984).

7. *See, e.g.,* Moore v. General Motors Corp., 558 S.W.2d 720 (1977); Vick v. Texas Employment Commission, 514 F.2d 734 (5th Cir. 1975).

8. *See, e.g.,* Zubulake v. U.S.B. Warburg, 2 Civ. 1243 (S.D.N.Y., filed 2002), (Opinion and Order of October 22, 2003).

Records Retention and Disposition

5

Introduction

As we will see, records disposition can mean different things in different circumstances. Whether we are dealing with dumping, transferring, shredding, recycling, or longer term preservation of selected portions of a file, circumstances drive the action. And, as usual, there are exceptions.

Case Files

All records have a lifetime and almost all will be disposed of within a defined period of time, following some event, as defined in the retention schedule. Destruction, however, is not the only method of disposition, particularly when we are dealing with matter files. Consider the following situations involving client files:

- ◆ Matter or case files, while held by the firm, do not really belong to the firm according to the majority opinion. This means that when the firm no longer has a need for the file, it must be offered back to the client. How do you manage that process? And what do you do if they actually want the file back?
- ◆ There will be occasional circumstances when the client decides to change representation before a matter is resolved. Another counsel, as directed by the client,

now gets the file. What controls do you have in place to manage this process? Which records do you send and which do you keep? And how do you minimize risk during the transition process?

♦ Sometimes the court will issue instructions regarding the destruction of some or all of the files involved in a piece of work. Sometimes these instructions involve some specific methodology. Are you prepared?

Administrative Records

If administrative records have been accurately identified by record series and date range, disposition of them is a relatively straightforward process. If records management software has been deployed, it can be used to generate a report identifying individual items due for destruction. Remember that these could be records in any medium: hard-copy files, boxes, tapes or discs, or even electronic records maintained on a server. If records management software is being used to track electronic data objects, they could include word processing files, spreadsheets, database objects, e-mail, Web content, and other electronic objects in addition to hard copy. If records management software is not used, essentially the same information must be tracked manually (not a very fun or easy process) on a record series level. In either case, the result will be a report to the effect that "records belonging to record series XYZ and created on or before date mm/dd/yyyy are now due for destruction."

Many firms find it advantageous to circulate reports to a select group of managers for review and disposition approval. This serves as a reminder that if any of them are aware of an audit, legal dispute, or other matter requiring an exception, this is their opportunity to initiate a legal hold. Contrary to an enduring and deceiving myth subscribed to by some, there is nothing inherently wrong with such a review and sign-off process. However, if the review and sign-off process is not to become a project in and of itself, and impose a serious impediment to the records retention program, the process must be carefully managed. The following are two of the major issues to consider when designing a review and disposition process:

♦ Requiring universal approval is a bad idea. Requiring an affirmative sign-off from everyone in management, or everyone involved with the files means that each of them holds veto power over the entire list. While initially this may seem like a good idea (Hey, let's spread the risk!), there are many reasons why the sign-offs may not occur. Political maneuvering, a personal dislike of the idea of destroying records, misplaced fear of the consequences, or just plain not getting around to reviewing the list are among the many reasons that the list may sit around indefinitely waiting for sign-offs that never come. A targeted approval procedure is generally a better and more productive approach since it places an affirmative duty upon a few designated and knowledgeable reviewers to act on the firm's behalf.

◆ Properly managing exceptions is important, but exceptions should only be permitted for specified or approved reasons, and should only apply to specific records in categories as narrowly drawn as possible for a specified period of time. In the absence of a legitimate and approved (and, of course, documented) exception, destruction is essentially an all-or-nothing proposition. Indefinite, enterprise-wide holds have a high administrative overhead, come with an increasing cost burden, and generally slow down the entire process. Ideally, within each record series, the firm should have well-indexed records, the retention periods for which have not expired, and no records at all for which the retention periods have passed. If exceptions for some record series must repeatedly be made, for some consistently recurring reason, something is amiss. Either the series must be broken into smaller series to accommodate the needs of some subset of it, or the period chosen for it is inadequate to accommodate all routine needs.

In centrally controlled hard-copy records systems, disposition should be carried out under the direction of records management personnel. If the system is well organized, it is a relatively simple task to segregate destruction candidates for disposition. If any of the records contain confidential or sensitive information, destruction should be carried out by a means that ensures confidentiality. Bonded and guaranteed destruction is available near most urban areas, and many vendors can bring a mobile shredder on-site and shred the records in your presence. Check with NAID, the National Association for Information Destruction, for a list of vendors in your area.

We encounter an analogous situation when dealing with a centrally controlled electronic records system. Highly functional contemporary records management software (particularly software that has been DoD 5015 certified) offers the capability of true purging and disposition of outdated information, and in a way that prohibits restoration.

Personal Filing Areas

Many paper and electronic documents are created that never get to the records staff. These include short-term records whose retention period is so short that they stay on the desktop their entire life, working files, convenience copies, printed versions of e-mail and attachments, and similar items. Like desk drawers and file cabinets, personal computers contain a lot of undocumented information, including multiple electronic copies of e-mail and attachments. In all but the most tightly controlled environments, this will occur regardless of any prohibition or preventative measures. Absent a disciplined workforce operating in a tightly controlled environment (not present in some law offices), it is usually necessary to conduct some sort of occasional compliance audit to ensure that uncontrolled records do not accrue in active workspaces.

While disposition of official records and original documents should be carried out under close direction of the Records Management Department, there are many other records that are not official—all of the duplicates, convenience copies, and old work files we have mentioned above that practitioners have collected. Left to their own devices and schedules, few lawyers will muster the discipline to get rid of these items. The usual way of managing the disposition of these unofficial records is a periodic "records clean-out day," wherein the records management staff encourages and cajoles lawyers and staff to dispose of old records from their desk, immediate filing area, and computers. Depending upon the culture of the organization, this can be quite an elaborate affair, with receptacles placed in strategic spots, or even wheeled throughout the corridors, and staff encouraged to take a few moments and rid themselves of excess paper and to delete old electronic files.

How effective this process is depends upon two factors:

1. *Staff buy-in.* If personnel are determined to defeat the system, they will figure out a way of doing so. Education and training are critical to making all end-users understand that working around or even avoiding the process hurts the firm.
2. *The degree of organization of information in the office and on the individual's computer.* The more success the records management initiative has had in bringing some semblance of order into personal filing areas and computer directories, the more effectively staff and lawyers will be able to utilize the small amount of time devoted to cleaning out old paper and electronic files.

Growth and change are facts of life in all records systems. As soon as a record clean-out is completed, additional records begin to accumulate, so the clean-out process must be a regular and expected part of the routine of every office. In organizations where this is attended to on a regular basis, it becomes habit. Lots of free pizza and sandwiches have been known to make the process moderately more attractive. Under no circumstances should "special" or out-of-sequence clean-out days be advocated, nor should any direction be given to pay particular attention to any set of records during clean-out activities.[1] As with other record retention activities, desk clean-outs should be incorporated into these regularly scheduled, normal-course-of-business processes.

Dealing with Mystery Boxes

All of the above assumes the organization of information in a way that permits easy and accurate identification of information that is a candidate for destruction. For information created or received after the initial implementation of a records management program, this process should continue on a regular basis. However, the reality is that many organizations and most law firms that have been around for any significant period of time find themselves with large volumes of disorganized and often completely unidentifiable legacy material that is completely unusable. If the records are not identifiable, they are not retrievable and all they really do is take up space and cost money. Once you start identifying these unindexed records, the typical haul will include boxes in off-site storage, computer tapes in off-site storage or vaults, unidentified archived data sets, old computer drives with no real indication of contents, rolls of unlabelled microfilm, and perhaps other items such as file cabinets in the basement, locked but with no key.

These items cannot simply be ignored, nor can they be destroyed immediately and the review of retention rules bypassed. Remember, a significant percentage of all records in any organization is governed by either explicit legal requirements or significant legal considerations such as tax audit considerations or risk management. Many others are needed for other purposes. It cannot be safely assumed that no such records are contained in unidentified or poorly indexed storage containers; just because they are not well identified, that does not mean it is safe to just chuck them. It is a common experience for businesses and law firms to have to cull through hundreds or thousands of such items seeking some record they know to exist but that they cannot locate.

Ideally, all files, hard copy and electronic, will be accurately inventoried as part of program implementation. As a practical matter, if the volume of a given collection is very large, and of any significant age, it may be impractical or prohibitively expensive to review and index all of it retrospectively. This is not to say, however, that these poorly indexed or unidentified records cannot be dealt with.

Triage

The first step is to determine to the extent possible what might be in the container. Several data points might be available to help in this determination:

- Boxes or other containers may be sent to off-site storage by a/an (administrative) department. If so, the name of the sending department gives at least a general indication of the types of records likely to be in them.
- Tapes, cassettes, disks, and other magnetic, audio, or video media may have at least a date on them, and boxes or other containers in

which they reside may well have a date recorded somewhere indicating when they were first sent to storage, at which time they were
presumably inactive.

Precision in assigning retention periods to records and information is
directly related to the level of detailed knowledge available about those
records. The more that is known, the more precisely retention periods can be
assigned and the shorter some of those periods can be. Conversely, the less
that is known, the more conservative the assigned retention periods must be
if we are to avoid the tedious and expensive file-by-file review process.

Triage must be carefully approached. For example, if we know that a
box contains internal accounting reports, our analysis may reveal that
those reports have no ongoing value and can be regenerated from the
accounting system at will. Such records are often listed on the retention
schedule with a short retention period to meet daily business needs, "until
superseded," or "active only." It may therefore be possible to destroy the
box immediately. If we know only that the box contains accounting records
from the year 2000, we must, in the absence of some more accurate indica-
tor, assume that they may be the sort of accounting record that might be
needed to support an open tax audit. In this case, we must assign a retention period based on the assumption of need.

On the other hand, if we know only that the box contains accounting
records and was placed in storage in the year 2000, we must assign the
longest period applicable to accounting records, and calculate a retention
period based upon the year 2000 date that they were placed in storage, even
though they may have been several years old at that time. If, on the other
hand, we have a full electronic accounting system, and have been scanning
invoices, receipts, and other paper items for the full period of our open tax
liability, it may be possible to conclude that all such boxes of accounting
records are either duplicates or unneeded, and so can be destroyed.

The worst-case scenario is that we know nothing at all about the contents of the box and have no confidence that the contents are duplicates or
are not needed for legal compliance or other important reasons. In this
case, it is still possible to assign a retention period to the box by assigning
it the longest retention period applicable to any record in the organization
(other than oddities such as partnership agreements and the like, which
may have retention periods equivalent to the life of the organization, but
which are highly unlikely to end up in this situation).

Essentially the same analysis applies to unidentified tapes, computer
servers, and microforms. Whatever information is available, when it is combined with some reasonable assumptions and some knowledge of the firm's
own business processes, will permit the assignment of a retention period to
many records, albeit sometimes a very conservative one.

When it becomes necessary to assign a conservative retention period to some set of items, it is worthwhile to track accession of these items along with the rest of the collection. Documenting the reasons for accession, the nature of the information sought, and the results of the search will, over time, give an indication of the value of the contents, and validate the initial decision about retention or indicate a need for re-evaluation of the retention period.

The first records purge of both departmental and personal filing areas is likely to be a painful proposition, but this should not discourage continued implementation. In most organizations, years of build-up and clutter must be dealt with, and in most cases this first effort can be a bit aggravating. Thereafter, however, things should run much more smoothly. After the first pass, the percentage of older and more disorganized material declines and we are left with a more manageable three- or six-month volume of well-organized records in the office.

Disposition of Matter Files

Matter (or case files or client files) pose issues different from those posed by the administrative records addressed above. The firm owns its administrative records and, subject to any legal requirements and current exception actions, may dispose of them as it pleases, without regard to the needs of any other entity. In contrast, in every U.S. jurisdiction the client or former client has significant property or possessory interest in the matter file, and the lawyer and law firm are under ethical duties to preserve confidences and secrets, and avoid prejudice to the client's interests. *There is no generally accepted definition of "matter file" or "client file" nor is there any law or general rule requiring any particular document to be in it.* Authorities governing matter files are commonly vague or indirect.

This does not mean, however, that matter files must be retained forever. *There is no rule of law in any U.S. jurisdiction requiring indefinite retention of closed matter files by law firms.* Those jurisdictions that have addressed the matter in ethics opinions are universally of the opinion that closed client files may be destroyed after a reasonable period of retention.[2]

"The basic principle is that the attorney may destroy a particular item from a former client's file if he or she has no reason to believe that the item will be reasonably necessary to the client's representation, i.e., that the item is or will be reasonably necessary to the former client to establish a right or a defense to a claim."[3]

Client Involvement

Early discussion with the client about the firm's matter file retention policy has long been recognized as an essential element of a sound retention program:

[L]awyers should encourage clients to participate in the decision-making process involving the ultimate disposition of files assembled for the representation of the client. Client participation may involve offering the file to the client, or reaching an agreement with the client about the disposition of the file after an appropriate retention period. If the client does not want the file, or is unavailable to give directions concerning the file, after reasonable, and perhaps repeated efforts at notice, the lawyer may determine the disposition of the file in a manner that preserves the confidential and secret nature of the details of the lawyer's representation of the client.[4]

Such communication and involvement not only avoids misunderstandings, but may also significantly alter the legal and ethical positions of the parties should a dispute later arise. The firm's matter file retention policy should therefore be communicated to the client in writing as early as possible in the representation. The notification should include:

◆ Notification that the firm has and abides by a records retention policy and supporting schedules that protect the interest of the firm and its clients;

◆ A statement as to the firm's procedures when the file becomes eligible for disposition;

◆ A statement as to the client's rights with respect to possession of the file—should they elect to take possession of it;

◆ A requirement that the client keep the firm informed of their contact information so that the firm may contact them prior to disposition; and

◆ A statement that, in the absence of specific instructions to the contrary from the client, the file will be physically destroyed after the notification.

An engagement letter or other communication addressing these matters will serve the interests of both the client and firm, and will permit the firm to avoid some potentially difficult and costly issues.

Determining Disposition Points for Matter Files

With the exception of any client-owned documents or objects contained therein, retention of closed matter files is not usually the subject of statutory law or court rule. Thus there are no explicit retention periods set forth as substantive requirements, except in rare cases involving specialized matters. Available authority is both helpful and vague:

◆ A few ethics opinions offer explicit retention periods for matter files, and all are quite reasonable.[5] The longest period opined as of this writing is ten years,[6] and this is based upon analysis of statutes of limitation.

◆ Other opinions generally admonish that the lawyer develop retention periods using their sound professional judgment, or some similar formulation involving a "reasonableness" standard.[7] Admonitions to give consideration to statutes of limitation in making a
determination are also common,[8] but in most cases, no indication of
which period (the period governing the substance of the matter, or
the applicable malpractice limitation) should be used is given, nor
any indication of how it is to be added into the mix of factors. This
creates a need to consider the actual period of risk as compared
with the theoretical maximum defined by the applicable statutes.

◆ Laws and rules addressing client-related documents in the context
of records retention may reference a variety of documents, any of
which may or may not be retained in the client file. Such laws and
rules may also be quite vague as to the precise records being regulated. The firm must therefore give consideration to what it actually
places in the matter file and be clear in defining what constitutes an
official record.

◆ Most ethics authorities, including those stating mandatory requirements, are applicable in only a single jurisdiction. A multi-jurisdictional
schedule requires some rationalization that accommodates this.

Statutes of Limitation

Two general categories of limitations periods may affect retention of a client
file—the limitations period for attorney malpractice, and the substantive limitations period for the underlying matter. In the first case, the statute in question might be an explicit malpractice statute. In cases where the jurisdiction
has no malpractice, negligence, or breach of contract statute, or possibly a
catchall general limitations period, depending upon the legal theory advanced
by the plaintiff and the local malpractice jurisprudence, may apply. In the
latter case, it could conceivably be any of a great number of limitations periods, either broad or very specific. In addition to the periods applicable to a
malpractice claim or other dispute arising from the representation, substantive limitations on the underlying matter may also affect the analysis.

Limitations periods over six years are generally (but not entirely) limited to enforcement of judgments, sealed contracts, recovery on bonds, and
suits involving improvements to real property. There are anomalies: Ohio,
for example, has a fifteen-year limitation on contract actions.

A related issue that might affect retention is the tolling of a pertinent
limitations period, or some issue that might arise long after any limitations
may have run, but which nonetheless substantially affects the client's rights
and requires access to the file. There are a few areas where this may be a
concern—habeas corpus appeals in criminal cases, and trusts and estates
work are two obvious examples. For most other representations, however,

the substantive limitations period will likely have commenced running prior to the representation, and will in most cases have fully run prior to the expiration of a seven- to ten-year retention period. The malpractice period, having commenced on the last day of the representation, will similarly have run at the end of the retention period. A similar analysis obtains for other applicable authorities:

- Abandoned property statutes, which may also affect a lawyer's duty with respect to maintenance of a file or its contents, also generally run under seven years nationally, particularly for abandoned property that is not some form of cash equivalent.
- Requirements for maintenance of client trust fund records under Professional Rule 1.15 range from five to seven years.

In any event, providing for a final review prior to disposition at the end of the retention period—several years after the close of the representation—offers an additional check to ensure that the matter is truly dead prior to destruction of the file.

Client File Retention Periods

Both ethics rules and ethics authorities admonish universally that the attorney must protect client confidences and secrets. Ethics opinions make clear that this duty attaches to management of the client file. Privilege attaches only to attorney work product and attorney-client communication, leaving a great deal of material in the file subject to discovery and other legal process.

The clients themselves may and increasingly do have and follow a records retention and disposition program, and any documents provided to the firm may be subject to that program. If a file contains client-owned original records subject to a client-mandated retention program, the document in that file must be retained for the period required by the client. This could require extensive discussions with the client to ensure that each party's responsibilities regarding this are clearly understood. Frankly, such discussions are unlikely to happen up front since both parties are far more concerned with addressing the legal issues at hand than talking about records retention. In the absence of such a discussion, the firm may find itself with an inadvertently acquired duty of retention, and may be unaware of the time frames that apply from the client side. If the firm's matter file retention period is longer than the client's retention period for those records, the firm may be exposed to malpractice or disciplinary liability for retaining the records too long.[9] In this case, a shorter retention period, based upon consultation with the client, is better. To avoid cumbersome and inconvenient discussions about which documents are to be retained and for how long, it may be more appropriate to include and emphasize text in the engagement letter, and in the follow-on correspondence relating to the matter of disposition, that goes to the issue of the firm's policy of offering closed files back to the client when the firm's retention period has expired.

Document-Specific Retention Periods

If a file contains other documents subject to topic-specific legal requirements, these must be identified and dealt with on a case-by-case basis. While there are relatively few document types that are subject to topic-specific legal requirements, examples of such documents are retainer and compensation agreements and client trust fund records.[10]

Other Considerations

If a file contains material of longer term legal significance, those significant documents should be maintained for an appropriate period of time that may extend beyond representation on a specific matter and even beyond the point where the firm has any relationship with the client. Specific examples of such documents include original wills and trusts, stock certificates, and the like.[11] Again, a workable strategy for avoiding the overhead associated with such long-term maintenance after termination of a client relationship is to offer the documents back to the owner.

Procedures for Accommodating All Considerations

This plethora of requirements and considerations requires the development of carefully crafted and well-implemented procedures. Those procedures can accommodate all current requirements in virtually every situation if the following points are observed:[12]

- ◆ The fact that the firm has and follows a records retention policy should be communicated to the client, in writing, early in the relationship.
- ◆ Originals of client-owned documents should be returned to the client promptly at the end of representation.
- ◆ The remainder of the file should be maintained in clean form by the firm for such period necessary to support the firm should questions about representation arise. Following this period, and absent any compelling reason for continued in-house maintenance, the file may then be considered for disposition.
- ◆ As part of the disposition process, a final review should be conducted to ensure that any documents that could be needed by the client are provided to them.
- ◆ Again, as part of the disposition process, and prior to destruction of the file, the client should be contacted, in writing, and given the

opportunity to (a) take possession of the file or (b) give the lawyer further directions with respect to it.

◆ If after repeated efforts the client cannot be contacted, or if the client has no further interest in the file, and so indicates in writing, the file may then be destroyed.

◆ The obvious exceptions apply to this strategy. If any documents are subject to independent legal requirements, these must be retained for the term set forth in that requirement. If the court has ordered a specific environment or level of security for maintenance of files, or a specific type of disposition, those instructions must be complied with as well.

As a practical administrative matter, it may prove easiest and most cost-effective to identify and deal with exceptions during representation. Some aspects will require only minor procedural changes, with little or no additional effort. Many problems can be avoided by establishing procedures for ongoing program functionality. For example, instituting a policy of segregating all originals that belong to other parties, including the client, and using copies (hard copy or digital) for daily work makes management and disposition far easier with almost no original investment. Instituting a policy of keeping no original client-owned documents or executed original documents in the regular client file, using working duplicates unless an original must be produced, and consistently sending clients copies of all relevant pleadings and other documents in a timely manner during the course of the representation will significantly reduce the amount of labor required at file closing or file disposition to ensure compliance with ethics requirements.

Other processes, such as segregating reference material, or culling duplicates and other extraneous material (to reduce the volume sent to storage) does require a modest amount of additional work, but it pays off in the end since to the extent that this work is accomplished in the normal course of handling the hard-copy and digital file during representation, the associated overhead is far lower and accessibility to and utility of the documents during active representation is greatly improved—and all of this is in addition to the lower cost of handling and managing the file after representation is complete. As with all files, the cost of retrieving and examining poorly identified records to examine their contents and define appropriate disposition on a case-by-case basis will prove a considerable drag on any records retention program.

Electronic Records and the Matter File

The destruction of a matter file extends to any electronic data of which it is a part. So too does the duty to provide it to the client if they ask for it. For a discussion of which, see the section on "Ownership and Possession of the

Matter File" in Chapter 3. Most clients and ex-clients have no interest in obtaining the matter file well after conclusion of the representation when the firm's retention requirements have been satisfied. Most, but not all. This need must be anticipated and planned for in all aspects of the records management program. It is particularly important in today's digital world that when developing your program you include all records in all media and make sure that the technology tools you have in play are properly integrated and provide collective, matter-centric control over document management repositories, other content collections, and e-mail, all of which are subject to the same retention rules. Remember that content, not medium, is king.

This means that the records management software (more about RM software later) a firm selects and deploys must be able to segregate or flag client-related data, and that indices and other metadata attached to electronic objects adequately identify client- or matter-related data.

The Vanished Client

Many law firms and lawyers that have been around for any extended period of time find themselves in possession of client-owned documents that are years—often decades—old, but which cannot be purged because the client cannot be located and the firm and client did not agree on any policy or practice regarding records retention.

The inability to locate the client may result from any number of situations:

- The client died and the firm does not know it—not uncommon in estates and trust work or other individual representation.
- Bankruptcy or closing of the business—the client may have gone out of business for any number of reasons and failed to inform former counsel.
- The client's name changed, not an uncommon practice in these times of corporate rebranding.
- Merger or acquisition—the client may have been acquired by another entity.

This dilemma could be resolved if at some specific point in time the file could be deemed abandoned by the client. At least one ethics authority has seized upon this and opined that when the client cannot be located, the file must be retained until it is presumed as a matter of law to have been abandoned.[13] The question then becomes, "When is a file presumed abandoned?"

Under common law, property is not presumed abandoned by the mere passage of time; rather, its owner must commit some act that constitutes an act of abandonment, or forego exercise of some duty that would demonstrate intent to retain the property.

Abandonment in law depends upon the occurrence of two, and only two, factors; one, an intent to abandon or relinquish; and two, some overt act, or some failure to act, which carries the implication that the owner neither claims nor retains any interest in the subject matter of the abandonment.[14]

Whether an act is sufficient to demonstrate abandonment must be based upon the totality of facts and circumstances of the case. Acts typically cited in decided cases are failure to pay required storage fees, and failure to retrieve property by some contractually agreed upon time. Mere passage of time is, however, not enough by itself to constitute abandonment.

> It is a universally accepted principle that mere nonuse of property over a period of time when unaccompanied by any other acts indicating an intention to abandon title thereto or ownership thereof, does not amount to an abandonment.[15]

When viewed in the context of client files, this is an important consideration. Ethics decisions make clear that client expectations are an important consideration in file retention and disposition. If, through lack of communication or otherwise, a client reasonably (or even unreasonably) assumes the attorney is maintaining the file for him for some period of time, common law provides no obvious relief from the burdens of that assumption. Communication of a retention policy to the client and placing them under an affirmative duty to maintain current contact information with the firm will serve to avoid the property-is-never-presumed-abandoned dilemma.

If the firm possesses old matter files from representations for vanished clients to whom it has not communicated a retention policy, it may find itself with a problem. Clients often mistakenly assume that their lawyer is retaining a copy of everything in their file indefinitely. Further, contrary to a popularly held notion, there is no "historical records" exception to the client-owed duty; thus the firm cannot pass off any duty of retention onto the local historical society. Doing so would violate the requirement to preserve confidences and secrets. If the file contains original client-owned documents, the situation is further aggravated. *There is no authority whatsoever for the proposition that client-owned items may be destroyed for any reason without permission.*

However, although the common law provides no default period after which property is deemed abandoned, it does provide for the determination of a period after which passage of time may be viewed as evidence of abandonment of property:

> Time is "not an essential element" of abandonment, although the lapse of time may be evidence of an intention to abandon, and where it is accompanied by acts manifesting such an intention it may be considered in determining whether or not there has been an abandonment. Nor is mere

nonuse evidence of abandonment unless it continues for the statutory period of limitations within which to recover the right or property.[16]

Thus, under the common law, failure to exercise rights in property for duration of the limitations period within which the property could be recovered constitutes evidence of abandonment. In the case of a client file, this serves to place a limitation on the period during which a client may assume the attorney is holding the file, without communicating that assumption, or specific instructions, to the attorney. One state has codified this as a rule, providing that a matter file is presumed abandoned by the client if they have not requested possession of it after ten years. This is, however, apparently the only such relief available as of this writing.

The firm that finds itself in this situation may have little choice other than to retain the matter files in question for an extended period of time unless specific and conscientious efforts have been made to contact the client. At a minimum, the following should be done prior to destruction of any such file:

- ◆ The client should be contacted in writing at their last known address by registered mail, return receipt requested. If the letter is returned, it should be retained as evidence of the attempt.
- ◆ The effort to identify and contact the client, if the first contact failed, should include documented research to determine what happened to the client and when. Law librarians are fantastic resources in this task.
- ◆ The file must be examined to ensure that no client-owned documents are in it. If there are, these must be segregated and preserved.

Depending upon the particular circumstances, more may be required. As with mystery boxes of administrative files, it may be useful to track any accessions to these files and the reasons for them. In addition to providing useful feedback on retention periods, tracking will serve as evidence of the firm's attempts to reasonably protect the interests of the client.

Only after reasonable and well-documented efforts to locate the client and obtain permission to destroy a file can the firm proceed with disposition and, even then, the disposition must be done in a way that preserves confidentiality.

Notes

1. *See, e.g.,* United States v. Quatrone, 03 - 822 (S.D. N.Y. 2003); and United States v. Duncan, Crim. Action H-02-0121(S.Dist. TX 2002), both cases in which out-of-the-ordinary memoranda urging staff to dispose of old records were characterized as veiled instructions to destroy evidence of wrongdoing.

2. *See, e.g.,* American Bar Association Informal Opinion 1387; Virginia LEO 1690. *See also* Alaska Ethics Opinion 95-6 (1995); Maine Ethics Opinion 74 (1986); Michigan Ethics Opinion R-5 (1989); Nebraska Ethics Opinion 88-3 (1988); New York Ethics Opinion 623; Nevada Formal Opinion 28 (2002); New Hampshire Ethics Committee Advisory Opinion 1986-87/3 (1986).

3. California Ethics Opinion 2001-157.

4. Michigan Ethics Opinion R-5 (1989).

5. *See e.g.,* Arizona Ethics Opinion 91-01, five years; South Carolina Ethics Opinion 92-18, six years; Michigan Ethics Opinion R-12, five years; Iowa Ethics Opinion 91-20, five years; Illinois Ethics Opinion 94-19, five years; Florida Ethics Opinion TEO 82507 (1982), six years.

6. *See* West Virginia L.E.I. 2001-1 (2001).

7. *See, e.g.,* Alabama Ethics Opinion RO-10; California Ethics Opinion 2001-157 (2001); Florida Ethics Opinion 81-8 (1981); New York Ethics Opinion 623 (1991) ("Ultimately, the disposition of closed files is a matter which will come to rest on the sound judgment of counsel.").

8. *See* New York Ethics Opinion 460 (1977); Utah Ethics Opinion 96-02 (1996).

9. *See, e.g.,* Alaska Ethics Opinion 84-9 (1984); Michigan Ethics Opinion R-5 (1989); New York Ethics Opinion 623 (1991); West Virginia Ethics Opinion L.E.I. 2002-1 (2001).

10. *See, e.g.,* ABA Informal Opinion 1384 (1977); Michigan Ethics Opinion R-12 (1991); Mississippi Ethics Opinion 98 (1984).

11. *See, e.g.,* Michigan Ethics Opinion R-12 (1991); West Virginia Ethics Opinion L.E.I. 2002-1 (2002).

12. *See* Arizona Ethics Opinion 98-07 (1998); California Formal Opinion 2001-157 (2001); Florida Bar Staff Opinion TEO 82507 (1982); Michigan Ethics Opinion R-5 (1989); Nebraska Ethics Opinion 88-3 (1988); New York Ethics Opinion 623 (1991); Nevada Formal Opinion 28 (2992); New Hampshire Ethics Opinion 1986-87-3 (1986); South Carolina Ethics Opinion 86-23 (1986); Utah Ethics Opinion 96-2 (1996).

13. *See* Arizona Ethics Opinion 98-07.

14. 1 C.J.S. Abandonment, 8.

15. 1 C.J.S. Abandonment, 10.

16. 9 C.J.S. Abandonment, 16.

Indexing

6

Introduction

Indexing is all about the file: What information about the file should be kept and how should that information be maintained to facilitate location and retrieval of the file and its contents? The indexing, taxonomy, and file structure discussed earlier, or any other structure, is merely a logical architecture built on a meaningful taxonomy so we can have an ordered set of place-holders for our information objects—it is a rule set to make things easier.

To make things a bit easier, let us assume that when we are talking about indexing we are talking about classification, cate-gorization, listing, naming—all of those descriptive activities that put titles to all of our records in all media, because index-ing does not apply to paper records only. As with hard copy, any useful electronic records system will require a well-thought-out indexing system if its contents are to be effectively managed and used. The principles for indexing paper and electronic records are similar, for a simple reason: there is no real distinc-tion in utility between the contents of paper and electronic information objects. For all purposes—matter management, billing and accounting, reference, research, and legal and ethics compliance—the contents of a document maintained in the two formats have equal value and should be treated the same. The difference is the ability to attach (and use) more and different descriptors to electronic documents—a process known as pro-filing when using document management software—and to retrieve those documents based on those descriptors.

Since the majority of law offices today include some users who are paper-centric and others who are techno-centric, we need a unified and consistent paper and electronic indexing scheme to serve both. Information about the acquisition and management of work done for clients, matter identification, and management data, once entirely recorded on paper, is now a combination of paper and electronic information captured in e-mail, spreadsheets, databases, word processing documents, workflow, and other electronic repositories. Since the client file is a unified whole, and is managed in the context of an enterprise-wide system, any indexing scheme must necessarily apply to all of it, with a single set of common rules that cross all aspects including intake, conflicts checking, marketing, records management, accounting, and billing, with the indexing system developed in consideration of electronic information objects as well as paper. In digital format a record, collection of records, or description may be called something else—a data structure, taxonomy, or a lookup table, but if the dataset is searchable by category and title, it's still an index.

If the firm is contemplating the use of records management or document management software (a really good idea these days), development of a sound index is a critical part of the implementation process. Contrary to what is often believed (or said by the vendors of such tools), neither of these technologies provides out-of-the-box search and retrieval tools and structures without some preparation in the form of, among other things, the development of indexing structures.

Building Indices

The Goal of Indexing

An index is a structured hierarchy of terms developed for the purpose of locating specific objects within a larger collection. An indexing scheme generally applies to a collection of records with something in common, and in our case it is client files. The terms or descriptors in the index provide information about the items to which they relate. Each term in the index represents a data point, or type of information, that may be useful to searchers as a way of identifying and retrieving one or more of the records in the collection. If it is not useful, it should not be there.

Hierarchical indexing schemes are built on logic and appeal to the (usually) well-ordered minds of lawyers. Each high-level topic represented by a term contains within it subtopics representing more detailed breakdowns. The deeper a searcher drills into the levels of the index or hierarchy, the more granular the topic. Our goal, as stated earlier, is to provide searchers with a logical and ordered decision tree, with intuitive and meaningful decision points at every topic and subtopic level that will quickly and logically lead them to the information they seek.

Potentially, any collection of items can be indexed in any number of different ways, as can any item within it. The choice of topics and terms, and the assignment of those terms to files or records, determines if your index is useful or not, and it cannot be assumed that any single indexing scheme will work equally well in every organization.

We need to define rules about what the index will be used for, what kinds of queries will be posed, what terms are responsive to the queries and so helpful to the users, and what decision path is most efficient and accurate in getting to an answer. The file structure or file plan discussed earlier is a type of index, as is the listing of document types embodied in the records retention schedule discussed in this book, and each is designed to suit a particular purpose. If other data about records, such as date of creation, author, or location, are captured in a manner that permits suitable organization, without incurring heavy administrative overhead, they will add to the value of the indices.

Creating Indices That Work

Let us consider two types of queries structured for identification and retrieval of records: queries designed to find a specific file or document (where are our current training and policy manuals?) and those queries intended to identify a large pool of records with one or more unifying attributes (as in a discovery response). While those two queries would be structured very differently, depending on the circumstances, it might be appropriate for records identified in the first query to also surface as a result of the second query.

This illustrates a key point, that an index that makes for an efficient query for one type of record may be of limited or no use for another kind, for any of several reasons: the terms may not be responsive to the needs of the requestor or the terms that work for one category may be meaningless for another. This is frequently the case when searching administrative records. Indexing systems keyed to common business records collections, if they are too generic, are often found lacking when litigation discovery is demanded of them. The discovery queries are simply too dissimilar to business-related queries to permit the index to be of much help. Indexing rules for administrative records should be created based on the specific collections of records and how they are most likely to be retrieved.

The kinds of queries that will likely be made of the system must therefore be carefully considered when designing it, or separate and parallel indexing structures may have to be created or maintained to meet different purposes. Many records management software vendors have improved the functionality of their products to the point that they can capture, and permit retrieval of, a wide variety of information about a record in addition to generic indexing terms, and this in addition to saving previous queries for modification and reuse. This added functionality is on top of the normal indexing terms such as date, author, and so on, and includes that which legal personnel have become familiar with when using tools such as WestLaw, Lexis/Nexis, and other research tools—Boolean logic, proximity searching, Soundex, synonyms, and keywords make it easier for the experienced user without getting in the way of the occasional user.

Search results using these tools can create parallel indices that can be chained together or filtered through each other. These additional indices share one key quality with a formal index: if the information they contain is of poor quality or is irrelevant, they will be of limited or no use to a searcher. Regardless of the strength of functionality provided by the most sophisticated software available today, some truths remain constant:

- Absent training and practice, searching will likely yield less than optimal results, and
- *Garbage in* still results in *garbage out.*

Since indexing is designed to provide information to the searcher about relevant qualities of the objects sought, it follows that indexing terms ought to be chosen with the goal of providing that information. If the index is to have value, the indexer must understand why people are searching the system, what they are trying to find, and what terms meaningfully relate to the things they are trying to find. It is more common for lawyers to do their own searching today than it was ten years ago, but it is still the practice for the lawyer to pass on instructions to a paralegal, secretary, records specialist, or database manager so that they can execute the search. Searchers commonly seek information objects based upon a number of criteria:

- *Informational content of the object.* "Show me records about perpetual trusts."
- *The class of the object.* "Show me stock certificates."
- *The relationship of the object to other objects.* "Show me records from the *Smith v. Jones* matter."
- *The creator of the object.* "Show me everything created by Jane Doe."
- *The date the object was created or received.* "Show me everything entered into the system between dates xx and yy."

And sometimes the query is based on the intersection of criteria, as in "Show me everything created by Jane Doe about perpetual trusts between 2002 and 2004 that ended up in litigation."

Many other search parameters are used, but in most real-world searches in businesses or law firms, the goal is to find records and information related to specific topics, events, or transactions. Although it would appear self-evident that index terms should relate to and describe such things, people do not always take the logical path—or any path at all that makes sense. Again, absent rules for using tools and creating responsive and usable indices and absent good training of end-users and appropriate follow-up, organizations end up with pseudo-indexing systems that place heavy or exclusive reliance on repeated use of meaningless and valueless indexing terms such as:

- Documents
- E-mail
- Records
- General
- Miscellaneous
- Reports
- Letters
- Binders
- Files
- Information

These are not good descriptive terms. They give no information about content, class, or relationship, and so do nothing to aid retrieval of whatever information they contain. Use of these terms (*This is pretty easy—call everything a document!*) tends to build a false sense of security based upon an assumption that information objects are actually being saved and indexed (*Where, how, and by whom?*) in a fashion that will make them retrievable and usable later on. In fact, using such terms results in large volumes of material that is effectively unindexed and largely unretrievable, and as a result is not usable in the normal course of business. To the extent that any indexing scheme incorporates these or similar terms, the responsiveness of that scheme will be degraded, as will the productivity of any related activities. Silly though it may seem, indexing systems using these and other equally useless terms, especially in document management profiling, are commonplace.

Structure and Terminology of an Index

What should an index look like? Recall that the structure will differ depending on the types of records to which it refers. First, since an index is an ordered hierarchy, it will contain topics, subtopics, sub-subtopics, and so on. There are times when taking an indexing structure to a level that lists every specific document within a hard-copy or electronic filing system may seem valuable, but it is seldom necessary to go to that level of detail in the records management scheme. In fact, the need for document level search and retrieval, beyond the higher level categorization addressed in a records management hierarchy, is very nicely handled by a well-executed EDMS and full text searching. And, in smaller offices where no EDMS is in play, clear categories and meaningful file descriptions within the categories, to which specific folder titles and documents are linked, will generally do the job nicely.

Let us look at an example. In traditional paper indices or their electronic counterparts, a portion of the first-level categories in the Accounting section of a scheme might include the following:

    ACCOUNTING
        Audits
        Cash Flow
        General Ledger
        Payables
        Receivables

The first-level categories in Human Resources might include the following:

    HUMAN RESOURCES
        Benefits
        Compensation
        I-9s
        Personnel files

and so on.

A deeper look might reveal some subcategories for the same two sections:

    ACCOUNTING
        Audits
        Cash Flow
        General Ledger
            Journals
            Ledgers
            Trial Balance
        Payables
        Receivables
            Adjustments
            Billing
            Collections and Aging

    HUMAN RESOURCES
        Benefits
            Benefits Files

> Plan Documentation
> Compensation
> > Bonus Structures
> Schedules
> Surveys
> I-9s
> Personnel Files
> > Administrative
> > Partner Files
> > HRIS Summaries

Remember, these are just a few samples of the terms that will appear in an enterprise-wide administrative records classification scheme.

When the classification scheme is loaded into records management software, the index may be displayed differently, depending on how it is configured, but the conceptual structure remains the same. In each case, the index levels continue down, until at last a terminal level is reached. Past this point the researcher must search through file and document titles until the correct item is found. In the best of the records and document management software products, this process is automated. The obvious question is, *"How many levels and sublevels are enough?"* There are competing tensions that must be balanced, and the balance struck depends upon several factors. Bear in mind that the same structure must meet retention scheduling as well as search and retrieval needs. Content and purpose will drive your strategy; there is no single hard-and-fast rule regarding the best way to create an index.

From the retention schedule management perspective, the fewer levels and categories we have, the better off we are. From the searcher's point of view, the more granular the index, the more precisely she can hone in on the desired information. For purposes of specificity, the searcher would like as detailed an index as possible. On the other hand, navigating through a large, complex, multilevel index (e.g., a West Case Digest or the index to the Code of Federal Regulations) can be confusing, difficult, and time consuming. Most needs are accommodated when depth and complexity are limited to the minimal amounts necessary to optimize searching.

When creating one's own index rather than using a commercial dataset, the question we encounter is, "What is a reasonable time investment when indexing in my own system?" The answer is very straightforward—If you are going to need it, index it in such a way that you and others who have a legitimate right to view the information can find it easily later on. *Do not waste time and effort indexing things for which you are not responsible and that you will not want to retrieve later.*

From the indexer's point of view, it may not be possible to optimize an index for every possible type of query required to meet every need. The index may often be the primary or only means of search and retrieval available. In such a case, it is a starting point for more detailed searches using additional terms for all purposes and all searchers. As a baseline rule, remember that every index and file listing should be machine searchable. When people actually *type* file labels and do not include classification (indexing) terms on those labels and then paste them on folders rather than using the most basic word processing utilities to generate labels, no electronic (and searchable) listing of titles within categories is generated.

Greater complexity requires more design time and increases the likelihood of logic flaws that lead to errors (such as, for example, conflicting or redundant index entries), which may reduce the utility of the index and require substantial time to track down and correct. Quality control in the design and original structuring of a system is a critical and worthy investment—it will make sure that your overall investment pays off. Invest the time and effort you need to get the detail the job demands, but no more.

Finally, once the index is designed, every object to which it relates must be indexed using it. Although in electronic systems this process can to some extent be automated, in most cases this means that a human being must analyze the object, compare it with the index, and choose a suitable slot for it. There are fully automated indexing systems for electronic documents that index by searching only for keywords, but such systems work with acceptable accuracy only with document types that use very specialized and precise terminology, and have lengths sufficient to permit the algorithms used to do sufficient analysis. Use of these systems in other environments has met with consistent failure as of this writing. Every such indexing operation requires time, and the time required for each increases as the complexity of the index increases, as does the likelihood of indexing error. All of this sounds like administrative and user overhead with attendant costs. The good news is that today there are tools available that know which categories you use most frequently and pop up a menu of those categories, making classification and indexing a relatively easy, on-the-fly, point-and-click type of process.

As a practical matter, workable indices more than four levels deep are difficult to develop and are cumbersome for most users to follow and use. This is particularly true if there are many entries within a level, since display limitations may make it difficult to visually browse and scan through the index and even to remember exactly where one is. More than four levels may also cause other display problems: In addition to the levels and terms themselves, the display, whether paper or electronic, must usually also show other information such as location, page number, and so on. Getting everything onto the page or screen at a reasonable type size and in a reasonable format may be problematic. Screens can appear far too busy and users can get lost in the detail. Be careful and exercise restraint; opt for simplicity wherever possible.

Terminology and Clarity

The only non-negotiable requirement for indexing terminology is that it be clear and meaningful to the searchers who will use it, and lead them down the correct decision path. Other considerations, regardless of their theoretical correctness or logical beauty, must yield to utility. If you really want clarity and ease of use, keep these points in mind:

Reading Ease

The eye is drawn to the left-most word in an entry, and scanning of an index normally takes place by reading down the left side of a column of entries. The left-most word of an entry should therefore be the most significant, with remaining words decreasing in significance sequentially thereafter. Unnecessary repetition does not gain anything except clutter, so a structure such as:

> Taxation
> > Taxation—income
> > Taxation—excise
> > Taxation—property

should yield for clarity's sake to:

> Taxation
> > Income
> > Excise
> > Property

Repeating the term *taxation* forces readers to read the entire entry to find a significant term, simultaneously slowing them down and annoying them. Index terms of more than two words should be avoided if possible.

Consistency of Terminology

Use of an index is a collaborative learning process between indexer and user. Regardless of how well-crafted an index may be, there is always a learning curve as users get used to the conventions and assumptions made by the indexer. Consistent use of terminology, and some mechanism for getting feedback from the user community, will minimize the learning curve, speed search times, and make the index more useful. If limitations periods are indexed as "statutes of limitation," they should be so indexed every time. If they are varyingly identified as "SOLs," "statutes of limitation," "limitations of action," "prescription," or something else, not only will the index be longer than necessary, but users will be forced to look in multiple places for a single class of item. Or, they may use a single term, not find what they are seeking, and think the index does not work, when in fact it is just overworked. Once again, users will be both slowed down and annoyed. Remember that in a small office, users may well know who created the problem index and with whom they should be annoyed.

Subject versus Object versus Relationship

It may be tempting to index all collections across an entire records system within a single, consistent conceptual framework, topically, for example. While it may be useful to apply some criteria to all objects, particularly at the most finite level (the document), as a practical matter, this will not likely be the most useful approach. In such cases, beauty and consistency must yield to clarity and practicality. Remember—different indexing schemes for different collections. Thus, *case files* should be grouped by client and matter and then subdivided by issue or document types to which they relate:

> CLIENT 1—ACE CORPORATION
>> Matter 1 XYZ Litigation
>>> Correspondence
>>> Attorney's Notes
>>> Court Papers
>>> Depositions
>>> Transcripts
>> Matter 2 Building Acquisition
>>> Correspondence
>>> Attorney's Notes
>>> Closing Binder
>>> Insurance
>>> Title Search
>
> CLIENT 2—ACME CORPORATION
>> Matter 1 Biggie Corporation Merger
>>> Correspondence
>>> Attorney's Notes
>>> Benefits Plans Analysis
>>> Due Diligence
>>> Executive Compensation
>>> Financials
>>> Players List
>>> Term Sheets
>> Matter 2—etc.

while *administrative files* are indexed functionally as we showed earlier:

ACCOUNTING
    Audits
    Cash Flow
    General Ledger
        Journals
        Ledgers
        Trial Balance
    Payables
    Receivables
        Adjustments
        Billing
        Collections and Aging

and the brief bank is indexed topically:

TRUSTS AND ESTATES
    Perpetual trusts
    Revocable trusts

Note that within a scheme for a particular collection, subtopics may sometimes be indexed in a conceptually different manner than their primary topic. Thus, matter files, indexed by client at the highest level, are sub-indexed by matter, and therein usually by document type—pleadings, client correspondence, and so on.

There may also be occasions when the proper topic-subtopic order is unclear. For example, should it be:

Limitation of actions
    Taxation
        Excise
        Income
        Property

or perhaps:

Taxation
    Limitation of actions
    Excise
    Income
    Property

Each will lead to the proper endpoint, but each makes an assumption about what term users will first search. In some cases this can be resolved by analysis of users' needs, but in many cases, the order will be arbitrary. In such cases, the goal should be to use the same convention every time—wherever possible be consistent in your approach to creating your indexing structure. As with inconsistent terminology, inconsistency here will make the learning curve steeper than need be, and waste users' time as they look in multiple locations and become annoyed with you yet again. Fortunately, as we move more and more toward the use of automated systems with the ability to scan across and through multiple datasets when searching, as long as terms are consistently applied within each collection, the software can usually find all occurrences, and the searcher can merely delete the hits he or she considers nonresponsive.

Planning and Development

Time spent planning an index is a great investment in continuity, consistency, and value. If time or staff resources for developing an index are limited, spend time creating the higher levels of the index and go back later to fill in the details. It is far better to develop the higher levels accurately and completely, and omit the lower levels, than to hurry through a detailed index that will require extensive revision later on. Quite possibly the greatest waste of time is the creation of the index while inventorying the records. It never works well and invariably results in having to reengineer the structure and reindex large portions of the collections later on. Sample, draft, design, refine—and then start matching up the records to the well-thought-out taxonomy.

In an information-intense environment such as a law firm, information accumulates quickly, and once an indexing system is applied against the items in a collection, it is difficult to change that indexing. Substantial changes may require reanalyzing every item in the system, and in the case of physical files, may require physically relabeling and reorganizing them as well. In large-volume indexing projects, this can be a very painful and expensive process.

With a conceptually correct high-level index, additional granularity can be added without disturbing what is already there. But when restructuring a poorly conceived system, everything, physical and digital, must be rehandled if it is to be redone. In cases where reindexing is not possible, or inordinately expensive, it might even be necessary to run dual indices until all records indexed under the old scheme have expired and been disposed of. This is obviously a less than desirable situation. But the most undesirable situation of all is to simply leave the bad system in place and add to it while ignoring records that were indexed before the index was fine-tuned. When this happens, you are just compounding the size of the problem that you will have to deal with later.

When developing an index, it is sometimes possible to start with existing resources. These include sample indices (often available from records management software vendors or handbooks) and standard vocabularies developed by industry groups and others. All of these are worthwhile as starting points, but none should be considered as a substitute for sound internal analysis. Standard or sample indices and vocabularies may or may not be well designed, and even if they are, they may not correspond to the information objects within a system or the way those objects are conceptualized or used in your organization. Use of these samples can save a great deal of time, but remember first, that they are only starting points, and second, that alterations can and should be made if it is going to work in your situation.

In the final analysis, an index is a tool for facilitating the conversation between the indexer and the end-user. The more the two know about each other, and their needs, the better the communication can be and the more useful the end product will be.

Application of the Index to Filing Systems

At some point, our index has been created, and we must apply it to our collection of information—we are actually ready to start matching categories/descriptions with records. When using records management software or some other automated tool, this means loading the index into the computer system as a data structure. The index entries (line items, categories, etc.) are then linked to information objects (files, documents, messages, etc.) as metadata by means of data entry screens, drop-down menus, or similar devices. Querying on a particular index term permits the identification and retrieval of all of the information objects tagged with that particular term. In physical file systems, the analogue of this tagging is labeling, and applying the index entries to slots in a file structure. Even if you are using the most manual of filing systems, make sure that you enter the taxonomy and the file titles into some sort of searchable tool (Excel, Access, even Word tables will do) that creates an updatable, manageable, and searchable master listing. And do not forget, make sure that the applicable indexing terms appear on the label, in a consistent format, along with the title.

Given the volume of objects in some existing systems, organizations sometimes decide to take a selective approach to building their well-indexed collection rather than committing to an extensive and expensive full retrospective conversion. A fairly common approach to this involves creating and indexing all new objects on a day-forward basis in the new system and indexing and saving legacy objects if and as they are retrieved from the old system. This works well in general research collections but not so well in case file collections where the full case file must be managed as an entity. However, it is possible to set some rules about which electronic objects (documents in an EDMS) are included in a conversion to a new taxonomy.

Is Automation Necessary?

For those who say, "We don't need any automation; our old filing system works just fine!" we say, "Welcome back to the Dark Ages!" At some point you are going to find yourself wondering how to manage or even find all of the e-mail and word processing documents that you and others are creating today. But before we leap into automation, a caveat is in order. While it is not possible to effectively and efficiently manage all of the different types of hard-copy and electronic information objects out there today without the use of some automation, it is not a process to be approached without thought.

How Much Will It Cost?

There are several aspects to the cost of acquiring and implementing an automated records management system and we could go into those in excruciating detail. For now, let us list some of these cost items so you can keep them in mind when doing your planning:

1. Software—You either already have it or you are going to have to buy it. If you are in a small office with a modest collection of files and you choose to go low-end and use an existing tool from the Microsoft or Corel suites, such as their word processing, spreadsheet, or database applications, you may have already made the initial purchase.
2. Design—You still have to design the taxonomy and classification structures, and that design takes time and time does cost money and takes people away from their other work.
3. Data Capture—The information must be gathered and prepared for entry into the system.
4. Data Entry—Once you have the system designed and the data ready to go, you must put it into the system.
5. Procedures and Controls—You are going to need document processes for all aspects of the process.
6. Report Development—Who will need reports, what reports will they need, and what will they look like?
7. Training—Those who manage the system will require training, as will those who are going to be using it. Yes, it is true—even the lawyers need to know the basics of how it works and what it does if they are going to benefit from it.

Actually, no matter what tools you choose to employ, you will have to go through a process that requires investment in steps 1 through 7. The beauty of it is that in your organization, while the cost and functionality of the tool you purchase or choose to employ in item 1 (software) may vary widely, regardless of which tool you employ, your investment in items 2 through 7 will be about the same. You cannot avoid doing your homework, and if you try, it will not work well and you will probably have to redo it later.

A number of law office-specific records management, document management, and other software programs on the market have well-developed functionality and to some extent have automated indexing capabilities. The prices on these tools are reasonable for most entities. Many small law offices, though, may not have the resources to build or purchase a sophisticated, automated records indexing system, and must therefore rely on a more manual indexing system built on a simple tool such as a spreadsheet or word processing program. For smaller offices, this is a workable and manageable first step toward a solution. It will not do everything that the fancy software does but, properly designed, and if it is well deployed and managed, it can make for a fairly efficient starter system and a great improvement over nothing at all.

Using any of these basic tools does not impose an insurmountable barrier to development of a sound indexing system. Again, use of any tool without a decent indexing system may cause more problems than it solves. Within certain parameters, manual and semi-automated systems can be very effective, and may take many forms. Successful use of a manual system does, however, imply certain assumptions:

- *Procedures*—Established and accepted procedures for maintaining the system are an essential element of a program that will provide consistency in the structure of information, integrity in the maintenance of the index, and accessibility to the users. In largely manual systems, procedures play a greater role in maintaining integrity and result in more overhead on the part of users—they are expected to do a bit more to make the system work right. Automated and manual systems alike require policies and procedures. One of the major benefits of using well-designed and more specialized records software is that execution of the procedures can be largely built into the system (as, for example, by requiring that certain fields be filled out, or that data be entered in a prescribed format or even by capturing some data automatically), so reliance on voluntary user compliance with rules is reduced.

- *Quality Control and Integrity*—Data elements must be consistently entered into the system in the same place, and preferably using the same format and terms. This applies whether using Excel or the most sophisticated legal records management software on the market.

- *Responsibility*—Assigned and documented responsibility for maintenance of both the files and the index, whether shared among numerous staff or assigned to designated records staff, is essential to a system so that consistency and compliance can be monitored and used as a baseline for evaluating performance.

- *Volume, Workflow, and Scalability*—Manual systems can work well only if well-thought-out and efficient procedures are followed, and if the volume of records and index entries is kept within reason. A collection of files for 1,000 clients with 5,000 matters, 20,000 folders, and up to 100,000 subfiles will prove an administrative and management burden that only technology—good records management software—can tame. Doing this in a homegrown system can result in a spreadsheet with over 125,000 line items—a headache to maintain and to use. If you are trying to do this with index cards, think about the cost of investing in specialized equipment to manage hundreds of trays of index cards and the cost of the labor required just to keep them in some semblance of order. The potential for error in the manual filing process, along with the likelihood that those errors will impact the office's work, increases with the overall volume that is being maintained. Most manual filing and indexing systems *will* have at least a 0.5 to 1 percent error rate. When you think about the direct and indirect costs that accompany a manual system in any but the smallest operations, it makes sense to use the right size tool for the job.

In-File Hard Copy Indexing

One of the older and (thankfully) now seldom-used approaches to indexing involves creating and inserting indices inside the hard copy files. In-file indexing systems rely on minimal external labeling, with the external titling often limited to just the client and matter numbers or names. The real detail, about which information is filed in which folders and subfolders, is found on an index maintained in a predetermined location for each of the files in the system. The favorite locations for this in-file index are inside the front of the first file folder, or in its own separate (usually first) folder with a special color or identifier on it, or as the cover document in the correspondence folder. All of these approaches to in-file indexing suffer a common flaw—you must go through several manual steps to find or retrieve the index before you begin using it. But if you have such a system right now, and it is fairly accurate—if not especially user-friendly or efficient—it can be used as a starting point for creating a solid index and better processes and controls.

On-File Only Indexing

On-file only indexing refers to labeling on the exterior of the folders and sub-folders, and using this as the sole indexing method. For retrieval purposes, this is a bit more efficient than in-file indexing. While labels can reflect a wealth of information, there are inherent weaknesses in using the on-file approach to indexing as the sole tool for file identification and retrieval:

- ◆ Access to the files (and the indices) is entirely dependent on the proper sequencing of the files on the shelves—there is no backup system; and
- ◆ The index provides a single method of access—the process supports very limited cross-indexing or referencing, and then only with significant administrative overhead required to create and maintain them unless you are willing to undertake significant duplication of records, a process that carries cost and space burdens of its own.

Master Indices

Having index information on files and folders is useful, but having it only there is a problem—you must go to the file to find out if there is a file, an obvious waste of time and labor.

If records management or database software is used, index entries for physical files will be recorded there, creating a single index with good integrity. If not, some sort of paper document, spreadsheet, or word processing file must be created to use as a master reference. For smaller offices, or those with limited financial resources, or those who want to take a more measured approach to converting to the enlightened world of records management software, a paper-based index can be a good start and certainly a step up from no index at all or just an in-file or on-file index.

Again, there are limitations, with the most significant ones being:

- ◆ Accuracy of the system is dependent on human error rates. Automated and process-driven indexing produce lower error rates by facilitating the use of hard-wired schemes and by capturing some information automatically. With a subjective, purely manual system, accuracy of indexing is entirely dependent upon consistent and intelligent use by staff, something that is hard to create and harder to maintain.
- ◆ If the document set being indexed is very large, maintaining integrity within the index and on the shelf may prove difficult because of the

sheer volume of work. It can be done, but it requires proportionately more bodies to achieve and maintain the same level of accuracy and integrity available from automation.

The lessons from this discussion are

1. There are trade-offs involving accuracy, integrity, efficiency, and cost to be considered when deciding whether to go with a manual or an automated records management solution.
2. A similar investment, particularly in index creation, data gathering, process design, and training, will be required at similar levels whether you go with a more automated or a more manual approach.
3. Finally, scalability matters since there comes a point when it costs more, in terms of dollars, time, and system integrity and usefulness, to maintain a manual system at an acceptable and usable level than it does to do so in a fully automated environment.

Each situation is different and requires some study, but much of the work that needs to be done to get results from either approach is the same.

Filing and Records Maintenance 7

Introduction

Like children and pets, records serve their owners best when given proper care and managed with a certain amount of discipline. In the case of files, this includes indexing and categorization as indicated in the last chapter. As we will see in this chapter, the care also includes discipline in the form of regular attention to details inherent in hard-copy filing according to established and proven procedures. The discipline has two elements: (1) creating the proper procedures, structures, and guidelines to support the maintenance and retrieval needs of individual practice areas and administrative functions in the practice, and (2) consistently executing the same tasks in the same way.

In this chapter we are going to talk about the issue of hard copy filing in some detail. For those of you who know in their hearts that paper is dead, we offer the following explanations:

1. There are a lot of lawyers out there who are far more comfortable with hard copy than with the digital world, and those lawyers are not going to magically disappear overnight. Whatever changes you make to your program, and regardless of the amount of technology and automation you apply to the records management discipline, you are likely going to have to serve a lot of hardcore users of hard copy for many years to come;

2. Hard copy is a great place to start your work. A review of format and structure best practices in a physical/

hard-copy environment has direct applicability to the digital world in terms of key data elements (remember the last chapter on indexing?) and internal file structures and contents;

3. Hard-copy file labeling formats translate almost directly into desktop presentation of file descriptions when building screens that are easy to understand by all lawyers, not just the techno-centric ones; and finally

4. When law firms prepare for the transition from the hard-copy world to the digital one, they quickly learn that it is not an overnight change—such conversions frequently take two or more years to fully implement for operational, cultural, and political reasons. If you do not have a good clean starting point for your transition from hard copy to digital records management, your conversion will be much more difficult, problematic, and expensive.

With these issues in mind, let us take a good look at filing.

File Room Organization

The key to proper maintenance of records is good organization. Good organization is what permits rapid and accurate identification, filing, and retrieval of all records. In addition, the file indexing and organization structure, as it was addressed in the previous chapter on indexing and is further explored here in terms of filing, serves as the baseline for a good records management program and drives virtually every other aspect of the program. While this may seem obvious, it is a point as frequently honored in its breach as in its observance.

If you walk through a law firm of any size at all that has yet to seriously address the issue of records management, a number of filing problems (they are not issues, they are problems) become immediately evident:

♦ Staffed or unstaffed, case file rooms (or workrooms, or war rooms, or . . .) are often in really bad shape. A charitable description of the situation in some firms might describe them as chaotic eyesores. Whether for a single practice (Litigation or Corporate, for example) or shared among several practices, if no one is responsible for a room it tends to deteriorate, and everyone who is assigned any responsibility for it on a time-available basis always has something far more important to do than keep things in order. If no one is responsible for the work and there is no one present whose job it is to do it, it generally does not get done well, if at all.

◆ Workrooms double as file dumping grounds where inactive work, duplicates, and closed matters pile up until they are so jammed that they cannot accommodate their original purpose.

◆ Empty space gets poached in a hurry. Empty offices, closets, and work stations attract paper—in piles, folders, binders, and boxes—and it tends to stay there as a way of preserving turf until it is forced out by the arrival of new staff. Then it is quickly (and usually inaccurately) indexed, boxed, and shipped to off-site storage.

◆ All of the spaces in and around offices and workstations, including file cabinets (built-ins and stand-alones), credenzas, overhead storage units, and deep drawers are jealously defended as lawyers look for more space. For some lawyers, influence and importance in some way relates to the amount of space they can commandeer.

◆ Files maintained in personal file space tend to be managed according to no rules except those of the individual who does what little filing actually takes place. It is common, particularly in personal filing areas, to discover poor filing systems or no systems at all governing records, most of which have not been accessed for ages, with the result that significant time and effort are expended on a daily basis simply to find space for more stuff and to locate information thought to be somewhere near at hand.

Centralized Records Operations

The discussion has been going on for years, "Should we centralize records or not?" Listen closely in firms where records management has been centralized in one or two staffed locations and, depending on the firm, you will hear comments that range from, *"It's a black hole and a waste of space, staff, and money"* to *"Best thing since sliced bread—what did we ever do without it?"* While centralization has its fans, and very correctly so, just putting everything together in one room does not solve a problem, create a solution, or improve service.

Even if there is a central filing area, if it is not well-designed and maintained, disorganization and chaos may prevail and all of the negative thoughts may very appropriately apply. In some older central records operations that have yet to transition to contemporary tools, it is not uncommon to find filing schemes (particularly older legacy schemes) that are so Byzantine as to make accurate filing and retrieval next to impossible, because nobody who works there today really understands how things are supposed to work.

To some users, centralization brings to mind visions of all active files in a single locked room with users lined up outside to request their files. While it may be a charming thought, in truth, this is not the case in a well-run operation. Centralization means, first of all, that the records are *centrally indexed* in one central database so that all the information about files in a matter is accessible. This means that, depending on the configuration of the office space, there may be one, or even several, file rooms.

Centralization may well mean one facility, but it can also mean multiple facilities, in different offices, run according to the same processes and controls so that the lawyers know exactly what to expect—consistent, high-quality service—from all records operations in all locations. And, if they know they can and will consistently get that type of support they are far less likely to hoard files in and around their own workspace according to patchwork systems only they or their secretaries or paralegals know how to operate.

So, at a high level, those things that make a centralized hard-copy records operation work well are

- Comprehensiveness and integrity of the database;
- Consistent and clear file titling;
- User-friendliness of the facility so users can find what they need, when they need it, even after hours and on weekends;
- Procedures and workflow designed to make sure the files are accurate and up-to-date at all times;
- Efficient process management to ensure delivery of services promptly;
- An ironclad rule that after-hours users can take files off the shelves but should never refile anything they have retrieved; and
- Staff with a positive, helpful service attitude.

We will take a more detailed look at some of these issues in a bit. But at this point, suffice it to say that when a well-designed and administered records program is in place, users attitudes are positive. When the program is well-designed and services are competently delivered in a timely fashion:

- Satisfied users give up daily control of all but their most active files;
- Secretaries, paralegals, and lawyers focus their own file maintenance activities on only the most active files;
- The overall workload on secretaries and paralegals goes down and their productivity goes up as their emphasis shifts to the most active and billable matters;
- The quality and integrity of active, semi-active, inactive, and closed files improves as it becomes largely the purview of trained records staff who do the work faster, better, and more economically than secretaries and paralegals;

◆ Movement of inactive and closed files from expensive prime office space to less expensive off-site storage space is faster and more efficiently managed;

◆ Space utilization and directly related costs are more manageable as efficiencies of scale are implemented—one or two large file rooms require less physical space than do several small ones containing the same volume of records; and

◆ Cost efficiencies related to enterprise purchasing strategies come into play for mundane consumables such as file folders, labels, and boxes.

Details, Details, Details

Let us look in some detail at the specifics of designing and administering a centrally administered filing operation if things are going to work as well as they must in order to support the lawyers:

◆ Facility and space allocation—The right space, properly designed;

◆ Equipment—The appropriate file equipment, properly configured;

◆ Layout and signage—That create a clear and very obvious path to what they want so the lawyers can, at any time, find what they need without feeling that they are wasting their time;

◆ Supplies—Sturdy, well-made folders, labels, and other supplies, designed to meet the needs of specific practices (where necessary) used in a consistent fashion;

◆ Procedures—Clearly documented process and workflow that keeps the files up-to-date and that identify what files are charged out, when they were charged out, and to whom;

◆ Technology—That facilitates:

  ◆ the prompt assignment of new client/matter numbers for incoming matters;

  ◆ the quick creation and delivery of clearly labeled, practice-specific folder sets for new matters;

  ◆ creation and management of a complete and clear index of all active and inactive files in all locations; identification, retrieval, and request for delivery of on-site and off-site files;

  ◆ the creation of clearly labeled new files for existing matters and their timely delivery to requestors;

  ◆ knowing where every file is at all times;

  ◆ fast and accurate transfer of files off-site while minimizing the burden on end-users;

- controlled review and disposition of records following firm-mandated retention periods, according to disciplinary ethics guidelines and firm-internal controls.
- Staff—Qualified, competent, well-trained, professionally managed, service-oriented staff who understand their role in context of the firm's overall mission of delivering high-quality client service.

Facility and Space Allocation

When a firm first starts to lay out a centralized records room, a number of issues will affect their decision to move forward with the work. Building a new facility is expensive, and many firms opt to delay the sometimes substantial costs associated with it until they are either moving to new space or doing a build-out, making extensive renovations to existing space. When doing the initial design, space economies are available because consolidating multiple file rooms allows creation of more linear file space that is far more usable and efficient, in less square footage. Production economies are also available since the new space can be better designed to facilitate the workflow of returned files, incoming documents for interfiling, data entry, and departmental maintenance of files. Cumulative costs are lower, so this means a net gain for the bottom line.

Movable Aisle File Equipment

Moving from small file rooms that have used stand-alone file cabinets in small offices to a larger, dedicated, consolidated records housing space allows for the use of high-density, movable aisle file equipment (aka tracked files) and shared access aisles. Some of the points to consider when selecting such equipment are

- *Stack height*—Depending on clear ceiling height and local fire regulations, maximize vertical stacking to achieve the ratio of linear file space to square footage occupied by selecting equipment that is six to eight shelves high.
- *Electrical assist*—If ranges (rows) of shelving are more than four units long, consider using equipment that employs an electrical range-opening capability. This should be backed up with manual opening capability, a standard attribute of well-designed systems.
- *Safety*—Make sure that equipment has (a) pressure-sensitive flooring that locks a system open when a worker is standing between two ranges and (b) kick-plates at the bottom of each unit that serve as a

backup. Also make sure that clear ceiling heights between the top of the equipment and the sprinkler heads meet local requirements.

◆ *Floor-load capacity*—Get an independent engineer or one that is familiar with the building to calculate the existing floor-load capacity before committing to design and equipment layout. It is not unusual in new buildings to encounter floor-load capacity of less than 50 pounds per square foot. Fully loaded high-density, movable aisle equipment can require floor-load capacity of 150 pounds per square foot or more. It is far more convenient and much less expensive to deal with the associated costs of reinforcement during construction than it is to retrofit a facility later on when you may well have to go in from the floor below, disrupting work in other offices. Make sure the building engineer and the engineer from the company providing the equipment agree to and sign off on the floor-load capacity requirements.

◆ *Number of openings*—Plan for one open aisle for every four ranges of shelving if the facility will accommodate a substantial amount of open matter files, and subsequently a higher number of accesses during prime operating hours.

◆ *Reference shelving*—Plan for one spring-loaded reference shelf in every third or fourth shelving unit in each range to provide a convenient workspace when staff are working in the stacks on interfiling and refiling tasks. In most cases, these should be mounted between the third and fourth shelves from the bottom for a convenient working height.

◆ *Shelf openings*—Allow for at least 12 inches clear space between shelves for easy insertion and retrieval of files. Make sure to consider depth of turned-lips on shelving since those can consume 3/4 to 1 inch of shelf opening space. Where turned lip shelves are used, plan on center-to-center measurements of 13 inches to allow adequate space. If binders that stand more than 12 inches high are to be interfiled with folders, consider this need as well. It may be more space efficient to design one shelf in each range with a 14 inches opening to accommodate these and other oversized items rather than making all shelf openings larger.

◆ *Aisle width between shelving ranges*—Most vendors will allow for a minimum of 36 inches between ranges when an aisle is opened. This allows staff space to open a reference shelf and stand in front of it when working and allows them to stand aside and safely let another worker pass behind them.

◆ *Main access or side aisle width*—To allow turn-in space for small file carts and longer wheelbase carts being steered into the stacks, allow for at least 48 inch-wide side aisles running around the periphery of the stack area.

Client-Matter File Sequence

Assigning separate file shelves and/or units for each practice occupies far more space than filing in a strict client-matter sequence. Assigning space on a practice-specific basis will eventually require expensive and time-consuming shifting of files. Client-matter file sequencing allows for expansion and contraction of space and so requires infrequent shifting of files as matters are closed and eventually moved off-site, systematically opening up space for new matters.

Alphabetic or Numeric?

Most firms that serve a large number of clients and have a correspondingly larger number of matters have figured out the obvious and use numeric systems. (There is no truth to the story that some firms like alphabetic systems because their people cannot count.) Alphabetic systems are base 26 and numeric systems use base 10. Fewer misfiles occur in numeric systems. Most financial and accounting software applications assign numbers to clients and then to matters within clients for very good reasons. These numbers should be used when labeling and sequencing files on the shelves. This does not mean that labels should ignore names and titles, but that the numbering should be included with the text on the labels to make tasks (like refiling) easier.

Signs, Signs, Everywhere Signs

Make it easy for the evening and weekend users. Mount an oversized map showing the file room layout, a graphic display that shows what files are on what shelves, in a highly visible location near the entrance of the file room so that it is the first thing a user sees when he or she enters the file room. Each range of shelves should be clearly labeled with signage that indicates the numbers of the files on them. The signs should be mounted vertically so they stick out from the ends of the ranges rather than flush with the end surfaces of the ranges. They should be large and easy to read and should be mounted high enough so they can be seen clearly from all points in the peripheral aisles. The records staff will generally know where things are; these signs are for the benefit of the users who come in after hours and on weekends. Use big numbers so middle-aged users can see them easily. Make it easy for your users to find what they need.

Supplies

Firms that have yet to convert from legal-sized to letter-sized supplies have a great opportunity to save a bit of space and money. The rationale and benefits of making this change are substantial and easy to accrue. Consider the following:

- Over 99 percent of all incoming documentation is letter sized today, and in fact, most courts now require it.
- Changing from legal to letter size means that every standard records box (10 inches high × 12 inches wide × 15 inches deep) that goes to off-site storage contains 20 percent more files, resulting in an immediate reduction in the number of boxes going off-site and lower total storage costs.
- Purchasing letter-sized pads saves money, as does resizing preformatted documents from legal to letter size.
- Letter-sized pocket files and other file supplies cost a bit less than the legal-sized equivalents.
- Planning file-room space around letter-sized media saves on equipment costs since fewer raw materials are required.
- Planning new file-room space around letter-sized media means a 15 percent reduction in stack space, with commensurate savings in square footage, space that can be devoted to staff rather than files, as well as annual cost savings.

Procedures

Lawyers as Users

Lawyers today are more portable than they have been in the past; they move from firm to firm and from office to office within their firms. New associates start in one practice and move to another as they move through rotation during their training. Senior lawyers and even partners move from one practice to another as the business climate changes, from corporate to bankruptcy and then back to corporate. In this environment, one of the great benefits that any firm can give its professional staff is consistency, the knowledge that records will be maintained according to a consistent set of rules no matter what office they are in or which type of law they are practicing. This does not mean that trusts and estates files look and are structured the same as are litigation files—they obviously are not. It does mean that a litigation file will have the same basic structure no matter where it is in the firm and that if it needs something special, there is a standard and time-efficient way of dealing with it. If users can rely on that one truth then they can concentrate more on their work than on doing their own filing. In order for this to happen, procedures must be clearly crafted, documented, and complied with.

Lawyers do not need all of the detailed procedures at their fingertips, but they do need basic documentation that tells them what services are available, and how to access and use those services to their benefit. This information can be in printed form (for those with an affinity for paper) or in digital form, easily accessible online via the firm's intranet. In larger firms that support both techno-centric and hard-copy using lawyers, it is worthwhile for user guides to be made available in both media.

Paralegals and Secretaries as Users

Similar, but slightly more detailed procedures than those provided for lawyers should be created for paralegals and secretaries—the staff who provide the most direct support to the lawyers and have the most direct daily interaction with them. They need to know how to provide the support the lawyers need, what their specific responsibilities are, and where to go for assistance should they need it. When records management services, retention schedules, taxonomies, and file structures are practice-specific, as they should be, and paralegals and secretaries are focused on specific practices, their procedures should be tailored to their work.

Records Management Staff

This is where the real detail comes into play. Records staff should have every step of every task detailed—task, process, responsibility, sequence, format, and so on. All of the manual processes, from internal file format and document sequence to document interfiling, file retrieval, charge-out, and refiling should be spelled out in minute detail so there is no room for differing personal interpretations.

Similarly, when records management software is deployed, or other automated tools or processes are in use, each step of each task should be documented with clear, supporting illustrations including sample menus and screen printouts.

Records management is an ongoing process for managing the life cycle of records in all media, and each procedure in each part of the records management continuum should be clearly titled and referenced by process:

- New matter intake
- New file creation and titling

- Initial data entry and records updating
- Document-level interfiling
- File retrieval and charge-out
- Refiling
- Matter closing and file consolidation (hard copy and digital)
- Boxing and transfer off-site of hard-copy files
- Retention review and disposition (again, for both hard-copy and digital files and documents)

. . . and for other specific tasks as appropriate. Where possible, online help should be context-sensitive so any user can go directly to help on specific tasks and processes.

Consistency

It bears repeating that processes and controls should be as consistent as possible across departments, practice groups, and offices. One of the great truths we have learned about records management is that services, processes, format, and structure should be centrally defined and administered but locally deployed and managed. In large, multioffice firms, we also know that differences in location, office configuration, staff size, practice profiles, and services are usually best delivered on a local basis according to established, firm-wide rules. In other words, define globally and deliver locally.

Education and Training

Failure to tell everyone who works in the office that there are specific records management services available, that the firm or office has invested substantially to make those services available, and that there are processes in place to get the most from those services, is an invitation for new hires and laterals to go their own way and to work outside of the system.

Orientation

All firm personnel, billable or not, from partners to clerks, should be informed when they come through the door that the firm has a records management program that provides specific services in a predefined manner. They need to know, for reasons of ethical compliance and client service, that if an individual goes his or her own way, the likelihood is that records will be created that (a) others cannot find or use, and that (b) may potentially put both the firm and the client at risk. Requiring new personnel to read and sign a one- or two-page records management policy statement outlining the firm's position on records management and detailing individual responsibility will serve the firm well.

Lawyers

Yes, the policy really does apply to the lawyers as well. Occasional mention of the importance of working in context of the firm's position on records management at partnership meetings, associates' luncheons, and practice or department level meetings is important. Such mentions help to reinforce the value of adhering to firm records management standards for reasons of ethics compliance, consistency in client service delivery, and to achieve productivity by virtue of information and work product sharing. Incoming laterals should receive the same message and be provided support in making sure that the active files and open matters they bring with them are quickly and efficiently incorporated into existing firm systems.

A brief overview by the records manager—the what, why, and how of records management—for summer associates, interns, and each year's new class of lawyers, will serve as a timely reminder that records management is there to help them. If new lawyers have a different system that they would like to pursue, they need to know who to go to before they wander off on their own path.

Paralegals and Secretaries

Mandatory training for these essential members of the firm's support structure is critical. Some support staff ally themselves with a single lawyer. While this was a pretty good idea years ago when one secretary for one lawyer was a common practice, creating different procedures and working in a one-lawyer vacuum is counterproductive in a multilawyer office in today's multidisciplinary firms. Even if the firm is small, just two or three lawyers, different procedures cause problems when one paralegal or secretary has to support more than one lawyer or fill in for another paralegal or secretary in cases of illness or unavoidable absence.

Records Management Staff

The detailed documentation mentioned earlier should serve as the starting point for creating a guide and developmental road map for training new records staff and retraining existing staff when they move to new positions and assume different responsibilities. Training should never be a matter of passing on a personal approach. This undermines the very concept and ensuing value inherent in a consistent approach. Good procedures and solid training also serve as an effective benchmark for monitoring compliance and providing retraining where necessary.

Technology

Law firms are fortunate that today there are several vendors providing records management software configured to the specific needs of the legal community. Some of them are widely deployed in law offices and have proven functional value. Most of them follow a path that includes regular (and often meaningful) changes to their programs and functionality based on user feedback.

Let us take a high-level look at this software, how it relates to other applications, and some of the considerations that should be central to this software's effective deployment and use.

- *What Should RM Software Do?*—Basically, records management software should tell users what has been created, in all media, for a given administrative record or piece of client-matter work. It should tell the user what is available (folders, e-mails, word processing documents, etc.) and if it is available for retrieval. The software should track the holders and location of hard-copy files and provide access to related electronic/digital records. It should provide some measure of security and control for restricted-access records and should serve as the primary tool for management of all administrative records in all media as well as matter-centric control of all client records according to a law firm's records retention schedule.

- *What About Conflict-of-Interest Checking Software?*—Most software vendors have recognized a basic truth—*that the details of a good conflicts checking software application are more closely aligned with records management software than with accounting software.* Checking for potential conflicts of interest has evolved into a complex and detailed discipline in most law firms for a variety of reasons. Lawyers and their practices change firms much more frequently than in the past. Clients are spreading work on the same matter or issue among several firms in an attempt to "conflict out" firms. The courts are more demanding than ever in their definition of what they consider due diligence in conflict checking. Many names and search terms are far more likely to show up in folder titles and electronic document metadata than in accounting software. As a result, the systems that have been built to support conflicts checking have become more detailed and often require the review of closed records indices and their contents. As a result, conflict checking software is today very tightly integrated with records management software and, in some cases, is built as an extension of RM software.

- *Accounting Software*—It makes elegant good sense that records management, conflicts, and accounting software applications should be integrated. Integration allows for less data entry, better data integrity, and tighter controls over processes, particularly when they are all tied together with workflow software to manage the full intake and work initiation process. One point has emerged as this integration between records and accounting has become more commonplace: *The old practice of reusing old client-matter numbers after a matter is closed out or a client relationship is terminated creates problems.* It makes the retrieval of old records more difficult when identical numbering schemes apply to more than one client and matter, and checking for potential conflicts becomes problematic if client-matter level information is deleted and numbers are reused.

- *Name Changes*—As law firms do more and more mergers and acquisitions and bankruptcy work for their clients, it becomes more and more evident that the organizations to which this work pertains do not remain static—*the names of clients change.* United States Steel becomes U.S. Steel becomes USX, and unless procedures and software make it possible to track and account for name changes, suddenly a law firm may be creating files under a new name, possibly under a new number, and likely to be indexed in different data locations. Neither records management nor conflicts searches on old records will yield a hit unless the search includes both names and because functionality built into the software facilitates such a search. Reliance on a single numbering system reduces the chances for mistakes in such situations.

Administrative Records

So far, much of our commentary has focused on client files, those that make up the bulk of the records in any law office. Administrative records, those that include everything that is not case files, the types of records every entity maintains, are important as well—just ask any firm that has had to respond to a discovery request. While administrative files are very different from case files, they are equally important in a very different way. These administrative records include:

- Accounting, Finance, and Tax
- Administrative Activities
- Business Development
- Firm Governance (or office management)
- Human Resources
- Purchasing

- ◆ Facilities Management
- ◆ Research and Reference

All of them should be logically arranged and with suitable categorical breakdowns that are accurately defined.

The best way to identify these records so they are easy to find and maintain is to create a logical and hierarchical list of terms that describe each type of record. In records management parlance this list is often referred to as a classification structure or file plan, and the categories listed in the classification structure are called records series.

A good classification structure is generally topic or subject-oriented and hierarchical in nature. In hard copy terms, it is a filing scheme; in all cases, its purpose is to allow identification and retrieval of files according to the topic of the specific records. It mirrors both the nature of the information it organizes and the queries that will be put to it. Classification structures should be developed for each major type of records. When creating the terms to be used in the classification structure, it is important to provide good descriptions, detailed definitions, and samples of the document types that are usually found in each record series.

When developing both structure and nomenclature, it is important to bear in mind the kinds of queries that users will make of the system. Classifications and nomenclature may be very detailed but not be particularly helpful because they do not correspond to the information the user is actually looking for. It may take some effort to develop a comprehensive classification structure that is reasonably responsive to most or all potential administrative, support, and management users. Just remember to keep terms as simple and generic as possible in the context of the records to which they pertain. As we said earlier when talking about indexing, meaningless terms such as "Daily Report" and the ubiquitous descriptors "General" and "Miscellaneous" should be avoided.

Titling Case Files

Titling of case files should be considered based upon the very obvious realities that more than one person may want to access them and more than one person may be asked to retrieve them. This alone argues strongly in favor of consistent enterprise rules and processes and against personal filing systems that only one person can use. If a file is titled *Depositions,* but the label contains no information about the specific litigation to which it pertains, the label will be of limited value to anyone except the person who created it, and then only so long as the creator remembers where the folder was put and the litigation to which it applies. Adequate titling on case files meets a number of needs:

♦ *Active retrieval*—The ability to find and deliver to the lawyer the one specific folder he or she needs from among all of the folders relating to a specific case or issue.

♦ *Maintenance*—Being able to find the file and add documents to it without asking the person who initially created the file to find it for you.

♦ *Tracking and refiling*—Knowing what a file refers to and where it belongs when it returns to central files or is discovered on a table after a meeting, or is inadvertently left elsewhere, or is discovered in the office of a lawyer who has left the firm.

♦ *Transfer*—Determining if the file is closed, or identifying the lawyer responsible for it, when the time comes to transfer files from expensive on-site space to less expensive off-site storage.

Many matters involve more than one file folder or item. Typically these items (commonly referred to as subfolders or inserts) are kept in a series of larger pocket files (folders). If a subfolder is separated from the main folder, it will be necessary to identify it in order to refile it.

To meet all of these needs, the label on each insert, when originally created, should reflect, at a minimum:

(1) Client number and name
(2) Matter number and description
(3) Date matter opened
(4) Practice area/type of matter
(5) Responsible lawyer
(6) Folder title and number
(7) A bar code (yes, even if you do not use them today)

It is also desirable to list on the outside of the folder in which the insert belongs the titles and numbers of all subfolders/inserts contained in the folder.

It is not necessary to maintain a separate client-matter numbering and indexing system for closed matters. Merely amending the existing database or master index with the official closing date of the matter and the box/location number in storage is sufficient.

While this sounds like a great deal of work (think of all that data entry!), consider that with an automated records management system, particularly one that is integrated with other applications, no data element needs to be entered into the system more than once and the result will be a comprehensive index of files and records that are fully and completely identifiable and easily retrievable. How difficult is it to generate the label? In most cases, after the label has been designed, all that is required is execution of the print command, generally a one-keystroke operation.

Grouping Records Within Case Files

The most productive way of grouping case file records is in a defined hierarchy. Some of this may sound simple but it bears repeating. As discussed earlier, most offices will benefit from grouping files in a numerical sequence—first by client, and within client by matter number.

> (example: 030215:0251, where 030215 relates to a specific client and 0251 refers to a specific piece of work for that client, a particular real estate closing, litigation, trust, etc.)

So, our hard-copy filing sequence or hierarchy looks like this:

> Client
>> Within client by matter
>>> Within matter, folders by document type (unless it is a really small file)
>>>> Within document type in reverse chronological sequence, or alpha sequence as appropriate

So, for a familiar type of folder in a litigation matter it might look like this:

Client	01234	Big Seafoods Company
Matter	0033	Big Seafoods v. Crawdaddy Catchers
Folder		Depositions—Vol 1
		Ahab Deposition, Starbuck Deposition, etc.

Unless a case or matter has generated very little documentation, the physical documents should be grouped so that similar documents are together in the same folder. This generally means creating a standard filing structure for the types of records typically generated for a particular matter type. The key in meaningful grouping of records for easy filing and retrieval is pretty basic—standardize the titles so that the same type of information will be found in a like-titled folder each time.

Many law offices attempt to create a single structure that covers all practice areas, assuming that the differences between practice areas are minimal. This does not work well. While it is true that similar document types are created among most practice areas, and these should be incorporated in the structure, the differences should be accounted for as well.

For example, almost every matter in any practice area will result in the generation of some records that can be grouped into:

◆ *Lawyers' notes*—handwritten notes by the lawyer(s), with separate folders or subfolders created for each lawyer working on the matter, with his or her name being incorporated into the title;

◆ *Internal memoranda*—generated by law office personnel and sent to law office personnel, with multiple volumes sequentially numbered broken into date ranges; and

◆ *Correspondence*—letters to the client from the lawyers and letters to the lawyers from the client, again with multiple volumes sequentially numbered broken into date ranges.

These categories should be part of the structure developed for most practice areas. Other categories that will be common to many, but certainly not all, practices are

◆ Duplicates—generally of printed matter (i.e., offerings), sometimes of reports or documents sent to the client and usually filed separately from the original in a single folder or subfolder so that the number of duplicates is easily discernable. Records clerks can be easily trained to understand that a document with marginalia is not a duplicate of a document without marginalia. People insist on creating and filing duplicate copies, so let us give them a home and make it easy to get rid of them when the matter closes.

◆ Drafts—generally of documents prepared for internal or client review, with the folder title reflecting the document title and each draft dated and numbered so the logic and development process leading to generation of the final document is understandable.

◆ Meeting notes

◆ Client documents

◆ Legal opinions and memoranda of law

◆ Contracts, agreements, and amendments

As with our first example of common categories, these will appear in the structure developed for many practices—but not all. Substantial differences do exist, however, among the practice areas.

For example, the practice of Trusts and Estates law will require unique categories for larger files, among them:

◆ Wills

◆ Death certificates

◆ Fiduciary bank accounts

◆ Fiduciary investment accounts

- Real estate assets
- Annuities
- Powers of appointment
- Estate tax filings
- Estate tax work papers

If the work done for a Trusts and Estates client is fairly simple, say a will, a medical directive, and a power of attorney and they can all fit nicely in one folder, that one folder may be sufficient. But with substantial work in a number of different T & E areas, you may need to create separate folders for each document type, or if the work is very involved and the resulting documentation is fairly extensive, you may even create separate matters for each endeavor on behalf of that client.

A far different set of categories would be developed to support the needs of a corporate practice group in a law office. Again, some examples of standard file titles for the structure to support such a practice might include:

- *Bidder Company Public Filings and Corporate Documents*—which might be further broken down into
  - Charter and by-laws
  - Loan agreements
  - 8-Ks
  - 10-Ks
  - 10-Qs
  - Annual reports to shareholders
  - Proxy statements, etc.
- *Target Company Proceedings*—which might start out with subcategories such as
  - Minutes of board meetings
  - Agendas
  - Bidder company Williams Act compliance
  - Target company Williams Act compliance
  - Communications and negotiations (such as bear-hug letters)
  - Offer documents

In addition to these subject-specific areas, each of our example practice areas would also include the common categories of lawyers' notes, memoranda, correspondence, and drafts.

When designing a structure for a particular practice area, the level of detail included (which may vary for different record types within the structure) should reflect the answers to the following questions:

- Will retrieval needs be for a single document or for a group of documents?

- Is the anticipated volume of records within a single category anticipated to be great enough that looking for a single document or version of a document will be impeded by the need to look through numerous folders?

What Do I Do with Great Work Product?

One of the more common questions relates to keeping track of documents that have a transcending value. Does a document or set of documents have value beyond this matter to the point that filing and titling it separately will make it easier to retrieve when it may be valuable as a resource for work on a similar matter or issue? The answer will likely be "Yes" in many situations, such as when dealing with opinions and memoranda of law or pleadings. Do not assume that you do not have to do anything except keep the file since you can go back and find that document later. In an automated system you can flag the document as having specific work product value or so indicate that value in the document management system. Today, many offices create either hard-copy or electronic copies of valuable work product and funnel that into the flow of a separate knowledge-management system.

Sequencing Documents in Case Files

The sequencing of documents within individual case file folders will vary by individual file and document type. Earlier we suggested the two most obvious sequencing methods, reverse chronological order and alphabetically. Suggested filing sequences for some of the most commonly used case file categories are

- *Correspondence*—File in reverse chronological sequence, with the most recent date on top. Transmittal or cover letters should be filed in the correspondence, but only the smallest attachments should be included. Larger attachments should be filed separately with like documents.
- *Internal memoranda*—Internal memoranda should be filed in reverse chronological sequence.
- *Lawyers' notes*—File in reverse chronological sequence, making sure that the date and the topic of the meeting or conversation are clearly identified.
- *Opinions and legal memoranda*—File alphabetically by topic, preferably with an index that includes a cross reference. Manual systems

should include the index as the first document in the folder; the index for automated systems should be maintained online.

♦ *Drafts*—Drafts should be segregated from final versions of the document, with each draft numbered and dated, and filed in numerical sequence. Unless a limited number of drafts are generated in a given matter, drafts of each document should be filed separately. A word of warning here—with the extended use of e-mail, many drafts are circulated as e-mail attachments outside the context of the document management system and are difficult to track.

♦ *Duplicates*—Duplicates should be filed in chronological order, separately from the original or record copy of a document. This makes it easier to cull out unnecessary duplicates when preparing files for transfer to storage at the close of a matter. When distribution lists are created separately from the original document, the distribution list should be attached to and filed with the original letter or internal memorandum.

♦ *Court records* (aka Pleadings, Litigation Binders, etc.)—Pleadings should be numbered, abstracted, and filed by case and venue in chronological order. The standard format index should be the cover document for each volume.

♦ *Depositions*—File depositions alphabetically by name of the individual being deposed and then by date of the deposition.

Grouping Records Within Administrative Files

For those categories of administrative records where the related documents are primarily correspondence, the preferred method of grouping documents within folders is by date, or by date within issue, with the issue or topic clearly reflected in the title.

Where the category is specific to a single document type or closely related series of document types, the grouping should reflect the method by which the retrieval of those records will most frequently be required. An example of the latter category is purchasing records. In the purchasing department files, a file might contain internal memoranda about a pending purchase, vendor evaluations, a requisition, a purchase order, the receiving report, related vendor correspondence, a copy of the invoice, and a copy of the voucher. In the purchasing department, hard-copy purchasing files are most useful when titled and grouped by vendor name. A closely related set of records will be maintained in the accounts payable department but they will likely be filed by purchase order number. In an office where the purchasing process is fully automated, all purchases may well be part of an information repository created from one or more systems.

The key is that documents must be grouped according to the needs of the users who are holding them and titled to reflect that grouping in a manner that facilitates retrieval.

A final note on the grouping of documents—the retrieval of files, and the identification of documents within those files, is facilitated not only when documents are properly grouped, but when those groupings are properly broken into smaller sections when volume dictates. Even if properly titled, a large file does not make the identification of records, and their ultimate use on a frequent basis, any easier. Unless documents in a folder are retrieved and used very infrequently, the folder should be divided into smaller increments (volumes), or a continuation file created, when the file is about one or two inches thick.

Titling Administrative Records

Titling of noncase files is relatively simple. The information on a label should answer two basic questions: (1) What is the subject? and (2) What specific information is contained in the file?

Consider a familiar example. Every firm has personnel files. Increasingly, more and more of the information generated about staff exists in soft (electronic) form as part of one or more data sets created by a human resource information system (HRIS), but we still see those ubiquitous hardcopy personnel files. A personnel file should obviously be titled with the individual's name, but it should also include the categories in which the file belongs. For example, for Joe Jones:

> Human Resources—would be the primary category
> Personnel Files—would be the record series under Human Resources, and
> Jones, Joseph—would be the title of the file.

And if Joe has a training file, then the information on the label of that file should include:

> Human Resources—would be the primary category
> Training, In-house—would be the record series under Human Resources, and
> Jones, Joseph—would be the title of the file.

Let us look at another example. Many lawyers deal with litigation, hearings, or investigations and rely occasionally on expert witnesses. One of the categories (records series) in the research files portion of the classification structure would therefore be Expert Witnesses. This category might be further divided into the subcategories meaningful to the firm's practices, such as Automotive Design, Construction, or Tax Law, or such details can be included in consistently formatted folder titles. The files for one set of these records, in a practice that deals with litigation involving the automotive industry, might include the following data elements:

Automotive Industry Experts
    Bumper Crash Tests
        Morrison, John J., ME
    Crumple Zone Efficiency
        Johnson, Ernest E., Ph.D.
    Electrical Systems Fires
        Simmons, Quentin Q., EE

This approach to titling allows the files to be easily grouped by like areas of concern, makes retrieval of records relating to a specific expertise easy and assures accurate refiling. A file on a specific expert witness might contain credentials, work experience, track record in testimony, and even copies of depositions or transcripts of testimony that might also be filed with the case files. The same applies to any other type of administrative files, such as accounts receivable.

Inactive Records

There is a tendency among many people to think that when records are changed from active to inactive status, the need for adequate indexing disappears. Perhaps this concept is rooted in the thought that when records leave the office, no one will ever retrieve them again. Whatever the rationale, the notion is incorrect. Indexing and control of records in their inactive state is just as important as when records are actively maintained in the office.

Another errant notion is that inactive records need an entirely different numbering and indexing system. This is a bad idea. All this does is create an additional and unnecessary administrative burden and the opportunity for error.

Records that have been changed from active to inactive status need the same handling as active records, with some minor differences. If the records management system is not automated, or does not include detailed indexing, an index of the records in each box should be created when the records are ready for transfer to storage, and copies of that index should be filed in different sequences to meet a variety of retrieval requirements. Regardless of whether an automated or manual system is employed, certain key data must be recorded to document the change in status:

- *Actual Status*—The file folders and the index should both be modified to reflect the change in status, from active to inactive.
- *Review/disposition*—A review date should be added to the file index to prompt a periodic review of the file to determine its continued value to the office, if the office has no formal retention policy (*not recommended—every office should have a good retention schedule!*), or to initiate the predisposition review when a formal retention schedule is in place.
- *Location*—The entry in the database, or the notation in the manual index, should be amended to reflect the new "assigned home" of the files. This notation can be as simple and brief as a box/location number if a single storage facility is in use, or it may include:
  - Storage facility name or code
  - Box number (from the storage vendor)—or—locator number if you manage your own facility (usually includes row, aisle, shelf, and position)
  - The physical file folders within the box also should be marked to indicate the facility to which they should be returned in the event they are separated from their container.

Remember, indexing should still be structured with retrieval in mind. For those who have a purely manual system and do not have access to software provided by a storage vendor, consider making copies of the index cards or other matter-specific or administrative topic indices and arranging them in different sequences:

- *By Client Number and Matter Number*—to support retrieval of records when the client and matter are known. This list should be centrally maintained by the records department as the master inactive records index.
- *By Administrative Records Series*
- *By Review/Disposition Date*—to facilitate timely review of records according to a records retention schedule.
- *By Practice Area and Key Issue*—To support issue-related research needs of individual practice areas. The definition of special indexing terms should be the responsibility of the practice area.

Additional Resources

A number of excellent resources for guidance on setting up classification structures and filing schemes for case files and administrative records are available. The Association of Records Managers and Administrators (ARMA) International (www.arma.org) is an association for records management professionals and those who support the records management discipline. ARMA has a Legal Services Industry-Specific Group (ISG) with a membership of hundreds of law firm and law department records managers, consultants, and vendors who meet monthly in local chapters around the country and who run seminars and educational sessions that are worthwhile educational tools for those interested in setting up records management systems and programs.

Many cities (New York, Los Angeles, Atlanta, etc.) also have local associations such as the New York Legal Guild. The members of these groups include experienced professionals willing to network and share their knowledge. See Appendix 4 for more information.

Filing and Managing Electronic Documents

8

Introduction

Electronic data is a fact of life in the twenty-first century. Everyone, including lawyers, is increasingly dependent upon it. Large firms have complex, integrated accounting and billing systems; intranets, extranets, and client portals; human resource information systems, conflicts checking systems, automated (sometimes enterprise-deployed) calendar and docket systems, and these days many lawyers seem to have the ubiquitous Blackberries or their equivalents. Even the smallest law office today has a computer or two, a lot of word processing documents, an e-mail system and the accompanying repositories, and an accounting program. These are the necessary tools of today's law practice. All of these tools have the potential to greatly enhance productivity and efficiency, and if they are correctly used they offer the prospect of significantly enhanced client service.

On the other hand, these systems and the data they generate pose vexing problems for those who have not addressed records management in a meaningful way. What kind of problems? Problems such as:

- Not being able to find information when it is needed
- Not knowing which is the most recent version
- Not knowing which is the official record and which is an information copy
- Not knowing what you sent to whom, and when

These problems are partly due to the nature of the systems themselves, but also partly due to the culture and nature of legal practice, the fundamental principles of legal ethics, and the traditions that have grown up around those principles. The result of this confluence of factors is that electronic systems and data, at least from the records management perspective, do not lend themselves particularly well to some of the historic and hard-copy-based aspects of law practice and legal ethics. This being the case, any lawyer using these electronic and digital tools in her practice will need to consider the impacts of information creation technology and of ethics requirements on the information management strategy in the practice. Failure to do so will result in a variety of problems like the ones mentioned earlier as well as possible ethics problems. Because you can find what you want, when you need it, and you get rid of excess copies according to a good retention schedule, a good records management system will help mitigate those problems and improve client service.

Ethics Considerations

Whether legal tradition and legal ethics are venerable or hoary depends upon your worldview. Regardless of your particular perspective, there is no doubt that they are old. The Anglo-American legal system runs in an unbroken line of descent from at least Anglo-Saxon England, and before that perhaps to the Germanic tribes of Europe. Along the way have come events, principles, and documents seminal to the development of human civilization—the Battle of Runnymede and the Magna Carta, the Declaration of Independence and the resulting war, the United States Constitution, *Brown v. Board of Education*—the list goes on and on. All combine and contribute to the development and extension of a great legal tradition, heavily influenced by lawyers at most stops along the way—twenty-four of the fifty-six signers of the Declaration of Independence, for example, were lawyers and jurists. Most lawyers see this lineage and tradition as venerable, and are justifiably proud of it. Few practitioners would be receptive to the idea of scrapping these traditions on the theory that such devastation would be a necessary step in bringing the practice of law into the twenty-first century.

From the information management vantage point, however, traditional legal practice can be a bit hoary at times—the practice of law is built around, and identified with, a very old information technology—paper. The stereotypes of the profession are of a lawyer carrying a briefcase (containing, of course, paper), surrounded by books and file cabinets, and of course, swimming in a sea of court filings, all on paper. Many lawyers today may see all of this as ancient history, but the mental image of a lawyer drowning in paper is pervasive. Combine this with the lawyer's trained eye for minutiae, and we have the situation where virtually every important event, action, or transaction—complaint, response, judgment, interrogatory, contract, will, the list is endless—is represented by its own unique document, to the point where the document and the transaction are virtually synonymous.

Ethics opinions, court rules, and similar guidelines in the past have by and large assumed that representations and other important occurrences in the practice of the profession are all memorialized on paper, even when they have not explicitly so stated. For example, when the documentation associated with a representation is discussed, it is a "case file" or "matter file," implicitly if not explicitly the traditional papers-in-a-folder document set, discrete, well-defined, and all in one place; and of course, all on paper. Today, it just does not work this way.

That is not to say that paper is bad. Paper is a tried- and true-medium, and in many situations and for many people, it is far and away the best and most convenient medium. Increasingly, however, the artifacts recording a representation, like many other lawyers' transactions, are not paper but electronic. They reside in word processing or document management repositories, spreadsheets and databases, and of course, e-mail. They exist not as paper in a manila file folder, but in a virtual folder in a virtual cabinet in a virtual file room. The problem is that the nature of these contemporary technologies and the types of records they create is in conflict with the basic assumption underlying both the legal ethics of records management and the way many lawyers view their records: that there is somewhere a physically separate, distinct, and complete hard-copy document set that is the "master case file."

In an earlier chapter we considered the question of client file ownership. There it was noted that most ethics authorities have progressively expanded the definition of "client file" and have expanded the right of client access to it after the termination of representation. Recent case decisions have ratified this majority position and have expanded in considerable detail not only upon what is owed the client, but upon the supporting rationale as well. Consider two prominent cases:

In *Sage Realty Corp. v. Proskauer Rose*,[1] the New York Court of Appeals examined the then-current state of law in this area, attempting to determine, not only the boundary of the client's ownership or possessory interests in records and information associated with a representation, but also the current doctrines and rationales in use. After a falling out between counsel and client, Sage Realty, an ex-client of the Proskauer Rose law firm, sought to obtain a wide variety of information related to its representation. Proskauer Rose turned over a great deal of the requested material, but refused to turn over some information, such as internal legal memoranda, drafts of instruments, markups, notes on contracts and transactions, and ownership structure charts. In requiring Proskauer Rose to turn over this material, the court concluded that the majority view, which it adopted, requires that virtually *all* material related to an ongoing matter must be surrendered to the client in order to avoid the potential of prejudice to them, unless the lawyer can "demonstrate that a particular document would furnish no useful purpose in serving the client's present needs for legal advice":[2]

> [A] former client is to be accorded access to inspect and copy any documents possessed by the lawyer relating to the representation unless substantial grounds exist to refuse.[3]

and

> We can discern no principled basis upon which exclusive property rights to an attorney's work product in a client's file spring into being in favor of the attorney at the conclusion of a represented matter.[4]

The court also observed that:

> [T]he minority position adopted by the courts below [requiring the client to specify the precise material needed from the lawyer] unrealistically and, in our view, unfairly places the burden on the client to demonstrate a need for specific work product documents in the attorney's file on the represented matter. Again, this case is illustrative that in a complex transaction where the file may be voluminous (commensurably increasing the likely usefulness of work product materials to advise the client concerning ongoing rights and obligations), the client's need for access to a particular paper cannot be demonstrated except in the most general terms, in the absence of prior disclosure of the content of the very document to which access is sought.[5] (bracketed text not in original)

A similar view of both the duty and the exceptions was taken by the court in *Swift, Currie, McGhee & Hiers v. Henry,*[6] which concluded that:

> An attorney's fiduciary relationship with a client depends, in large measure, upon full, candid disclosure. That relationship would be impaired if attorneys withheld any and all documents from their clients without good cause, especially where the documents were created at the client's behest.[7]

In disapproving a theory that material created during a representation was the property of the attorney and so immune from client access, the *Swift* court observed that:

> [T]he work product doctrine does not apply to the situation in which a client seeks access to documents or other tangible things created or amassed by his attorney during the course of the representation.[8]

The *Sage* court did carve out exceptions to their requirement of general surrender of records and information to the client:

> [The ruling] should not be required to disclose documents which might violate a duty of nondisclosure owed to a third party, or otherwise

imposed by law. Additionally, nonaccess would be permissible as to firm documents intended for internal law office review and use. . . . This might include, for example, documents containing a firm attorney's general or other assessment of the client, or tentative preliminary impressions of the legal or factual issues presented in the representation, recorded primarily for the purpose of giving internal direction to facilitate performance of the legal services entailed in that representation.[9]

This narrow exception conforms to preexisting authority as set forth by Arizona in an advisory opinion:

[The attorney's obligation to turn over documents to his client] does not, however, extend to such things as the attorney's own notes and memos to himself; nor to his myriad scratching on note sheets; nor to records of passing thoughts dictated to a machine or a secretary and placed in the file; nor to ideas, plans or outlines as to the course the attorney's representation is to take. Those recorded thoughts remain the property of the attorney and, in our opinion, he need not release those even though his bill has been paid in full.[10]

As such, like the entire holding of *Sage v. Proskauer*, it represents not an extension of existing authority, but merely an exposition of it. In considering the holdings above, and the other ethics authorities covering client access to matter files, the lawyer should consider their applicability to electronic records and data, and the potentially enormous scope of their impact on the electronic data maintained by lawyers and law firms. Analytically, there is no meaningful difference between say, a formal written letter to a client and e-mail sent to them.[11] Both objects have the same legal status for virtually every purpose, and to the extent that an ethical duty attaches to a data object created in one medium, there is no reason to believe that the same duty does not attach when a comparable data object is created or transmitted via another medium. "Information shall not be denied legal effect, validity or enforceability solely on the grounds that it is not contained in the data message purporting to give rise to such legal effect, but is merely referred to in that data message."[12]

These legal realities force a simple conclusion: The concept of a single physical case file is simply outmoded. The "case file" is now a complex dataset containing not only traditional paper documents, but a wide variety of electronic data objects likely to be distributed over at least several platforms. This, in turn, points to the need to consistently organize those data objects if ethical and client service needs are to be met. The above references lead to the likelihood that *any* data object created during the course of the representation may well be viewed by a court or other authority as presumptively belonging to the client, thus requiring an affirmative demonstration by the lawyer that it is not in order to withhold it from the client. And, to the extent that the lawyer is bound by an ethical duty to manage her records and information effectively, that duty obviously extends to electronic information.

For the lawyer, this trend, and its extension to electronic data objects, poses a substantial records and information management issue. Aside from the pure question of ownership, DR 2-108 (D) and many following authorities implicate sound management of records and information associated with a representation: part and parcel of the duties of protecting the client's interests and delivering records to the client is the obligation to maintain the records and information in a manner that will facilitate their effective use on behalf of the client, and ultimately, their delivery to the client. If the records are not well organized or lost, the lawyer may well be unable to comply with these needs, thereby subjecting the lawyer to the potential of malpractice or disciplinary action.

This requirement has generally posed few issues for the formal hard-copy matter file itself beyond cost and annoyance. But the hard-copy file, if not particularly well organized, is at least more or less in one place and all labeled as a single collection. For electronic data objects associated with a representation, however, the situation is likely to be considerably worse. Most computer users create and maintain their electronic data in a manner inconsistent with sound records and data management principles. Indeed, they frequently fail to apply even the most basic of hard copy filing and control principles to the digital counterparts of the information contained in hard-copy files. Structured electronic file systems and directories, with well-indexed contents, are the exception rather than the norm, and formal taxonomies and naming conventions for electronic files are all too frequently nonexistent.

The problem is exacerbated in those organizations where every individual has his or her unique (and frequently poorly conceived) system for naming and saving files, and in reality it is often no system at all. Unfortunately, the larger the organization, the worse the problem usually is. Law firms pose particular challenges, since most have a culture of independence with little or no central direction over the way a lawyer does anything except bill time. Handling of electronic records, even though the records do not belong to the individual lawyer but are the charge of the firm, is almost always up to the individual, and this one issue is in large part responsible for the situation in which we find ourselves today. Even when the firm has purchased and implemented tools such as document management software, these tools are of little help when people do not use them or use them improperly. These tools are pretty much useless unless workable, responsive, and utilitarian indices, taxonomies, and other data management structures have been implemented and consistent processes enforced. In such circumstances, the chances of a lawyer quickly and accurately finding what she needs to do her job, let alone respond to a client's demand for all data objects relating to a representation, pose a formidable, billable-time consuming, and expensive challenge.

In cases where a firm uses e-mail to transact significant matter-related business, these challenges multiply. The content of most e-mail systems is poorly organized, and may be subject to policies that make it almost impossible to manage the content while creating clear conflicts with ethics requirements. E-mail protocols that delete all e-mail after 30, 60, or 90 days are a very clear example of this. If, as is usually the case these days, e-mail is being used extensively to conduct client- and matter-related business, a short-term e-mail retention and quick disposition policy will usually result in deletion of significant amounts of relevant material, including client communications that are not being maintained elsewhere or that might require inconvenient and costly restoration from sources such as backup tapes. Compounding this problem is the truth that attachments to e-mail, often marked drafts of documents circulated between client and counsel, seldom if ever make it into document/content management systems and so are not captured, version controlled, or available later if the firm needs to reconstruct the evolution of a transaction.

Data objects such as voice mail or instant messaging logs, which are notoriously disorganized, or data from unified messaging data systems (systems that capture voice mail, e-mail, and sometimes instant messaging in a single electronic data system) may prove even more burdensome if the installation parameters and ongoing management of the system are not carefully thought out and implemented.

The Need for Effective Data Capture and Retrieval

It would be nice if electronic data were self-organizing, but that will not be the case unless well-thought-out processes and controls are in place and users have received good training. The data in some programs, such as accounting, billing, or conflicts checking software, are often highly and effectively organized within their own structures. Others are not. If, for example, one uses the Microsoft suite of office software products, she will by default save her output into the "My Documents" folder. This is an improvement from the past, when the default folder for Word was "Word," the default folder for Excel spreadsheets was "Excel," and so on. However, for purposes of say, retrieving items related to a particular client, this is not effective. A lawyer may have hundreds of clients, and co-mingling all of their documents in a single directory is hardly efficient. If software tools creating similar objects from other vendors are used, they do not necessarily follow the Microsoft convention, and the result of using the default setting for each means the creation of multiple and inconsistent directories, with each containing some material from multiple clients. And since data structures from different applications are not necessarily consolidated, the problem is exacerbated. Even within the Microsoft world, not everything goes to the same place. E-mail goes into an "inbox," regardless of sender or topic, making for one more general repository within which a particular client's information may be found.

This distributed storage of information objects is contrary to the notion of a master matter file, and thereby contrary to the underlying assumption of most ethical duties surrounding client-related information. From an ethical standpoint, matter-related data, regardless of source, repository, or medium, should be considered as a unified whole, and logic and good practice dictate that it be managed as such and indexed appropriately. That management should utilize tools that facilitate its retrieval in its entirety, and also at a very granular, document-specific level, at a reasonable cost and with minimal effort.

Managing the Dataset

The question then becomes one of how this structuring and organization can best be accomplished. We have discussed the value of records management software that organizes both paper and electronic information, and physically manages and retrieves electronic information. We have also talked about records management software, which is indeed part of the solution, but that software is not *the* solution, nor is it even the first piece of the solution. The garbage-in-garbage-out rule applies to records management software in precisely the same manner as it does to any other software. So even when use of records management software is contemplated, it is important to take those first steps that will ensure that the input is not garbage.

In some cases, however, the use of records management software may not be on the table, and for valid reasons. The office may be too small or the budget may not include resources for acquiring the software right now. (Organizational ennui in large firms is *not* a valid reason.)

This does not mean that nothing can be done. On the contrary, most of the steps that are a necessary precursor to effective acquisition and deployment of records management software have enormous potential value to the small law office and can, when used in conjunction with appropriate procedures and controls, be powerful aids to a well-managed and successful practice. Even in the absence of records management software, well-defined processes and workflow, combined with good organization, may offer substantial relief to any lawyer suffering from both hard-copy and electronic information management headaches. And, much of their value can come at minimal or no direct, out-of-pocket cost. All that is required is the investment of a small amount of time to think through some concepts, and the discipline to apply them consistently.

Data Structures

Elsewhere in this book, we have discussed data structures and taxonomies—indices, file plans, and the like. The first step in management of electronic data is the application of the concepts that help you build a good taxonomy for your office's records.

The initial problem confronting management of electronic data is that the default data structures in most software are poorly designed from the records management perspective. The good news is that, in most cases, these default structures can be altered. Doing so, however, requires careful consideration of the design of the data structure and a modest time investment.

Consider, for example, the question of word processing documents created in a small law office that does not have the luxury of a well-configured and deployed document management application. Virtually every law office, regardless of size or its use of technology, will create large numbers of word processing documents in the course of business. These documents will encompass administrative matters as well as client work. Within the client sphere, there will be an assortment of document types, the precise makeup of which is dependent upon the nature of the practice, and of course, many that are common to any type of representation.

An obvious first step is to create multiple directories or folders (and within them as needed, subfolders or subdirectories) based upon client identity and piece of work or administrative record type. The second step is to apply a standard, universal naming convention to those folders. These concepts are not difficult, and their design is not particularly complex. All that is required is a bit of thought, and the asking of a few simple questions *before* creating and loading a master data structure. Consider:

- *What is the most intuitive and meaningful structure for my data?* Should it be segregated by client? (Probably) Matter type? (Probably) Business function? (Again, probably so) Document type? (Maybe) Note that for different types of records, the convention may be different. Client matters may best be identified and categorized by client name and nature of the representation, while administrative records may best be organized by function—accounting, business development, human resources, and so on.
- *What are the most intuitive and meaningful naming conventions for my electronic (and hard-copy) folders?* Client name (Jones, John)? Matter name (*Smith v. Jones*)? Matter number?

◆ *Within any folder, what subfolders, if any, should be created that will provide a meaningful and logical path to any document I will look for? Pleadings? Correspondence (and within it, breakdowns for client, opposing counsel, and so on)?*

Developing a data structure after consideration of these questions will yield (surprise!) a file plan or index like those discussed earlier in this book. In most cases it will closely if not exactly mirror the organizational approach for managing hard-copy files. The same basic conventions and rules apply— the structure and terms should be almost intuitive, the number of choices at any decision point should be limited to a reasonable number, and the number of levels in the index hierarchy can and should be limited to three or four. Once developed, the investment in time needed to apply the rule to a folder set for a new matter is measured in seconds. The question then becomes what should go into these folders.

File Naming Conventions

All electronic files get named something. The problem is that many of them get names that are useless or nearly so. This alone is the source of many records management issues—even within a well-designed directory structure, poorly named files create uncertainty and force users to open and inspect multiple files in order to confirm that the file they have retrieved is indeed the correct one. In the absence of a well-defined and well-executed structure, poorly named files can mean they are effectively lost.

As with directory and file structures, file naming is primarily a question of logic and consistency. If complaints are called "complaints" within the firm, the file must be named "complaint" every time, not "complaint" here and "comp" there and "pleadings—comp" somewhere else. To this simple consistency can be added other data points that will significantly facilitate the retrievability of electronic documents. The first and most obvious choices are

◆ *Client Name.* If you have a large volume of clients, describe each with its formal name and assign each a unique number. It makes things a lot easier.

◆ *Matter Description.* Be concise, be clear, and again, if your practice dictates that you may represent the same client multiple times, create a clear and descriptive name for each representation and assign a unique number to each matter.

◆ *Version Number.* If you draft documents and revise them more than once, number the drafts and indicate which were forwarded to the client for review. Consider using a code to indicate which drafts *went to* the client and which *came from* the client.

◆ *Creation Date.* Do not confuse this with the date in the word directory detail—that doesn't necessarily indicate the actual date on which the document was created.

A file might thus be identified as:

03 William B. Jones
02 Smith v. Jones Litigation
Complaint v2
2005-02-03

Shortcuts—To Chaos

And while it might be tempting to shortcut the naming a bit and simply call the file, say "complaint 2005-02-03" or "2nd complaint," *don't do it.* You may know right now that this refers to the *Smith v. Jones* litigation, but what happens in four months when you are dealing with the *Smith v. Brown* litigation and you are creating the second complaint for that case?

The implications of such shortcuts should be carefully thought out. Even the most diligent and accurate of staff using a manual file naming and processing system will make a mistake occasionally (purely manual filing systems yield 0.5 to 1.5 percent error rates). Avoiding shortcuts (or giving in to laziness, as the case may be) means not having to deal with the panic that sets in when a document is inadvertently saved or moved to the wrong directory. Remember, it can most easily be found if it is described so that the file name contains full information about the document. If portions of the naming conventions are left out, then a later search of the directory— or of multiple directories—is likely to turn up a number of candidate documents that must be inspected to determine which is correct. The few seconds required to apply a truly meaningful and helpful file name will be repaid bountifully in time saved locating files.

The order of terms in the file name is dependent upon the way documents are searched, and may also be dependent upon the structure within which they are placed. A client document might be "complaint 02-3-2005 Jones John" while an employment tax return might be "//client name// Employment Tax 2005 941 Q2." Different file naming conventions will result in different on-screen sort orders, and this may make a difference as well. This does not mean that everything must have and follow the same rule set; it just means that different practices and file sets may require different protocols. A few general rules do, however, apply. Within a case folder, all documents will be from that case, so leading the title with document type or some other parameter will make for a more meaningfully sorted display. For tax documents, date followed by form number may often be best. If a full date is used as a primary naming term, beginning with the year may be helpful.

Documents named according to the convention "03-13-2005 941 Q4" will sort by month, then form type, then quarter. If named according to the convention "2005-03-13 941 Q4," they will sort by year, then by form type, and then by quarter, which is normally a more desirable sort. Obviously, the same convention could also be arranged for quarter to immediately follow year, to get a real chronological sort.

For example, a file structure containing your firm's tax filings might look like this:

Accounting
   Tax filings

       2004 941 Q1
       2004 841 Q2
       2004 941 Q3
       2004 941 Q4
       2004 1120

       2005 941 Q1
       2005 841 Q2
       2005 941 Q3
       2005 941 Q4
       2005 1120

In a small-office environment with relatively limited volumes of documents, such a structure may well be a complete solution, without the need for record management software.

There exists no comprehensive master plan to overlay all of the varieties of law offices' client and administrative file structures, and while designing one to suit the needs of a particular law office takes a bit of focus, it is not an insurmountable challenge. As noted earlier, the keys are

- Intuitive and logical structure;
- Intuitive and meaningful terminology; and
- Consistent use.

Frequent users will quickly learn the details of any structure and naming convention, and will be able to navigate it effectively provided that it is logically structured. A meaningless rule set or taxonomy is as bad as random naming and indexing, and will cost users a great deal of lost time as they attempt to guess the places where an item might be filed.

E-mail

E-mail poses many of the same problems as other electronic data, and it responds well to many of the same problem-solving organizational strategies. If records management software is in the plan, it may contain a relatively comprehensive grouping and indexing functionality. Normally, this involves dropping e-mails sent or received into predefined client/matter/ issue folders along with all other electronic and paper documents. With a bit of training and conformance to a few rules, some of these e-mails can actually file themselves. Properly applied, this can be a complete solution.

If records management software is not being used, other solutions are available. Within the e-mail program itself, directories and subdirectories can be created for e-mail that mimic the hard copy and word processing file structures so you are, in effect, creating one normalized taxonomy that applies to all information in all media. As an alternative, many e-mail programs permit an e-mail to be saved, as either a text or .html file, to a location other than the e-mail program-defined .pst file, thus permitting its filing directly into a subfolder within a single matter folder or other directory to which it relates, along with everything else concerning that matter. Some e-mail programs also permit automatic sorting of e-mail based upon sender or other parameters, although these may, if not configured correctly, have the disadvantage of sending e-mail directly to multiple in-boxes, rather than a single location where it can be easily perused on a daily basis.

Although e-mail messages do not have names, and so there cannot be a naming convention for them, they all have subject lines and a similar concept can be applied to that subject line. A significant problem when attempting to locate a particular e-mail is that, even when the sending or receiving party is known, the subject header does not contain useful information about the contents of the e-mail. If multiple e-mails are received from or addressed to the same party, this requires the searcher to read or scan multiple e-mails until the desired one is found. This can waste a considerable amount of time.

The solution to this problem is to develop a standard subject line convention similar to that used for naming files. It could be client-matter number, client-matter names, or any number of things, provided only that the terms of the convention are well thought out and meaningful, agreed to by the user community, and consistently applied. If e-mails have important attachments, these should be covered by the convention as well.

Combined with either a directory structure within the e-mail program or a policy of saving e-mail directly into matter folders (or better yet, into records management software), a naming convention is a powerful tool. Its goal and outcome are the same as those of a directory structure and file naming convention: to attach meaningful and consistent summary information to electronic data, and to provide it to searchers as quickly and as easily as possible within the data structure in which it resides.

There are many possible file naming conventions. The key to making them work is consistent use. Time spent tinkering with them in order to develop a truly useful format is time well spent. Once developed and applied, good rules, consistently applied, save both time and frustration for the user. Applied within the context of a simple file structure, they make consistent filing and easy retrieval a matter of habit.

Regardless of the technology used, consistent application of a well-thought-out set of naming and filing conventions saves time, aggravation, and money and makes for better client service.

Notes

1. Sage Realty Corp. v. Proskauer Rose LLP, 689 N.E.2d 879 (1997).

2. *Id.,* 91 N.Y.2d 30 at 37.

3. *Id.,* 91 N.Y.2d 30 at 35, quoting Restatement [Third] of the Law Governing Lawyers § 58.

4. *Id.,* 91 N.Y.2d 30 at 36.

5. *Id.,* 91 N.Y.2d 30 at 36.

6. Swift, Currie, McGhee & Hiers v. Henry, 276 Ga. 571 (2003)

7. *Id.,* 276 Ga. 571 at 573.

8. *Id.*

9. Sage Realty Corp. v. Proskauer Rose LLP, 91 N.Y.2d 30 at 37.

10. Arizona Ethics Opinion 82-30.

11. *See, e.g.,* Armstrong v. Executive Office of the President, 1 F.3d 1274 (D.C. Cir. 1993).

12. United Nations Commission on International Trade (UNICTRAL) Model Law on Electronic Commerce, Art. 5 bis. See also United States Electronic Signatures in Global and National Commerce Act, P.L. 106-229.

Systems and Technology | **9**

Alternatives

Remember, records management is a set of systems, processes, and tools that combine to make possible the efficient use and maintenance of all the records and information in an organization. It also provides a framework and structure that facilitates (a) application of the firm's records management policy and (b) compliance with records retention requirements. Each element in the combination that makes this possible—systems, processes, and tools—is equally important to effective records management. For all the reasons covered earlier, and particularly for the effective management of e-mail, word processing documents, and other electronic and digital objects, automating the records function, applying technology wherever possible, makes elegant good sense.

Once the decision is made to automate the records management function, the next questions generally have to do with how to go about it and what software to use. The options available are varied, as are the costs, but there is an approach for virtually every law office that will save time and improve efficiency. Prior to building, purchasing, or deploying any software, records management or otherwise, it is a good idea to consider in some detail the functional needs of the firm, the expectations being made of the system, and the desired outcome of its deployment and use.

Commercial records management software applications are built based upon assumptions about user needs that derive from vendors' experience in the market and their assumptions about what will sell. A custom-developed or homegrown technology solution will be designed based upon assumptions about the needs of the individual firm for which it is developed as translated by the team that establishes the rules and the programmers that write the code. In both cases, commercial and custom, if those assumptions do not match user needs, the system will not deliver the desired performance.

Before You Do It Yourself

The situations under which the "do-it-yourself" approach is appropriate are somewhat limited, but there are times and places when it makes very good sense. A homegrown or custom-developed records management software program, with very limited functionality, might be appropriate for:

◆   A solo practitioner,
◆   A very small office, or
◆   A highly specialized practice with unique or very specific, non-mainstream requirements (rather than a multipractice firm).

A word of caution, however, is appropriate. Almost any firm of any size that relies heavily on e-mail and word processing documents—and that is pretty much every firm beyond those described as *very* small firms—would do well to use one of the commercial solutions that have been proven productive and efficient in the legal-specific market. The daily operational and compliance needs of most firms are so demanding that the time, effort, and resources necessary to develop a custom system that will come anywhere close to meeting their needs, and then keeping it up to speed with necessary changes over time, will be so extensive that a commercial solution becomes the obvious one for both functionality and cost reasons.

It does not make sense to design your own word processing software—and in most cases it does not make sense to develop your own records management software.

The Upsides and the Downsides of a Home-Built System

The reason most law offices try the "do-it-yourself" road is cost. (After all, it *is* just a filing system, isn't it?) This is absolutely the wrong reason; first, the time required to create an application with any real functionality is not short, and second, trying to avoid costs today by taking the do-it-yourself path generally means incurring far more costs later on. Since there are, however, a few reasons for some offices to take this road, let us look at the positives and negatives of doing it:

On the Upside

- *Getting Started*—When a law office is first getting started, making a minor investment in building a system yourself allows for exploration and experimentation in determining how a system should look and function.
- *Low Cost*—Designing your own system is an inexpensive way to invest in the development process. It is also, for some do-it-yourselfers, the only opportunity they have to apply automation to the management of the office's most precious resource if budget dollars are difficult to come by. Something is better than nothing, particularly if the features that are included in the homegrown system are those that the lawyers find most useful.

The Downside

- *Time Commitment*—Programming even a modest database is very time-intensive. Programming a database with even elementary records management functionality is likely to take a significant number of hours. A highly functional, fully tested, error-free, and user-friendly database that can be trusted to handle a significant number of real records management activities, and that can be used by lawyers and support staff lacking in technology experience, is likely to take several hundred hours or more of development time.
- *Expertise*—A little bit of programming knowledge *does not* go a long way. The less proficient the programmer, the more time that must be invested, both from an initial design and programming standpoint, and later on correcting the errors inevitably ensuing from inexperience that would not otherwise have arisen. Hard-to-find mistakes like logic errors that give plausible but incorrect results may drive your part-time or amateur programmer, as well as any users, to distraction. Very small law firms and solo practitioners are unlikely to have the in-house expertise to create records management software, and few law offices of any size are likely to have experienced and competent staff available, with time on their hands to learn a new discipline.

If either of the above considerations is applicable to your situation, and you are still set on creating a custom solution and the numbers tell you it is a possible way to go, hiring a good programmer on a one-off basis may be a workable option. Even if a firm takes the option of hiring outside expertise to create a custom solution, there are still significant issues to consider:

◆ *Lack of Regular Upgrades*—When contracting to build your own system, it is generally a one-time shot. You design it, you build it, and you use it. The programmer then goes on to something else and does not have time to devote to staying current with the discipline, investigating new functionality or capabilities, and issuing upgrades to the system—and that is assuming you know where the programmer is in two or three years.

◆ *No User Population Driving Changes*—Commercial software serves a wide user population. The impetus for change comes not just from one organization, but from a range of law offices with a variety of needs, which a wise vendor will translate into regular enhancements. The custom program has no such population driving changes.

◆ *Upgrades and Migration*—Most law offices change or significantly upgrade their automation platforms every few years. Firms that have old custom applications developed in-house that run on old systems are then faced with deciding whether to recreate their old system in a form that will function in the context of the new architecture, or purchase software from a reputable vendor with an established track record.

◆ *The Programmer Lacks Records Management Expertise*—If an in-house or even an experienced outside programmer is assigned the responsibility of creating a records management application, that programmer may have to learn the records management discipline from the ground up in order to fully understand and then translate the firm's needs into functionality and code. Such an approach puts a tremendous burden on any programmer who is new to the discipline.

◆ *The Programmer Has Other Projects*—A custom programmer seldom has responsibility for a single application and often has to split his or her time among several systems and programs. This may delay delivery of the program or result in less than desired functionality as the programmer has to limit the development time available for the project. If a firm uses an outside custom programmer, because of competing demands for his or her time, that individual may simply not be willing to take the time to learn records management, or they may feel that the time investment is too great. In either case, a program designed without a sound understanding of records management is likely to be of limited or no utility.

◆ *The Hostage Factor*—One of the greatest factors weighing against a homegrown program is the potential for loss of the person who developed the system—and that is the same person who will be needed to fix it when it breaks. The nightmare version of this scenario is when the in-house developer of the new system departs (without having created any documentation) and offers to sell his or her services back to the firm as a consultant. Even though this person may not be an expert in the software used, or an expert in the discipline of records management, he or she may well be the only resource available for making changes because he or she is are the only one who knows what was developed and how the program was structured.

- *Lack of Documentation*—While independent programmers may write pretty good code, they may not create much in the way of usable documentation. Creation of thorough documentation is an absolute necessity, and this documentation, along with the code, should be escrowed as a hedge against future situations where the programmer may not be available.

- *Training*—We may admire and respect our programmer's skills, but is he or she the right person to be doing the training? Remember that training should be targeted to the audience. Unless you do the programming yourself, for your sole use, and you do not care what happens after you are gone, you are going to want some sort of training program so each new person can understand what is happening, and why, and be brought up to speed on the new system. Learning as you go, without any help, is a bad idea.

If the homegrown route is chosen, the keys to making the investment one that will meet expectations are not to invest too much money or too much time, and to be prepared to:

- *Document It*—Adequately document the system so you cannot be held hostage. You should know how it works and you should have suitable documentation available so another programmer can step in and make changes.

- *Protect It*—Escrow both the source code and the documentation. This will provide protection and assure the office access to the software in case something happens to the programmer or the firm that develops your custom application.

- *Create User Documentation and Training Materials*—It does not have to be sophisticated, but it does have to do the job.

Other Do-It-Yourself Approaches

Not every do-it-yourself approach requires deep programming expertise. There are tools that lawyers use every day that have the potential to create and manage file lists. While these tools do not provide the ability to create the functionality of the sophisticated (and expensive) commercial systems, if properly used, they can help the solo or small office greatly improve control over their records.

Primary Tools—Word Processing and Spreadsheets

Most of the word processing systems and suites of office products currently in use in law offices, and all of the leading products, have attributes that can be leveraged as tools for developing records management systems. As we said earlier, although systems developed based on these tools will not have anything approaching the functionality of the most basic off-the-shelf records management applications, a basic and helpful records system can be developed using standard word processors and spreadsheets.

For our purposes, a standard office software suite includes the two applications, a word processor and a spreadsheet, that are most useful to the minimally trained user in creating records management tools. Other important tools are the e-mail program (most typically Microsoft Outlook in today's law office) and for the more adept user, a database like Microsoft Access. And although lawyers as a group are highly intelligent, if they do not already know how to program in Access, this is not the time to shut down the practice and learn how.

Although many of these applications have built-in defaults for data storage locations and other parameters (such as the Microsoft "My Documents" directory), these are user-configurable to a high degree. It is this configurability that offers the prospect of using them as basic records management tools. This lets us take advantage of a few simple facts:

- The computer operating system uses a hierarchical folders-and-files data structure similar to that of a standard records indexing scheme.
- The intercompatibility of the software, along with its built-in configurability, permit the unified management of data objects from more than one program.
- The operating system will have a rudimentary search function supporting queries based on content or titles.

Keys to a Successful Design

Using standard software for records management requires that the features in these applications be leveraged and their value extended with development of basic conceptual tools: a suitable index and file structure hierarchy, file naming conventions, and so on. These tools, combined with their careful and consistent use, let the everyday user develop a basic but workable records management capability in their office provided that the number of data objects under management is fairly small, and consistently titled.

The "My Documents" folder in Windows can be modified or replaced by a file structure similar to those outlined in previous chapters. In a similar manner, e-mail directories can be configured to mirror the overall scheme, or substantive e-mail can be saved directly into the subject matter directories to which it relates. So we take a big, and very useful, first step by creating and using the same hierarchical structures for managing both our word processing documents and our e-mail. Combined with suitable file naming conventions that are consistently used for all data objects created in the course of work, this first step provides a surprisingly powerful baseline records management capability. Our next tasks are careful development of the data structure and the file naming conventions, and making sure that we maintain a high degree of consistency in their application.

On the other hand, if software is used that does not permit user choice of file-saving location, or if hardware platforms with no cross-talk capability are in use, this approach may begin to break down—fixed data structures may be unpredictable, may not meet your specific logic requirements, and documents will not be easy to find. Thus, if accounting software or time-management software is used that saves its data to a subdirectory of "program files" or some such place, and this cannot be reconfigured, this data resides outside of the records management hierarchy and must be manually tracked and managed. Fortunately, there is less and less of this minimally functional—and minimally useful—software in the market these days.

Spreadsheets

If functionality beyond creating consistently structured lists is desired, but no one is interested in or capable of database development (see above discussion regarding Access), a spreadsheet, properly used, can be a fairly powerful development tool. A spreadsheet can be particularly helpful in creating and organizing structured lists of files and other objects that relate to a specific matter and tracking changes to the location of those files or the boxes when they are moved as activity slows down.

If, in a spreadsheet, every row represents a record or folder (aka a data object), and if every cell represents a useful bit of information (aka a metadata point) for that item in some standard order (e.g., column 1 = date the object was created, column 2 = the highest level index entry, and so on), careful and consistent design and use will yield a solid file-tracking tool. The sort function of the spreadsheet permits items to be sorted by any of the metadata points represented by the columns, or by some combination of them in a nested sort. So if your indexing and other data entry tasks are consistently executed, this alone results in a useful query tool. Advanced spreadsheet users may also be able to create and use other search and sort functionality through the use of macros, links to other documents, and similar features. Further, should the firm ever move up to database or records management software, all of the efforts to this point in categorizing, indexing, and organizing are not wasted—the spreadsheet will be a useful, easy, and economical way to load a great deal of data into new records management software that would otherwise have to be keyed in manually.

It is important to remember that whether you are using basic tools and approaches or sophisticated off-the-shelf tools, and whether you are doing it yourself or using third-party experts, the primary records management tools are the same: a well-designed data structure, a logical hierarchy, and consistent naming conventions. Your basic set of office software applications has value in and of itself, but unless serious thought is given to data structure, logical hierarchy, and consistent naming conventions, its potential value as a tool for records management capabilities is extremely limited.

Databases

The next step up from the basic set of office applications with which most users are familiar is the use of a commercial database program such as Access or SQL for development of a home-built records management system. Commercial databases are attractive tools for developing systems if you have the resources—the time and skill—to make full use of their potential. Since most records management applications are created using commercial databases, it might seem to make sense to use a commercial database to build your own system. Be very careful before you go down this path. Building a good, fully functional records management application takes a substantial amount of time in design, testing, debugging, report writing, and other areas. Before you start with this approach, make sure you have the skill to do it or oversee it, the time to take away from revenue-producing work, and the attention to devote to nonclient service issues.

Records Management Software

Records management software refers to software developed specifically to meet the records management needs of users. It comes in two primary forms:

- *Commercial Off-the-Shelf*—This is the software you buy in prepackaged form. This commercial off-the-shelf (COTS) software has usually been developed for a specific market, in this case law firms and law departments, and presumably has functionality and capability that will spur its selection by large numbers of happy buyers.
- *Custom Systems*—For purposes of our discussion, a custom-built records management software program is one developed to meet the specific needs and requirements of one user by a third-party

developer. Many COTS software packages started out as custom systems. The programmer then saw that there was probably a more general demand and went to market with it after making a few changes to make it more attractive to a broader range of users. Custom-developed systems are far less the norm today than they were just a few years ago, for very good reasons as described previously.

Off-the-Shelf Software

There are substantial functionality and cost differences among the COTS records management (RM) software packages available today:

- *Original Specifications*—First in importance is the quality of the original list of functional requirements on which the base product was built. If the product was built based on requirements developed by a highly qualified, experienced set of records management and systems professionals, the odds are good that the system originally met most of the requirements of discriminating buyers and that it has continued to evolve. If it was not designed by a well-rounded team, some desirable functionality was likely missing from the original application, and the product today may be clumsy and inefficient. The greatest difference today among COTS RM software products is the elegance, comprehensiveness, and ease-of-use with which they handle digital/electronic records such as e-mail, word processing documents in multiple content management applications, spreadsheets, and databases.
- *Frequency and Quality of Upgrades*—Vendors that do not frequently improve their software products based on user input and according to an established schedule tend to lag the field in today's competitive market.
- *Complexity*—The more sophisticated the package, the more it is going to do, and the more it is probably (but not always) going to cost.
- *Size of User Base*—All other factors being equal, pricing often depends on the number of users the system will be supporting. Licensing costs for a system supporting half a dozen users on a small, one-office network are going to be far lower than that same system running on a network that supports hundreds of users in multiple offices.
- *Platform*—Rarity plays a role. Vendors develop their software to run on the most widely installed computer platforms and operating systems, and to interface with the most commonly run programs. If you have an unusual or custom system, the software may not run well on it without significant additional work. If you run esoteric or

unusual software, it may not interface with some or all records management packages. The records management software vendor may be able to resolve compatibility issues or write a custom interface, but this is not usually free, and may be quite expensive.

We list (see Appendix 5) but are not recommending specific software vendors or applications for a number of reasons:

- *Vendors come and go.* A vendor may well be in business when this book is first printed but may not be around when you read this, while a vendor not previously in the market may enter it, and enter it with an excellent application.
- *Software changes.* Vendors (the best ones, anyway) are constantly working on enhancements to their existing products, so any rankings published today, if based purely on functional capabilities, might be out-of-date as soon as one of the contenders issues a new version.
- *Software selection should not be based solely on technical issues.* There are many factors aside from functional capability that should affect your decision to acquire software from a particular vendor. It is important to establish an objective evaluation system for other factors such as how long the company has been in business, how many installations it has, how well it integrates with other applications, the depth of the vendor's staff in legal records management expertise, and the quality of their support team—all factors that may affect your satisfaction with the product.
- *The importance of specific criteria will vary from one law office to another.* A law firm with an IBM mainframe or an aging AS/400 computer may not care how many installations the vendor has in a networked client-server environment. A general counsel's office evaluating records software probably will not care how well the conflicts checking module operates. A plaintiff's firm may have very different requirements than a full-service corporate firm. And, a law office with substantial in-house systems expertise may not give heavy weight to the fact that a vendor offers deep and comprehensive conversion support. So a factor that is worth 10 points on the 1 to 10 scale for one law office might not even register on the scale of another.
- *Ratings are subjective.* Of necessity, ratings reflect the biases of the rater, if not in the ratings, then in the categories and the weightings given them. Hopefully, these biases reflect those that should be in place to reflect the needs of the acquiring law firm. Sometimes it is

worthwhile to pay for experienced and knowledgeable objectivity and subjectivity.

If you are not sure of the criteria upon which to base your evaluations, it is worthwhile to get experienced, high-quality assistance from someone who knows legal records management well. Borrowing someone else's list of qualifications and applying it to your situation without careful thought, without full consideration of your own situation, and without an understanding of records management in general and your firm's requirements in particular will lead to a poor outcome.

Custom-Developed Systems

As used here, a custom-developed system is one that is developed by a commercial vendor. There are few situations today in which the development of a sophisticated customized records management system from a commercial vendor is warranted. Earlier, we discussed the downside of developing your own records management software. Most of those issues apply to custom-developed systems as well. At the current stage of development, COTS RM software is very robust and highly configurable. The development costs for any mature application have been spread over a large user base by the vendor, and unless the software is a completely new product, the reputable developers will have fixed most bugs and deployed many user-driven enhancements. A custom program that matches this level of performance will be very costly, and since it is new, will have the usual teething problems in terms of bugs, compatibility issues, and so on in far greater number than a mature COTS package. Only the most compelling and unusual requirements are likely to outweigh these disadvantages.

Timing and Selection of Software Acquisition

Whether purchasing software from a vendor or developing it in-house, software acquisition and deployment should be something that occurs later, rather than sooner, in the process of building a records management program. It is tempting to purchase and install software early on for several reasons: the urge to have a new toy is strong; the buyer may assume that having the new software will somehow make other predeployment tasks easier, or even do away with the need to complete some of the required preliminary work; it may seem desirable to have something tangible to show early on in the form of running software; and besides, buying sophisticated software is much more glamorous than building a pedestrian file plan.

Giving in to these urges is a mistake. Unsuccessful records management software installations are generally the result of responding to these urges. Since value does not accompany the unplanned purchase, money is spent too soon. Proper preparation and attention to detail will substantially impact the decision about actual software that will be acquired and its ultimate cost, and will pave the way for a successful installation. The question then becomes, *"What are those preparations?"*

The Functional Specification

Since software is supposed to do something, it is important to understand exactly what it is you want the software to do. Of course, we know in a general sense what we want records management software to do—it must manage records. Presumably, every reputable commercial package is capable of doing so. There is far more to it than this, however.

Within the limits of its configurability, records management software manages records in accordance with several built-in limitations, including:

- *Philosophy*—The developers must subscribe to a basic theory about what records are and how they should be managed. Ask the vendor to define a record and to differentiate that definition from the definitions of information and data;
- *Intended Users*—Specific functionality may derive from the needs of a particular industry, or particular users—in this case, law offices and lawyers. Find out how many law firm or general counsel installations they have and when they were last updated;
- *Platform*—The software may run on a particular platform, operating system, database, etc.;
- *Scalability*—The software may be intended for small installations with relatively few users and a small volume of records, or for large installations with hundreds or thousands of users and millions of records. Find out if the software can handle millions of objects. You would be surprised to see the number you come up with if you count all the documents and e-mails in your office and how much that number grows every day;
- *Hard-copy and Electronic Records Functionality*—The software may be designed to manage and track only hard-copy files in a file room, only boxes of records in a storage facility, or only a specific type of electronic records, such as e-mail—ask for proof; and
- *Compatibility*—The software may be compatible with and interface easily with just one type of financial system or document manage-

ment software from a single vendor. If a vendor owns and sells both records management and document management software, and makes it difficult to integrate with any other vendor's document management solution, it might not make much sense to purchase that vendor's records management software if you do not have or are not committed to getting that same vendor's document management software.

These factors result in software that is intended to do certain things in certain ways. If skillfully programmed, it will do them well. It may not, however, do other things as well, or at all. This is not necessarily a flaw in the software; rather it is a result of the design philosophy of the developers. Since it is not possible to do everything for everyone, the developers have identified a prospective user base and attempted to craft a product that is responsive to the overall needs of that user base, within whatever other limitations—programming resources, budget, and so on—the developer must live with. And of course, the success of the outcome depends first upon the viability of the developer's philosophy and second upon the skill and insight of the designers and programmers in accomplishing the goals embodied in that philosophy.

The choices the developer makes and the solutions they craft may or may not be compatible with the actual needs of prospective buyers. If buyers are to choose software prudently, not only must they understand the design choices made by the developer, they must also understand their own needs. It pays for buyers to develop a strong and comprehensive functional specification of their own needs against which software can be vetted.

A functional specification is simply an ordered and structured listing of the user's needs. It need not be a technical document, and does not require a deep technical background to prepare. What is required is a sound and detailed understanding of what is possible in the records management discipline, the actual needs of the prospective user community, the actual demands that will be placed on the software, and the limitations of the environment within which it must run.

Technical Specifications

The functional specification may be broadly broken into two parts, technical and user-based. In a functional specification, the technical aspects are of a general nature, but are critical. If, for example, a law firm runs on Apple computers, or uses the Oracle database platform, a records management software package that cannot support them is unlikely to be well-received or successfully installed, regardless of its other merits. General factors of this sort include:

◆ *Database*—as discussed previously, Oracle, SQL, Access, or something else;

◆ *Operating system*—Windows, OS2, Apple, and so on;

◆ *Software*—Microsoft Office, WordPerfect, accounting software, conflict-checking software, etc.

◆ *Scalability*—one location, ten locations? Three users, a thousand users? Ten thousand objects, five million objects?

Know Your Needs

In a large-scale environment, there may be many other such factors, some of which will be effectively non-negotiable—either the software meets the need or it does not, and if it does not, it must be stricken from the list of candidates. Purchasing incompatible software and then attempting to pound the rest of the organization into some makeshift fix to accommodate its limitations will not only be unsuccessful, but it will make the firm's staff and the users exceedingly unhappy.

Work with the Computer People

All of this, of course, requires that this list of factors be in hand when vetting candidate software. Do your homework and get expert help from those who know your technical environment and parameters. It is imperative that, prior to and during the vetting of any software, technical personnel be consulted to ensure that these factors are properly considered, so that the software will function correctly in the preexisting environment with a minimum of difficulty and expense. The firm's technical staff, whether an in-house IT staff or an occasional on-call consultant, should have an in-depth understanding of the full array of important issues within the firm's particular computing environment. Since they are the ones who will be charged with making the software work and keeping it working, and ensuring that it does not compromise the rest of the system, they are in most cases highly motivated to participate in the software vetting and selection process.

Firm and Individual User Considerations

Once technical factors have been accounted for, user needs must be considered. These will encompass a wide variety of issues, including:

◆ *Indexing and File Plans*—The software should support any indexing scheme and file plan that the firm has developed for both administrative records and matter files without complicated work-arounds. If, for example, the firm uses a four-level index, the software must permit at least a four-deep index, while allowing for additional titling and subfiling levels. If the firm has a document collection with unusual indexing parameters (e.g., maps are often indexed by township and range or some other system which permits querying by maps of physically adjacent parcels of land), the software must support this as well or integrate with a document management system that allows this specific capability.

- *Query and Search Strategies*—When not using targeted indices, or in conjunction with them, users will conduct various types of searches specific to their needs. Examples include simple keyword searches, Boolean (using AND, OR, NOT, and similar operators) searches, nested and similar searches (using parentheses and other advanced operators to create complex Boolean searches), date range searches, searches by document creator, and many others alone and in combination with one another. The software must support all of these.

- *Media*—The firm may be all paper (some still are), all electronic (not yet), or a mixture of both (almost all of us). Does the software support management of whatever media the firm has? As the firm moves more and more to a digital workspace, does the software have functionality that will aid in the transition? What about less common data objects such as .wav or MP3 files? The software should support at least the most important, and preferably all, of the media and data types used by the firm today and anticipated for use over the next five years.

- *Policies and Procedures*—If the firm has policies and procedures on such issues as privacy, ethical walls, data ownership, and similar matters, can the software support enforcement of them?

- *Security*—Does the software support flexibility in assigning data security and access rights commensurate with the firm's needs?

- *Containers*—Does the software manage single documents without a huge administrative burden? Does it manage complete hard-copy as well as virtual or combined folders? If the firm has boxed records either on-site or off-site, and in multiple facilities with differing number schemes, can the software manage all of them? The software must offer choices and granularity options that match the practice needs of the office.

- *Ease of Use*—This encompasses many things:
  - Are default, full user RM screen layouts easy and intuitive to understand?
  - Can different screen layouts be easily designed and deployed for different types of users?

- Is navigation from one function to another easy and intuitive?
- Are menus and drop-down boxes configurable to limit the display to a reasonable number of choices or favorites, or must the user scroll through long lists to find the correct item?
- Are data entry screens configurable for maximum user ease and efficiency, as, for example, by permitting users to tab through data entry fields rather than having to use the mouse, and by customizing available fields?
- Are the fields appropriately sized to support the index entries and file names being used by the firm?
- Is the help system context sensitive and modifiable by the firm so you can insert your own examples and specific instructions?

- *E-mail*—Does the software manage e-mail and other electronic/digital objects, and does that management capability effectively meet the needs of the firm's own e-mail management philosophy? Is it easy enough to use that staff will actually use it or does using the application in reality add a huge administrative burden?

- *Workflow*—If the firm is contemplating automated workflow, does the software support integration with workflow software? If so, which type, the vendor's proprietary workflow software or a variety of proven COTS products?

- *Configurability*—How easy or hard is it to configure the software to do all of the above? Once configured, how hard is it to change any of the settings? Must every user adopt the same configuration or can the configuration be modified based on individual or group needs?

- *Bells and Whistles*—In addition to basic functionality, records management software commonly comes with the potential for a variety of add-ons such as bar-coding capability (which reduces data entry and may permit more effective tracking of files), printing of color-coded labels, and other features. Any or all of these may or may not be of interest to the firm.

Get Other Input

A thorough analysis of the firm's actual user needs is likely to reveal other factors of varying importance, and collectively, these and the technical specifications will, when suitably structured, form a substantial part of the specification. Additionally, the developers of the technical and functionality specifications will do well to compare their documentation against that developed by other firms and against industry best practices to get a fuller understanding of the benefits such software can bring and what functionality is necessary in order to deliver it.

The point to bear in mind is that the most effective and compatible software cannot be selected until these things are known; and they cannot be known with any certainty unless and until the firm knows a great deal about itself, about records management in law firms generally, about its specific needs, and about the technical and cultural environments in which it will have to operate. Rarely does the firm's records management committee know this *a priori*. This means that prior to, or concurrently with the software selection process, a considerable amount of data collection and analysis must be performed, and some conceptual tools such as file plans and indices, if not fully developed, are at least fully designed. This means that much or all of the data collection and analysis for the entire records management initiative should be performed before making any decisions about software and probably should be done even before evaluating the software products. Do not invite the vendors in for demonstrations until you are well educated and prepared to evaluate their offerings or they will make the decision for you.

Utilizing a Functional Specification

Take Control

When all of the relevant technical and user factors are gathered and ordered, they must be ranked. Some requirements may well be deal killers—the absence of some key functionality may exclude a particular software product from consideration. Other requirements fall into descending categories from very important to slightly important or even, *"Gee, that sounds nice but we don't really need it."* The ranking is important—it may be that no COTS product has every feature desired, so the various vendors' offerings must be ranked according to their ability to meet a prioritized set of requirements. In custom programming, and to some extent in COTS packages, more features means more programming and therefore more cost and time, so unless the budget is effectively unlimited, desired features must be ranked in order of the value they bring, the availability of funds to pay for them, and the necessity to see them actually in place in the near future. There is no hard-and-fast rule here—a deal killer for one firm may be irrelevant to another firm. The trick is to know what you actually need. Rather than relying on a canned set of specifications that someone else has determined is relevant, *you* must determine what *your office* needs or the vendors will try to make the decision for you. Get help if you need it, but make it *your* help, not the vendors'.

Educate the Vendors

After determining what features are needed and wanted, the next step is to discuss them with prospective vendors. The key here is to have a detailed understanding of your most pressing needs (if necessary, create a multi-level outline, with charts or diagrams or whatever else is necessary to effectively and in detail represent *exactly* what you want) and to construct detailed and pinpointed inquiries to determine just how close to that *exact* desired outcome the software can get. Thus, you should not ask "Can this software do workflow?" Almost certainly, every software package vetted will do something that could be characterized as "workflow," so the answer to this question is likely to be "Yes" regardless of what the software actually does. A specific question should be posed, something along the lines of "We are contemplating an automated routing of documents from A to B to C to D, with routing depending on a variety of rules the system must abide by based on specific analysis of information drawn from multiple systems and repositories, in each case after an on-screen review and sign-off that must be captured and recorded." This should be followed by additional questions such as:

- *Does* your software do this now? (Note: This is not the same as "*Can* your software do this?")
- How does it work?
- Is it standard functionality?
- Will you demonstrate it for me?
- Do you have installations where this is in place and where we can see it actually working?

These questions are much more likely to lead to a useful answer than a single generic question in response to which a vendor can shape a meaningless reply. Even more detailed requirements and analysis is needed when designing custom software—a good product will require a very detailed description of exactly what is wanted for every feature. Telling your custom programmer that you need workflow functionality, and leaving your explanation at that, will lead to surprising and disappointing results, all at considerable cost to the firm.

Having determined that one or more COTS packages meet actual requirements closely enough to merit further consideration (and in the case of custom software, once a beta version is up and running), it is desirable to set up a test environment. Once again, the technical staff must be a central part of the process. Although the test environment should mimic the actual and live operating environment insofar as it is possible, it is prudent to completely segregate the test environment so as to avoid any chance of crashing or damaging the working system.

In the test environment, the new software should be vetted for stability, compatibility, security, and other technical issues, and in general tested to find out what it takes to break the software. Dummy datasets should be loaded into the system and both the records staff and test users given the opportunity to evaluate it for ease of use, responsiveness, navigation and configuration, search capability, and other important features. All of this adds considerably to overall knowledge about whether the software will actually work as advertised in the real world of the firm's business.

It may be tempting to skip this step, particularly in a small firm with a simple computer system, but again, that temptation should be resisted. Avoid adopting a system based solely on an effective sales pitch and demonstration. Software will almost always look good during structured demonstrations, and will be running on a vendor-owned computer that is likely configured to maximize performance while running with a small test database that falls far short of the reality of your system. Remember, once a purchase is made, any limitations or compatibility issues are there and may be hugely expensive to correct, and if compatibility or stability problems cause crashes or data corruption in the operating environment, the small savings accrued in bypassing the testing phase will result in an expensive headache indeed.

Other Issues: Vetting the Vendor

In most cases, the vendor is just as important as the software. A vetting of software may well reveal several candidate packages that appear to be suitable, and in a test environment at least, *are* suitable. In every case, vetting of the vendors will prove useful. When you start your evaluation with the vendor, rather than just with the software, you are making sure that you do not fall into the trap of "Good software, lousy vendor—wish I had chosen something else." Key questions to ask and issues to investigate with other users, absent the vendor's smiling influence, include:

- *Installed Base*—Do they have a significant installed user base for their product in the legal community among like-sized and configured firms? Are they willing to let you contact those users and visit installed sites without the vendor actually tagging along?
- *Help Desk*—What are the vendor's help desk hours, who staffs it, where are they, and who do you go to if they cannot fix things in a hurry?
- *Responsiveness*—How responsive is the vendor when you actually have a problem? How long does it take to resolve a problem and what is the tracking process?

- *Upgrades and Changes*—How frequently are upgrades and fixes issued? Are fixes packaged as "new versions," requiring substantial additional investment instead of being included as part of routine maintenance?

- *Professional Services*—Who does the work? How much ownership do they take? Does the vendor actually do the work, do they oversee the work of others, or do they farm out everything to a third party? How big should you expect the bill for professional services to be relative to the licensing fees? Experience says that you should budget at least as much for professional services and related fees as you do for licensing.

- *Installation and Configuration*—Who is responsible for what during installation, testing, and configuration? How long does that take and how much does it cost? Do they have a checklist of data configuration issues you need to deal with that they will provide to you before you actually sign the contract so you can get an idea of whether they have a structured approach or need to redesign things every time they go in to a new client? Who among their client base can you talk to about this?

- *Technical Depth*—How many programmers and other technical personnel does the vendor employ? If you have SQL Server questions, do they have the depth to deal with these issues or do you have to figure them out on your own? How many technical staff will be devoted to your project, where will they be, and when will they be available? Do they usually spend some time on-site? If the vendor says they handle everything remotely, confirm this with several other clients that have operations similar to yours.

- *Customization*—If custom programming or integration is required, does the vendor provide it, is it usually handled by a third-party integrator, does the vendor even care, or is it totally the firm's responsibility? Does the vendor have a full set of application program interfaces (APIs) and a proven tool set for doing imports and integrating with your financial, contact management, conflicts checking, and docketing applications?

- *Pricing*—How is the software priced, by overall firm size, number of end users, or some other criteria? Will they consider an open-end site license? Does each utility, even if used only once, carry an annual maintenance fee? Do maintenance fees start at purchase or will the vendor prove out the quality of the installation and get a sign-off from the buyer indicating satisfaction before starting the clock on maintenance? On what percentage of licensing has maintenance historically been calculated? What is it today? Do they cap maintenance fees? If so, at what level?

- ◆ *Who bought it and who left?*—Talk to other buyers. What were the key factors in their decision-making process? Are they happy with their decision? What would they do differently? Are there questions they did not ask but wish they had? Who bought the product and then dumped it and why? Remember that the initial list of references you get from the vendor will be their shining stars. Ask the shining stars who you should talk to about how the vendor handles problems. Ask to go to a user meeting to see how happy the users really are. There are no perfect vendors or products, but there are some very good ones that are not in a constant war with their users and that know how to address and fix problems when they occur— and they will.

Summary

There is a records management technology solution for every law office or practitioner. Vendors have developed and improved their offerings for law firms over the years, and custom solutions are available if you are willing to pay for them. Whichever strategy is pursued, it should be undertaken from a perspective that is both informed and prepared. If the decision is made to purchase a COTS solution, do not buy until you are ready: do your homework, check your options thoroughly, make sure you get the right product from the best vendor, and ensure that everyone clearly understands their roles in the acquisition, testing, configuration, and deployment continuum. Solid research into proven COTS solutions should result in a choice between the two best options, not in buying the lesser of two evils.

A software installation and data conversion in a large or complex environment may require considerable help from the vendor or a qualified third party during installation and afterward. Your ability to manage and control all steps in the process can make the difference between a successful and unsuccessful installation.

Staffing and Training 10

"Who manages the system and makes it work so that we can find what we need, when we need it, to deliver the right service to our clients on a timely basis?"

The questions are the same in most law office settings and the answers, depending on the size of the office and the records management program structure and tool set, may be surprisingly similar and different at the same time. Breaking down the topic into manageable pieces yields a very specific set of issues and questions:

- ◆ Where in the firm should records management report?
- ◆ How many people are required to run a good records management operation?
- ◆ What skill set is required by a contemporary law firm records manager?
- ◆ What are the responsibilities of the secretaries and the paralegals in all of this?
- ◆ What kind of training do we need?
- ◆ Can't we just outsource the whole thing?
- ◆ As a lawyer, now that I have made the investment, won't things just happen the way I want them to?

The Lawyer's Role

Let us start with the last of those questions and a very basic truth. Most lawyers do not want to be records managers, but a good many already are. If you have a solo practice, or work in

199

a small firm without personal support staff, you undoubtedly already do a good deal of physical file handling—retrieval, refiling, and very likely even some file creation and labeling, and of course, you have a great deal of information in your computer that you personally title, classify, and manage. Even if you work in a large firm with an extensive support staff and an electronic document management system, it is likely that you do at least some ad hoc filing around your desk and on your computer.

The Lawyer as Records Manager

The question in each of these cases is not "Are you a records manager?" since the obvious answer to this one is "Although you may not be *the* records manager, you are *a* records manager." Our truth is that when you have physical possession of a file, you cannot expect it to maintain its integrity and structure, nor can you expect it to shout out "Hey, here I am!" without some care. So, our questions become "How good a records manager do I have to be?" and "What is the easiest way to get that good?" The answer is that you just have to recognize that while you have a file, you are responsible for it and you need to act accordingly. Unfortunately, if you are like most people who do personal filing around some other main job, and you did not inherit a well-developed filing system from someone else, then your filing skills might not be good enough to get you a starting file room job.

The average personal filing system is a bit of a jumble, with no real organization or structure. Files are titled according to whatever seemed meaningful at the moment, and inserted into the cabinets (or just as commonly, added to the pile) wherever there is room, to be retrieved later by trying to remember where the file was likely stashed, scanning the tabs on each file folder in that location, and identifying likely suspects. Lots of time gets invested in searching for information, and so less time is available for using it.

Making Things Better

If you read the rest of this book before reading this part, it has probably occurred to you that improving upon this state of affairs is not really all that hard. To be sure, implementing everything we have discussed in this book in a large firm can be a bit of a challenge, but you, as an individual, do not need to do everything yourself in order to gain real benefits. Consider how much time you have spent in the last week or month just hunting around through those piles on your desk and going through those file cabinets in and around your immediate office area looking for things that you knew full well were there, but that you just could not find. Your immediate problem is fixable in quite short order, regardless of what the rest of the firm does.

Figure Out What You Do

Regardless of the kind of work you do, a quick check will usually reveal to you that most records and information-oriented tasks fall into a narrow range of topics and activities. You have some finite number of cases immediately active (*I am working on it today*) on your desk; you do certain predictable things with them: draft a pleading, compose a letter, and send an e-mail. In most cases, from an analytical standpoint, there really are not many of these things, nor is there a particularly complicated workflow to them: you read the file, do some research, draft a pleading, put a copy in the file, send off the other copies, make a phone call, take some notes, put them in the file, close the file, and move on to the next one.

For the solo or small office practitioner without a support staff to assist with such issues, this is good news—it means that the effort and time needed to develop a filing scheme adequate for your own desk and your other immediate surroundings is probably quite small—a few hours at most, and probably much less. All of those piles and a couple of file cabinets could probably be organized and labeled according to your file plan in a day or less, and the important files on your computer similarly arranged and organized in a day as well. That is a 16-hour investment of time, perhaps less. The return on that investment is likely to far outstrip your investment. If you now spend an hour a day looking for documents in your immediate office area—and you may be spending much more—you will discover that this time is dramatically reduced, perhaps almost eliminated. If you rid yourself of most of that futile searching, you will recoup your investment in two or three weeks. Thereafter, you gain five or so hours a week as a result of investing just a few minutes a day. Whether that extra time is invested in business development, billable work, golf, or family, it is a pretty good return on your investment.

That small additional and ongoing investment in maintenance is an important one: you have to *continue* doing things the new way, otherwise things revert to their previous chaotic state. That means labeling files according to your scheme, naming files appropriately, and dragging e-mails to the right folders. At first, this will be difficult—in the crush of the daily workload, old habits die hard, and you will forget, or use the wrong term, or will simply feel so hurried and harried that even dragging and dropping an e-mail will seem a burden. But over time, it will get easier, and soon, it will be second nature, an actual habit, and you will wonder why you ever did it any other way. You will end up spending far less time on the task and achieving far better results than you do now.

In the solo or small office practice, it is likely that *you* built the conceptual tools, *you* created a basic file plan, and *you* developed **some rules** for their implementation. This was your records management initiative. Making yourself implement the program consistently is your own private training and education program for the staff of your personal area—you. *You* made sure everyone (that would be *you* again) understood the rules, *you* implemented them, and then *you* enforced them until they became a habit. And it worked. So now, not only have you become a records manager—and a pretty good one within the scope of your mandate—but you have also become an education and training specialist.

In so doing, you have touched upon and resolved most of the issues that you or your firm will face in designing and implementing a larger-scale records management program. There may be more tools, more rules, more people, and a great deal more in the way of records and electronic data, but the fundamentals will not change. The rules will be conceptually simple and the tools by and large easy to use—once people are familiar with them and get in the habit of using them correctly.

The real issue with making the program work is the same one faced in our hypothetical desktop initiative: people and habits. In a larger initiative, each of the people involved must overcome the same mindset and obstacles to change that you did: they will feel imposed upon by naming conventions; they will not immediately and intuitively understand the records management software; they will forget to do this or that; and every time one of these things happens, they will be tempted, just as you were, to forego the new program and, just this once, do things the old sloppy way. Regardless of the size and scope of your records management initiative, you will face these other people, you will deal with the culture and habit issues, and know that by resolving them you have created an environment and a program that helps everyone.

The Need for Lawyer Involvement

There are three reasons our personal desktop records management initiative worked:

1. The person in charge of it (you) knew what the lawyer who would use it needed;
2. The person in charge of it (you) had a personal investment in its success or failure; and
3. The person in charge of it (you again) knew she would have to live with the results, good or bad.

These three ingredients are a pretty good recipe for success. Like the other attributes of the desktop initiative, they also have value in a larger setting and so make a powerful argument for ensuring that the lawyers in your firm are actively involved in many aspects of a records management initiative, including the training component:

- ♦ It will serve to educate the lawyers in the fundamentals of records and information management—this is valuable training for them.
- ♦ It will serve to inform others of precisely what lawyers need out of the initiative in order for it to have value.
- ♦ It will facilitate education of support staff in what the lawyers need and expect in the area of records and information management.

These interactions are critical. The goals of most law firms are the practice of law and the providing of client service, and every process and operation in the firm should be optimized to support those goals. If records and information management activities are to do so, not only must the information creation and management processes be optimized, but so too must the practices and habits of support staff, for they are charged with the day-to-day implementation of it. They can only do this if they are made fully aware of both the needs and demands of the lawyers, how those needs can be met by managing and delivering the right records and information, and how the new tools they have been provided with can facilitate this.

The Right Reporting Relationship

Larger Firms

In firms where records management was traditionally a *box and store* type of operation, it frequently reported to the Manager of Facilities. Where the program was more sophisticated, involved with active records, centralized support, and centralized records and filing operations, and particularly if it also controlled conflicts checking, it might have reported to the Controller, Director of Accounting, Office Administrator, or in some cases, directly to the Executive Director. As RM has become more sophisticated, with responsibility for records retention and disposition, electronic records control and the management of large-scale databases, we see some of the old relationships fading away, others proving their worth, and some new ones emerging.

Global and Local Considerations

Overall, records management is a discipline that should be defined and administered globally but delivered locally. This means that in firms with more than one office, the RM function, the set of services it delivers, and the standards by which it is judged in that delivery should be centrally defined. However, the firm will generally find that accommodations in the methods of delivering RM services are necessary to account for differences in culture, office size and staffing levels, and even physical layout.

Who Should Be in Charge?

With the increasing emphasis on electronic records, there are those who say the obvious reporting relationship for Records Management is up to Information Technology (or Technology Services, or Information Systems, etc.). In those firms where the head of IT or IS is enlightened beyond plugs, cables, operating systems, and architecture, where he or she truly understands the rules, influences, and compliance issues surrounding the management of records in all media, and the personal, high-touch delivery of services, this reporting relationship will work. In most sizable offices, however, records management can and should be bundled with a different set of services and should report directly to the individual charged with the office's administrative management, generally titled Administrator or Executive Director (ED) or Chief Operating Officer (COO). In the largest law firms the Records Manager should have the title of Director and report to a high-level administrator who then reports to the ED or COO.

Organizational Responsibility

What are those other functions with which RM should be bundled? Recently, with the increasing importance of risk management, conflicts checking, and the appearance of workflow technology as a standard component of many large firm operations, some or all of the following functions are coming together under a single umbrella:

- *Records Management*—Our obvious starting point.
- *Conflicts Checking*—The conflicts checking database is largely the same as the records management database and offers depth well beyond the accounting database.
- *Client Intake Management*—A good intake system starts with conflicts checking and ends with records management. This is a good place to put intake management in order to avoid the temptation to have the intake process forced into a structure that is biased toward the demands of some functions while downplaying the very pressing and most important demands of conflicts checking and ethics compliance.
- *Calendar and Docket*—More and more firms are going with enterprise calendar and docket systems that have value to more than just the litigators. (Note: Specialty Intellectual Property applications are another story.) When an amended complaint and new par-

ties are added to a case, a new/updated conflicts check must be executed. This means the conflicts checking and calendaring applications must be integrated, the processes must be part of a single flow, and oversight to assure compliance with ethical requirements must be operationally centralized.

◆ *Library*—Some librarians prefer to remain in the library where they find challenges enough, with the conversion from books to online services and other changes to the library and research world. Other librarians extend their reach with relish and successfully manage extensive operations that bundle library, records, docketing, and intake as part of a single function that meets firm-wide demands for risk management and individual lawyer's demands for records management services.

Job Titles

Take your pick—depending on the scope of operational responsibility—but make sure that all titles accurately reflect the level of responsibility and authority. RM was once a backroom filing or boxing and storage operation. Now it has to do with technology, personal services to lawyers, risk management, and ethics compliance. Because of the old connotation—dusty back rooms and people schlepping boxes—we prefer Records Services to Records Management as a department name. A little respect goes a long way, so do away with the term *clerk* and change it to *specialist* when you modify job descriptions. Do not give the person who manages all of these functions the title of supervisor when their peers in other areas such as accounting, marketing, technology, and human resources are titled managers and directors.

Some job titles currently in use are

◆ Information and Records Manager/Director
◆ Manager/Director of Client Intake and Information
◆ Manager/Director of Conflicts Checking and Records Services
◆ Client Information Services Manager/Director

There are some job titles that should not be applied to the person running a records operation in a law office (all taken from real life):

◆ File Supervisor
◆ File (or Records) Clerk
◆ File Specialist
◆ Box Boy

How Many People Do You Need?

Large Offices

In a large/main office with 200 lawyers who are educated about records management, and who are supported by a hundred secretaries and a hundred other staff, a well-conceived and administered records department with good procedures and a thoughtfully assembled tool set should be able to deliver a superb level of service with just seven or eight well-trained and managed staff. In an office of the same size where the lawyers have received no training, where the records manager is a clerk promoted past his or her competencies, and where poor tools and procedures are the norm, a staff of 18 to 20 will likely struggle to deliver even marginal services. It is in organizations like the latter where records management is referred to as *"the black hole."*

Years of seeing both good and bad procedures, both creative and uncaring managers, firms with good technology tools or with no tools at all, and those that have well-trained staff and users and those whose staff have received no education and training at all have taught us something. If investments *are not* made in records management tools, staff, training, and procedures, a ratio of 8:1 to 10:1, lawyers to RM staff, will not deliver acceptable services and the failure will be accompanied by a high annual cost and an almost complete lack of trust in RM. If the right investments *are* made, a ratio of 20:1 or even 25:1 is possible, records management services are excellent, are highly valued by the user community, and annual costs are reasonable.

The larger an office is, the greater the opportunity to accrue and take advantage of economies of scale. So in offices with 20 to 50 lawyers the RM staffing ratio might range from 15:1 to 20:1.

Smaller Offices

In smaller offices the work needs to be shared out more, but the importance of service delivery remains the same. With the need to share responsibilities among staff, the smallest offices, those with less than 12 or so lawyers, and particularly if they are a branch office of a larger enterprise, can seldom justify someone devoted solely to records management. The obvious needs for backup and cross-training provide a strong rationale for extending records management expertise and the ability to deliver related services to users to more than one individual. So if the person in the main office is the Records Manager, the person in this smaller (but still sizable) office might appropriately be termed a Records Administrator or Records Supervisor. The important thing is that RM not be relegated to *"We'll get to it when we get to it"* status. That is an invitation to return to chaos.

Organization Structure

Competence and Turnover

- ◆ Changing Perceptions—Some law offices resign themselves to incompetence among the RM staff—they assume it is the standard in the industry. It is not that way in many firms and it does not need to be that way in any law office. There are real reasons why in many law offices the records management function fails to deliver and the people who work there are perceived as a drag on profits, or worse, a danger to efficient lawyering and client service.

- ◆ Low Expectations—In many law offices the firm's expectation is that the records person is there for the short term. The staff person's expectation may well be that it is a dead-end job, and so why work at it? Stay out of the light, draw no attention to yourself, and hope to survive. Not a lot of criticism comes your way when nobody knows who you are.

- ◆ Dumping Ground—Some firms still have a problem getting rid of the dead wood. *"Hey, he couldn't cut it in the mail room, so why don't we transfer him to records?"* This is effectively dealt with by hiring competent people to start with. Some ask *"Why bother?"* but the truth is that a well-structured and managed records management function will present opportunities to records management staff and result in substantial benefits to users.

- ◆ No Chance for Advancement—In many firms the organizational structure, even in large records departments, is flat and it is obvious that any opportunity to develop and advance from the position into which one has been hired is effectively nonexistent. Most human resource or personnel department professionals, when made aware of the problem, can assist with creating new opportunities to provide incentives for staff to move up in that department or to transfer laterally to another department when an opportunity opens up. In offices where there are as few as five records personnel, the records management department structure can be reorganized in a hierarchy to provide advancement opportunities. For example, in a five-person department, all of the staff could report directly to the records manager but two of them could be designated as records specialists and two could be designated as senior records specialists. Alternatively, two could be designated as records specialists and two as records coordinators. Career paths must be created or the absence of advancement opportunities will foster the idea that effort leading to superior work and service are not worth striving for since they will not be rewarded.

Staffing, Hiring, and Training

◆ The Right People—Finding the right people to staff records management takes a bit of skill, but nothing beyond the scope of a good recruiter who knows what to look for. The first thing to do is set aside any notions that just anyone can do records work or that records is a fine place to put folks who could not cut it elsewhere in the firm. We are, after all, talking about the people largely responsible for managing one of the firm's most precious resources and making sure that services surrounding those resources are delivered promptly, reliably, consistently, and in a fashion that facilitates client service. Some firms require a college degree for all records management staff beyond entry level.

◆ Skills and Attributes—When evaluating people for positions in the records department, certain preferred skills and personal attributes rise to the top of a list of desirable characteristics. Among the characteristics you should seek in records management staff are

　　◆ A sense of *order and neatness* since working in chaos is what you are trying to avoid in the first place;

　　◆ A *high degree of literacy* since you are not going to believe that someone who has trouble reading can understand what depositions are and then correctly file them;

　　◆ Good *interpersonal skills* since you want someone with a good attitude who can comfortably communicate with driven professionals and the variety of staff who support them;

　　◆ *Courtesy and patience* since the user community does not always show their most highly developed social skill set;

　　◆ *Physical strength* to lift 50 pounds since at times records management still means moving that jammed records box (the standard is 10 inches × 12 inches × 15 inches) or helping to lift a full transfer case (typically 10 inches × 15 inches × 24 inches).

　　◆ Willingness to work as *part of a team* since everything is process driven and what each person does affects what the next person in the queue has to do; and

　　◆ A devotion to *quality* since "almost the right file" just will not do.

◆ Managerial Skills—Today's records manager, the person leading the team, should be a highly skilled professional or he or she will not be able to deliver.

- ◆ *Strong communications* are at the top of the list since your leader needs to be an advocate for new systems and processes and must be able to carry their message to a variety of user communities in the organization;
- ◆ *Technologically savvy* so they can work well with the IT folks, with vendors and consultants, and supervise management of a large and intricate database (possibly more than one);
- ◆ A *motivator* since they need to push staff to perform at consistently high levels, and possibly motivate them to make major changes in their attitude; and
- ◆ *Forward thinking* since the RM discipline, the tools, and the processes are changing and will likely continue to change for the next decade.
- ◆ Managerial Training—Some firms are amazed that an individual promoted to a records management managerial position just does not measure up or have the skills to do the job. It may not necessarily be that they were a bad choice, but simply that they have never been trained as a manager and do not know how to manage people or deal with lawyers. Given training and the opportunity to develop their managerial skills to excel, most will rise to the challenge and do a fine job.
- ◆ Staff Training—The same applies to all of the other staff in the records department. Seminars, conferences, and custom training opportunities are available through local and national records associations and consultants. Given the cost of bringing a new person into the firm and getting them up to speed, some counseling and a modest investment in training can pay off better than seeking, hiring, and training a replacement.

Job Descriptions

As RM has changed, so have the skills and the expectations put on the staff and the users. Creating and issuing a policy statement is a good first step at setting expectations. Training helps as well, but until people know that they will be evaluated and judged based on how well they manage the records in all media, and their job descriptions are modified to show their responsibilities, most will wonder why they should care.

The old job descriptions may have been pretty thin for RM staff—"Give it to 'em when they ask for it and put it back when they are finished with it"—but today's RM staff person has duties that involve a range of processes, tools, technology, communications, reporting requirements, and service delivery responsibilities. Each position in the department should be considered separately based on its responsibility. Some of the skills and duties will be generic, running across all positions in the department, but some will be more specific. An intake specialist will have duties that differ from those of a storage coordinator. All of these need to be specified in job descriptions and staff must understand that their performance relative to this job description in serving the firm is what they will be judged on—not on how cleverly they can bend the system to minimize their own workload or to accommodate the demands of a single vocal and unpleasant user.

End-User Education and Training

The end-user community in most law offices comes in a number of flavors, and the larger those communities are, the more targeted the training has to be in order to meet their specific and changing needs. Broadly speaking, education and training have three overall goals: to inform, to train, and to habituate. Each is important to overall success.

Informing

A records management program will have rules governing its operation. These will range from high-level policies such as those on information ownership (your enterprise records management policy statement), to lower-level policies such as e-mail handling, to very low-level procedures such as those governing how to pack and label a box for storage (workflow and procedures). A large-scale, large firm initiative will have a number of them, but even the smallest operation will have a few—even our earlier hypothetical desktop initiative had rules on filing.

Obviously, users cannot obey these rules if they do not know why they exist or what they are, or if they are not aware that there are even any rules to obey. If you do not want your records management initiative to wind up like some—as a binder on a shelf—it is necessary to publish your rules to the firm and to train end-users in how to get the most from them.

Passive publication is inadequate. Most people are barraged with things they are supposed to read but for which they do not have time so they prioritize. Almost everyone in a high-pressure job where a lot of e-mail crosses their desk has done it at some point—many lawyers will admit that they routinely delete or ignore e-mail from anyone except their clients, their immediate supervisor, and the managing partner. Passive publication will result in most personnel not reading the rules at all, a few people giving them a cursory review, and very few people actually reading any part of them in depth. Publication must therefore be active. Staff must understand why the changes are necessary to them and to the firm, they must focus on the rules in a structured manner, consider their impact on their daily work routine, and begin the process of mentally adjusting to them.

Training for the End-User

Even with all the tools available today, effective training still most commonly occurs in face-to-face education sessions where records management personnel or trainers run meetings and seminars. This tried-and-true approach has many advantages—you know who is there, you can be at least nominally assured that they are paying attention, and you have the opportunity to answer questions and dispel misconceptions in real time.

The approach of getting a group in a room where the likelihood for interruptions is limited (turn off cell phones and Blackberries) and training them can work well with some populations. Today, however, training programs must come from a variety of directions and education must be delivered through a number of tools to cover all the bases. There are some interesting options available to help achieve your training goals.

Training on how to use records management software is essential. In the absence of formal, supervised, and structured hands-on training, most people will learn only enough about any software tool to solve the problem most immediately in front of them. In the process of doing so, they may use features incorrectly (e.g., by entering data into the wrong fields) or omit important steps. The end result when structured training is not available is a user base that complains about how bad the software is, when in fact, they just do not know how to use it,

Training must also include the here-is-the-button-to-click issues, and other issues such as proper use of indices, standardization of terminology, and similar consistency issues. Although it is usually possible to configure the software (e.g., through drop-down menus) to minimize user errors in these areas, no such configuration is entirely foolproof. When these errors are perpetuated by uneducated users, the integrity of the records repository in which they reside is compromised, and the utility of the software and its data are degraded. And since most users will self-learn only a small fraction of a program's functionality, much of the power of the software will never be utilized. Ultimately, staff training and habituation will be necessary to ensure full and consistent use of the software. Any commitment to implement records management software must therefore be coupled with a commitment to thoroughly train all concerned staff in its correct use:

- ◆ Large Group Sessions—The concept behind this sort of education is simple enough—you gather a group of like employees in a room, give them each a copy of the rules, walk them through the rules, show them how things work, and answer their questions. Such sessions should be limited to 60 to 90 minutes wherever possible—two or three hours of a talking head will cause many minds to wander, diminishing the value of the session and wasting time. PowerPoint presentations, other visual aids, and workbooks all add variety and value. One caution is appropriate—always plan for a certain amount of interaction and try to keep the tone light. Delivering a training session but not being able to answer questions sometimes creates the idea in attendees' minds that things are not well thought out. Do not let an uneducated person with no real knowledge of records management deliver your training message. If you want to keep things interactive, use a knowledgeable person as your trainer.

- Teleconferencing—It is also possible to conduct this sort of session via video or teleconference. If this route is chosen, however, it is wise to make sure that your technical and production standards are high, and the presentation is designed to capture and hold their attention. Expecting staff in remote locations to pay close attention and understand new concepts while someone drones on over a speakerphone or on a video link is unrealistic—they will rapidly lose interest and spend the time checking e-mail, reading documents, and otherwise not paying attention. If audio is garbled or otherwise poor quality, and video is of the talking head variety or absent, this will simply happen sooner.

- Click to Accept—This tool has gained wide acceptance for deploying and making sure people read relatively short documents such as policies. When issuing a new, firm-wide RM policy statement, click-to-accept can be used to distribute the document and capture the names of the individuals who read through it and to date and time-stamp the record. Check with HR—they are likely already using click-to-accept during orientation or to manage the distribution of changes to policies and may well be familiar with it.

- Interactive Training—Another training tool that is gaining popularity is self-paced computer-based education. This approach eliminates the need to gather staff in a room, and permits individuals to participate in training at a time and place convenient to their schedules while making sure that the delivered content is consistent across the population. Such education need not be passive—in addition to reading whatever text is placed on-screen, users can be required to interact with the program, answering questions, providing feedback, and actually using an electronic workbook to learn new procedures. Not only does this make the session more enjoyable for the employees, but it prompts the employees to pay attention, and by not permitting them to advance the program until key questions have been answered correctly, ensures at least a minimum level of comprehension of the concepts being taught.

The cost of developing such a training tool escalates in relationship to the complexity of the training. For those who want to pursue use of this type of training aid, but are somewhat budget constrained, it can be deployed to explain the concepts and content of something fairly manageable, like records retention schedules.

Interactive computer-based training has been very effectively used in bringing users to a basic level of understanding about new technology tools. It stands to reason that this concept can be applied to training on records management software.

Face-to-Face Training

- ◆ Small Groups—While getting large groups of secretaries and paralegals to sit down together for a training session may be a challenge, getting large groups of lawyers together may be more difficult unless they are first-year associates who are being broken in and who can be brought together by a management summons. Small groups present a workable alternative to the large group format and have the benefit of creating a fairly intimate environment where the users can feed off each other in discussion, something not always achievable in large groups.
- ◆ Personal Training—One of the benefits of being a partner in a law firm, or the general counsel in a non-law firm setting, is that people actually pay some level of attention to you and understand your importance in the hierarchy. Many senior equity holders and management personnel expect to be and should be handled differently. Getting them to understand and use a new tool set, even nominally, has great precedent value. The records manager or the firm trainer should have a separate training outline and script prepared for personal, one-on-one training sessions.

Compliance with other parts of the records program, some quite mundane, will benefit from training as well. It may seem at first glance a bit silly to have a training session on how to pack and label a box for storage, or how to properly label a file, but the simple fact is that end-user failures in areas such as these are extremely common and are major contributors to records management program breakdowns. Most end-users will not perform these everyday tasks right unless they are given explicit instructions. Lapses on these most basic of tasks, if uncorrected, are the bane of effective records management, since these simple processes and artifacts are the hooks upon which other processes depend for success.

RM Staff Training

In addition to knowing the rules, the RM staff will be required to know the nuts-and-bolts of everything they need to do—each step in each new process. They need to know what happens before their responsibilities kick in, what happens afterward, and how each step is to be executed. The most obvious need for this is when a system has been substantially overhauled and when records management software is being installed. Regardless of how user-friendly the software is, if RM personnel are to hit the ground running when using it, there must be a certain amount of *click-here-to-do-this* and *click-there-to-do-that* training on it.

Handing out training manuals or printing and issuing system documentation is cheap, but it simply does not do the job. Records management staff are comfortable with how things used to be—that is the world they know. If they are going to transition to a new world filled with new processes, they will need the chance to see how each new process compares with the old, what the changes are, how those changes affect their jobs and the overall flow, and to ask questions about the changes. Training of this sort must occur at the computer with a live program if it is to have much value. In a small environment, it may be possible to do one-on-one training, but in a larger firm, it may be most practical to educate and train records management users on new processes and technology in a well-equipped training room.

Periodic Refresher Training

Most tasks require some amount of repetition before the student really absorbs and understands them well. That is why musicians spend hours practicing and football players hours drilling—flawless execution of a concerto or a football play requires hundreds or thousands of repetitions in order to truly habituate the desired sequence of activities. Regardless of intelligence or motivation, people (even lawyers) simply do not remember everything about a new skill or concept if they have only been exposed to it once. If they did, they would remember why Brownian motion works, since almost everybody was exposed to this in high school, but nobody does. So it is with records and information management.

Employees attending a training class will learn the basic steps of creating and classifying a document and then performing basic queries in records management software. In a typical half-day class, they will perform the steps required for each task a handful of times—once or twice perhaps, while being walked through with the instructor, once or twice on their own, and then on to the next topic, which will tend to crowd out whatever they learned about the first topic. Having completed the course, they will correctly remember perhaps 75 percent of what was taught for a short period of time. The other 25 percent or more will be fuzzy at best, or will have escaped them entirely. If they start using the software immediately, the part that they remember correctly—and that they use regularly—will be reinforced. Everything else will gradually recede into the realm of *I-know-there's-a-way-to-do-that-but-I-can't-remember-what-it-is.* Some people will take the time to relearn how to do it, but most will not—many will simply not have the time to stop work, read help screens or manuals, and attempt a trial-and-error process until they hit upon the correct solution. Even those who do may find themselves in a cycle of learn-and-forget. If you have ever found yourself wondering how to do something on a computer and realizing that you figured it out once before, but cannot remember what you did, you understand only too well how this works.

The solution to all of this is to supplement initial training with additional training to reinforce the desired habits and skills. If additional classes are held, they should be held within a relatively short period of time after initial training; otherwise people will have forgotten much of the initial training, and you will be starting all over. Supplemental training can build upon initial training with more advanced concepts, but it should also have a significant component of review and reinforcement. Repetition works.

One more comment is appropriate here. Some of your users will be very occasional users and training, even on a regular basis, is not going to work. In cases like these, stress those tasks that they will likely have to perform and then run them through those tasks a few times and then give them a cheat sheet. A senior lawyer with a single laminated, bullet-point instruction sheet that covers the basics of how to search for a file, request a folder, get a box from storage, and ask for a new folder to be created and delivered may not express a lot of gratitude, but he or she will have the tools needed to work through the few records management tasks most frequently performed.

Habituation

Once everyone knows what they are supposed to do and they have been given as much training as the firm can afford, the question becomes one of making sure that they continue to do it. At the conclusion of education and training, compliance is likely to be relatively high, within the limits of people's ability to execute newly learned skills—people are motivated, they have new tools to play with, and everything they have been taught is fresh in their minds. If they can be made to do things correctly for long enough, after a time doing so will become habit, and continued success will be much easier. There is, however, an interim period, while they are still learning new habits, that presents the most danger. Initial enthusiasm will fade before new habits are set in place, and the temptation will arise to revert to old ways just because they seem easier and more natural, or because people simply forget. The training and education program must be prepared to bridge this interim period in order to build and reinforce new habits. Habituation can be accomplished in several ways.

The first is simple nagging, or more politely put, providing a continuing series of reminders. As mentioned earlier, once out of a training session, a person's attention is directed back toward other activities, and memory of records management training starts to flag. Occasional reminders (productive and well-delivered reminders are really nagging) will serve to refresh users' memories and to bring records management back to mind. Reminders can be general—"Remember to put a date range on the label of any box sent to storage"—or specific—"Bill, you forgot to put a date range on that box you sent to storage." Periodic reminders of what needs to be done, how it needs to be done, and why will not only raise awareness and bolster compliance, but specific feedback on errors will serve both to give precise feedback to employees on known problems and to gently let it be known that these things are being monitored. The fact that staff know you are monitoring performance will increase overall compliance.

Another approach is the do-it-until-you-get-it-right method. Rather than reproaching Bill for not putting on a date range, you send the box back to him and make him label it correctly before you will accept it. When this approach is possible, it is highly effective—sending something back for rework very effectively calls attention to the mistake. Further, people do not like to do things twice, and if having to do so is a likely consequence of mistakes or laziness, they will soon learn to take the path of least resistance and do it right the first time. This approach does, however, require management support.

A third approach is the cheerleader method. Training and habituation are approached from a positive we're-all-in-this-together standpoint, and compliance is encouraged through sloganeering, staged events such as "records cleanout days," and other activities designed to heighten awareness and compliance in a benign and nonthreatening way.

Which approach is best depends upon several factors. If the firm is supportive of the development of a good records management program, nagging may work well in any environment. The tone of the nag may, however, need adjusting depending upon the identity of the person being nagged. If Bill is a senior partner, the nag may have to be a good deal more circumspect than if he is a paralegal.

The get-it-right approach is most obviously available in the case of physical objects such as boxes and file folders—sending back an electronic document will in most cases mean sending back a copy of it. When the corrected item is resent, it will be yet another copy. This copying and recopying is not sound records management, and so should be avoided. As with nagging, the identity of the offender will probably count. You will probably not be sending that box back to a senior partner with orders to relabel.

The cheerleader approach is highly popular in corporate settings, and if appropriate, can be quite effective. In many law firms, the tone is likely to be a bit too bubbly to be compatible with the culture and atmosphere that the firm is seeking to cultivate.

A combination of these approaches is likely to be necessary in most settings. Regardless of the culture or environment of the office, it takes time and reinforcement to get people to change habits and embrace new processes. And while training is directed at the end-user, it may not be perfect. If the trainers or program auditors detect consistent trouble among users with a particular facet of the new program, or if the details of a particular process seem to escape users despite training, then it may be an indication that the training needs to be reworked or even that the process needs a second look.

Additional Resources

Regardless of the education, training, and general nagging done, people will have questions about many things: "How do I make the software do this?" "What's the retention period for this document?" People are far more likely to deal with an issue or question promptly and correctly if they can turn to a friendly and knowledgeable person for answers. Informal networks of such resource people already exist in any work environment—the guy who really understands spreadsheets or the woman who can do fancy things in the word processing program are both likely to be well-known and highly valued colleagues in any office. Making an approachable expert available for records and information management questions thus taps into a process that people are already familiar and comfortable with. Although a good program will have the answers to these questions in place somewhere in a policy, procedure, or instruction manual, some version of a records management help desk that is easy to access will probably pay off. It need not be staffed by an additional body; indeed, it may not need to be staffed at all but rather take the form of an e-mail address supported by a voice mail box where users can call in with questions or suggestions. The records department in one firm has a voice mail box answered with a message, "Hi. This is the records guy. Tell me what I can do to help or leave a message and I'll get back to you."

Some of this can be managed via the firm's intranet. It is a good idea to create an FAQ section—Frequently Asked Questions—with the answers. It should also make available to users the names and contact information for all of the records management subject experts in the firm—the records management software guy, the records retention guru, the file plan maven, as well as providing a link to the enterprise RM policy statement discussed earlier. These persons, as part of their mandate, should understand that their responsibilities include being available to answer questions and respond to user concerns and questions. Their availability will ensure that the concepts and skills taught in the rest of the education and training programs will continue to be reinforced and refined.

Outsourcing

Many firms, once they get to a certain size, consider outsourcing, and in some situations it makes sense. Outsourcing is merely turning over an existing operation to some other entity, usually a proven provider of specific services, so the organization that is divesting itself of an operation can concentrate on its core business. Outsourcing does not necessarily fix things, it just turns over management of those things to someone who is supposed to run the current system better and more economically than you can do it. Outsourcing has worked well for large and not-so-large law firms and law offices in mail room operations, janitorial services, food services, courier operations, facsimile services, and other areas. Be aware that the mere process of turning a poorly run but important operation over to outsiders does not mean that it will get any better. The only thing worse than running your own black hole type of records operation is writing a monthly check to someone else to run that black hole records operation.

In most cases, success in outsourcing a function or operation depends on a few basic factors:

◆ *The process must be fairly simple and straightforward.* Collecting, sorting, and delivering mail, making copies, serving and cleaning up after meals, and cleaning offices are all good examples: the simpler an operation is, the better the odds that outsourcing will work.

◆ *The process must work pretty well now.* If the idea is to take a proven operation and tighten it down from a management perspective and make current processes run smoother, outsourcing may indeed work.

◆ *The vendor must be expert at the discipline.* Easy disciplines like mail, copy, and fax have lots of experts; more complex, analysis-centric disciplines like conflicts checking, accounting, records management, and technology management have few. Be aware that a few of the less reputable outsourcing vendors work very hard at learning on the job on your dime rather than coming in with established credentials. You do not want to pay for the mistakes they make while they are on their learning curve.

◆ *The outsourcing vendor must have the firm's best interests at heart.* All will say they do, but many are looking only for reasons to justify the addition of more staff, at higher fees, to their operation.

So, for more complex, expertise-based operations where flexibility is critical and response needs to be tailored to the situation, outsourcing may not work well at all. That is not to say that there are no situations where outsourcing has not worked well for active records management (read central file room management here), but many firms choose to retain control of this operation where the firm's greatest active assets after its lawyers reside. Remember that outsourcing firms may not be the best choice for upgrading and reworking service delivery or for designing new and more efficient and responsive processes and controls or for defining records retention schedules based on laws and ethical considerations.

Records Storage

One aspect of records management where outsourcing shines in law firms is in management of the inactive records and their ultimate disposition—the off-site storage and destruction markets. Commercial records storage operations come in many forms: the big national and international firms like GRM, Iron Mountain, and Recall; regional operations like DataSafe in the San Francisco Bay area and Fireproof in Ohio; and local companies with just one or two facilities all can leverage their facilities to get economies of scale at lower unit costs than can a single law firm. Whether or not they provide excellent performance at a competitive price is another issue.

Most commercial records storage operations concentrate on their core services of picking up, storing, retrieving, and delivering files and boxes that are maintained in a warehouse. Delivery schedules and elapsed time between request and delivery are all subject to definition and negotiation. Most commercial records centers prefer to put the burden of indexing boxes back on the customer—that way, if it is not done right, then it is not their fault. If they do take responsibility for indexing, they charge a healthy per-line fee for capturing the information and a per-character fee for entering the information. It is all basic inventory control wrapped up and delivered as a business service.

Many storage companies offer one or more ancillary services as well, including microfilming, imaging, indexing, fax on demand, workrooms, recycling, and destruction. The best are an irreplaceable and smoothly functioning cog in the records management engine.

Records Storage Contracts

Another word of caution is appropriate, this one having to do with the contracts some storage vendors put in front of their clients. Some vendors have yet to learn that it is not nice to create egregiously one-sided, no-risk-for-them, all-risk-to-the-client, no-responsibility-for-anything-at-all on their part even if it is a fire or major security breach, we own the data and you do not, type of contract. Some continue to prey on the unwary. When presented with a contract, look it over closely and if it is not equitable and fair, if they are not taking responsibility for delivery of services, safety, and security, if anything makes you feel uncomfortable—then give it back to them. Those who say, "But it's the industry standard! Everybody signs it!" are not telling the truth. See Appendix 4 for information about PRISM, the association for records storage companies.

Records Destruction

Another aspect of records management, and the one where outsourcing pays off the best, is in records destruction. In investigating the controls that must be in place when arranging for destruction of documents, many firms have made some interesting discoveries. Among the most interesting is that different companies define *destruction* in different ways. Consider these:

♦ *Sell 'em.* We charge you to pick up your sensitive documents and then sell them to someone else for recycling. Those documents may sit out in the rain or wind in loose piles or poorly secured bales and get blown around in the process before they actually get destroyed by someone in another city, county, or country—after they, or the local investigative reporter, take a look at them.

♦ *Dump 'em.* We charge you to pick up your sensitive documents and then dump them in a landfill, where again they may sit unprotected and get blown around until they can serve as a wonderful starting point for some journalist looking for a story.

♦ *Hold 'em a bit.* We charge you to pick up your sensitive documents and then store them at our facility until we have enough of them to make it worthwhile for us to destroy them. Your documents may or may not be secured, from our staff or other curious folks, while we stage them until destruction and they can be held for quite a while.

♦ *Really destroy 'em.* We send this huge vehicle to your place of business and grind up the records right there in front of you. You can watch every step of the process and see your files turn into strips, confetti, or powder—whatever you choose. We charge you for it but it is done right. Needless to say, this is the best approach to destroying client files (once the client says it is OK) and other sensitive documents.

See Appendix 4 for information about NAID, the association for records and document destruction companies.

Record Management Program Implementation

11

Program Attributes

As you move toward implementation, bear in mind that a good records management program, one that will support the firm's records management and risk management needs, has specific attributes, and the inability to prove that a program has these attributes puts the firm at risk. A firm that is moving toward the implementation of a good program knows that it will be judged on a number of criteria:

- Inclusiveness—All the information in the firm is included, not *just* client files or *just* administrative records;
- Media Blindness—It addresses hard-copy and electronic records, including e-mail, Web content, word processing document repositories, spreadsheets, and databases;
- Operational, Legal, and Ethical Focus—The program supports the day-to-day operating needs of individual users and departments while it addresses firm-wide legal and ethical compliance issues and deals with enterprise issues such as knowledge management;
- Assignment of Responsibility—The program clearly defines exactly what shareholders and staff are expected to do;
- Consistent Application—No one in the firm is exempt; all users from partners to clerical staff use the same system and operate according to the same set of rules.

No collection or set of information is purposefully excluded from the system; and

♦ Accommodation of Necessary Exceptions—It allows for defined records sets to be temporarily moved outside of standard records retention controls in case of claims, audit, investigation, or litigation, without bringing the entire program to a standstill.

Program Components

By this time, the knowledgeable firm also has learned that a good records management program, one that manifests the above attributes, has specific components:

♦ Records Management Policy Statement—This document provides a definition of a record, clearly articulates ownership, and details management, support, and operations staff's responsibilities relative to the care and maintenance of records. It assigns formal responsibility for records management program definition, support, auditing, and compliance.

♦ Active Records Controls—These procedures govern how both hardcopy and electronic records are created and identified, how and where they are housed, and how they are indexed and tracked during their active lifetime.

♦ Inactive Records Controls—These controls specify how and where firm records are maintained in the period following their active use until final disposition.

♦ Retention Schedules—These schedules define all of the firm's records and information, state the official retention periods for each type of information, identify the function that is responsible for compliance with the retention periods, and present the laws, statutes, and policies on which the stated retention periods are based.

♦ Records Purging and Disposition Guidelines—These guidelines define those records that must be offered back to the client (yes, it is true) when the firm no longer needs them. They define which records must be destroyed and how they are to be destroyed, depending on the nature of the information they contain, whether it is an original or official copy, and occasionally based on specific guidelines laid out by third parties.

♦ Technology Tools—This is the collection of technology and software applications and the structure that ties them together. It includes records management database software for identifying and requesting files, bar code software, readers and printers for file and box tracking, integration software for linking record and content management applications, retention scheduling software for applying the rules in your retention schedule, and more.

◆ Exception Management Procedures—These include the processes and controls to make sure that when specific records are needed to support the firm's position during a claim, audit, investigation, or litigation, they are properly retained and maintained, without increasing risk to the firm in other areas.

◆ Education and Training—These programs increase awareness of the firm's position on records management among shareholders and staff, provide answers to their frequently asked questions, and provide clear, step-by-step training for all users based on their individual professional needs and those of the department of which they are a part and the firm as a whole.

At some point the preliminary design work on the components of a records management program is substantially complete. When that happens, the next task is the development of an implementation strategy for putting all of the pieces together.

The time that the project will take, the complexity and level of detail that is necessary in the implementation plan, and the amount of outside help a firm needs during implementation will be driven by a number of factors:

◆ The number of offices in the firm;

◆ The number of lawyers in each office;

◆ The services the firm delivers to its clients;

◆ The current condition and integrity of file lists or databases;

◆ The current state of integration among applications;

◆ The experience, expertise, and availability of project support staff and trainers in the office; and

◆ The availability of in-house resources and expertise to attend to the project over its full term.

In any event, as with the development of the program, the implementation process should be fully documented in case the program is ever called into question. Solid documentation that explains what was done, when, by whom, and in what sequence can be critically important.

In a small law office or solo practice with a handful of file cabinets, the entire document collection that explains and tracks the development and implementation process might be a few pages long. In a large, multi-jurisdiction firm with a sophisticated records system, the documentation set might be so extensive that the only reasonable way to collect and manage it is electronically.

An important caveat is in order as you move forward with implementation. Each of the basic issues involved with implementation may be subject to revision and supplementation during the implementation process. Implementation provides a reality check on each step of your workflow, and it is common to discover that indexing, procedures, or retention schedules need modest tweaking or modification. So implementation should, in addition to its primary purpose of actually rolling out and commencing formal records management, also be viewed as a continuing test environment for the fundamental operational elements of the records management program with a view to continual improvement. That improvement should continue indefinitely. In a large and sophisticated records system, many opportunities for fine-tuning are likely to exist, and when identified may in turn provide real opportunities to improve client service and efficiency, perhaps even to reduce costs. These should not be overlooked; many of them will be in the nature of free or inexpensive improvements, correcting some point that was overlooked in the initial design of the system.

Commencing Implementation

Project Management

The best way to meet multiple needs—building the project task set, identifying who is responsible for each task, specifying deliverables, establishing time frames, documenting changes to all of this and tracking progress—will require the use of a real project management tool, something like Microsoft Project. Back-of-the-envelope project management or allowing one person to keep it in his or her head (*"Hey, don't worry! I have it all in my head and it's not that big a deal!"*) can create serious time, cost, quality, and integrity problems.

What Is Involved?

The question now becomes, *"What do we do, and how do we do it?"* Implementation of a records management program is not a single discrete task, or even a single process. Rather, it is a number of processes, some linked and sequential, some independent. Depending on the condition of the current records program and the sophistication of the program being contemplated, the more significant high-level tasks, which will likely be broken down into smaller and far more detailed subtasks, might include

- Reindexing and relabeling the files;
- Reorganizing the files according to a new file plan;
- Purging active and inactive files (hard copy and electronic) according to the records retention schedule;

- Implementation of imaging or microfilming operations;
- Purchase, installation, and configuration of records management software;
- Data conversion and loading of data into the records management software;
- Integration of the records management software with workflow, conflicts checking, accounting, and marketing applications;
- Training and education for end-users, including lawyers, paralegals, and secretaries; and
- Training and education on hard-copy and electronic/digital aspects of the program for administrative/support personnel, both in records management and other parts of the firm on policies and process.

Which of these tasks or others is actually needed depends upon the prior state of the system and the extent of the initiative. Some aspects may already be in place and functioning satisfactorily, and the project at this point may only extend to implementation of a retention schedule or new filing procedures. However, unless the implementation consists of a single activity, significant thought should be given to the order in which it proceeds.

The Need for an Ordered Process

As a practical matter, unless the implementation is very simple, it will not proceed all at once. Limitations on internal resources, the need to gain experience by proceeding incrementally, and the need to avoid excessive disruptions of business activities will require that the implementation be planned in stages. Careful planning and the use of a good project management tool will help avoid chaos. The precise stages chosen, and the order in which they should proceed, will be partially dependent upon the tasks, and partially dependent on the organization. Proper planning will make for greater efficiency, lower costs during the implementation, and result in a better records management program.

Should We Buy the Software First?

Although it is tempting to consider the purchase of records management software as the first step in building a records management program, doing so is likely to yield poor results. An inconsistently indexed, structured, or managed electronic or hard-copy record system or repository, whether for management of files, word processing documents, e-mail, or other content, likely contains a large amount of useless and duplicative information and outright garbage. Without foresight, planning, and clean-up, the information in any repository that has not been consistently maintained according to strict rules will inevitably be poorly organized. Data capture, data mapping, and the ensuing data conversion are usually expensive and time-consuming processes in the best of situations. Cleaning up and preparing data in many cases requires the use of costly outside resources in addition to substantial in-house resources. Conversion of data prior to a thorough clean-up of existing data will mean spending considerable amounts of time and money to convert data that is not only valueless, but will have to be purged in short order anyway and will result in delays before the system is usable.

Further, if the software installation is executed prior to development of clean indices and other consistent data structures, and without the context of established procedures, education, and training, RM staff and end-users may both perpetuate the bad data entry habits described elsewhere in this book, resulting in the rapid accumulation of large amounts of poorly identified and structured *new* data, defeating the whole point of having the software in the first place. This is in fact a major reason for failure of records management software, document management software, and imaging installations—the technology works fine, but the installation and implementation process was poorly thought out and managed, and indices and data structures were poorly constructed or simply ignored.

Bear in mind that a similar caution holds for physical files. Relabeling and physically rearranging a filing system can be a major and labor-intensive project involving a detailed set of tasks. It frequently requires in-house and third-party personnel to come in after hours and on weekends, at premium rates. Doing all of this for files that may be purged wastes a great deal of time and money.

The volume of information to be converted in both paper and electronic conversions can be reduced, often substantially, by conducting as extensive a cleanup and purge as possible before conversion. Each file that is purged before data capture will result in savings in data entry, handling, and consumable supplies. Since the purge may substantially reduce the size of the dataset, the needed infrastructure—shelves, floor space, servers, and so on—may also be proportionately reduced, again avoiding costs.

Analysis of other aspects of implementation will generally lead to similar conclusions—ensuring that everything happens in the proper sequence will make the process as efficient as possible while ensuring accuracy of the process and integrity of the information set.

Reduction of Volume

The electronic dataset to which any process is applied should be reduced as much as possible by weeding out data, the value or integrity of which does not justify the cost and effort of conversion. This means that (a) the retention schedule should be completed prior to implementation and then applied insofar as is possible against the firm's records and information as discussed above, and (b) bad data should be expunged.

The same concept also applies, however, to the question of backfile or retrospective conversions. In any preexisting file system, paper or electronic, that has been in existence for a significant length of time, the question will arise whether or not to convert everything in it to the new system. Generally, the older information is, the lower retrieval rates for it will be, and the less urgent will be the need to identify bits of it on a granular level. At the same time, converting it to a new system may be a very costly proposition. Determining how much information should be captured and converted depends on two different issues.

Information Value

Most firms, when faced with the initial project planning, want all data converted to the new system. Budgetary considerations or other factors will usually make this unrealistic. If a backlog is sizable, old, or of questionable integrity, the cost of converting all of it will usually be prohibitive. In such cases consideration must be given to some sort of triage that will make the conversion manageable from perspectives of both cost and utility. Active information, created last week and last month, that is needed in current work is accessed frequently, so a clean-up and reorganization of it brings obvious value. For last year's information, value and utility may be more difficult to assess. For information relating to files a decade old, or even older, value is difficult to substantiate.

Potential Risk

Strict utility and value of information generally declines substantially with age; very few closed files are actually referenced, either by the lawyers or the client. However, closed files will need to be maintained for that period specified in the retention schedule following closing, and that means that matters must actually be closed.

Unless the firm is in a position to commit to a full backfile conversion, it will be necessary to create marker points in the past beyond which either less complete or less granular conversion is required or no conversion at all is required. This *does not* relieve the firm of any responsibility it may have with respect to those records. It is, instead, recognition that, past some point, rates of access are so low that it is easier and cheaper to retrieve and reorganize those records on a case-by-case basis as and when the need arises than to convert the entire group up front. The trade-off is a simple one: pain avoided now for what will hopefully be less pain later.

Past the time frames indicated in the records retention schedules, there are no hard-and-fast rules for what this cutoff should be—conducting a preconversion purge is one obvious way to create a cutoff point—a determination that has been made that purged records have *no* retrieval value—but the rest are less obvious, and in some cases, a day-forward conversion may be the right approach. Only a real analysis of the firm's actual client service and risk management needs on a practice-specific basis, combined with accurate cost estimates for various conversion scenarios, will reveal the proper cutoff points. However, when considering triage in data capture and conversion, calculations should not assume that all conversion costs for data older than the cutoff points have been avoided entirely. In all probability, they have not, and the firm will periodically find itself having to pull from storage and sort through old files (or the electronic analogues of this) that were not initially converted. The expectation of this cost and inconvenience should be built into the calculation—if it appears that it might be excessive, a more extensive conversion may be warranted.

Organization Should Precede Action

Any activity that requires application of an index or other data structure, or matching of data objects against a structure, should not commence until design of the structure and taxonomy is complete. The temptation is to take draconian steps in order to put tangible results on the table as quickly as possible, particularly if powerful stakeholders in the organization are expecting results, but this must be resisted if the results of the implementation are to have the desired quality. A system conversion of any kind requires the handling, physical or virtual, of a large number of individual data items, perhaps more than once. Any tinkering with the structure after data conversion will require rehandling these items, many on an individual basis, and that is expensive. While the incremental cost of rehandling a single item may be small, if multiplied by thousands or tens of thousands of items, the time and cost rapidly become significant and may delay implementation.

Make sure the data is as clean and consistent as possible and that the retention schedules have been implemented against existing hard-copy and electronic collections before proceeding with acquisition, implementation, and deployment of the software.

Pilot Projects

There are ways to show results, and one of the best is to pilot the new system with a friendly group. If the firm does not have extensive experience with sophisticated records management controls and wants to test procedures, workflows, or other aspects of the records management initiative prior to its firm-wide deployment, a pilot or demonstration roll-out has real value.

A pilot project can encompass some or all of the aspects of a records management program: indexing, refoldering, conversion to open-shelf filing, implementation of an indexing system, software implementation, or retention scheduling. When handled well, a pilot implementation is extremely helpful both to the project team and to the user community:

- *Controlled Test Environment.* Properly managed, a pilot project involves the users and allows for testing with the understanding that fine-tuning will take place.
- *Vetting.* Policies, procedures, workflows, training, software installation, and many other aspects of the program may require fine-tuning. Doing this in a controlled environment prior to an organization-wide roll-out is far easier than trying to analyze and fix things on a global basis with a live system and makes subsequent roll-outs much easier.
- *Learning Curve.* It allows for the development and refinement of targeted training tools and permits the creation of time projections *("How long should this step take?")* that can be applied to the rest of the firm, improving expectations and management of roll-out to other departments and offices.
- *Results.* It provides quantifiable and measurable results that can be viewed by the rest of the firm.
- *Credibility.* It proves value and increases overall buy-in.

Where Do We Start?

When dealing with the installation, configuration, testing, and deployment of records management software, start with the records department. The records staff are presumably versed in records management practices and service delivery, training should not be as complex as for end-users, and their own administrative records, generally structurally simple and modest in volume, will provide a test for other administrative departments. Management and oversight are simplified since staff are generally centrally located and the requisite authority for doing whatever needs to be done is likely to already be in place.

The choice of candidate entities—department, location, or business function—that will serve as end-user pilots is in part dependent upon which aspects of the program are being tested. If the firm is inexperienced, selection of a small operation whose processes are well-understood and that does not control large volumes of very diverse data may be a best choice. The goal in this case is to gain early experience and success, without excessive difficulties and delay.

If the goal is to gain visibility within the firm, or if political considerations dictate the order for a roll-out, another unit may be a better choice, so as to make the desired splash—assuming, of course, that the pilot can be done well. In most cases, however, since the goal will be to gain experience and fast success, a small and conveniently located pilot will provide the best results.

Approaching Specific Implementation Tasks

Policies and Procedures

Polices and procedures are simply instructions about what to do and how to do it. Implementation of procedures is essentially a process of informing personnel of the details, providing solid education and training on those details, monitoring personnel in the initial testing and revision processes, and following up to ensure that the results are meaningful.

As simple as this sounds, in practice things can be a bit more complicated. Most people are change averse when presented with alterations to their long-established habits and behavior patterns. Many employees view new records management and filing policies and processes as an intrusion on their personal domain, inconvenient at best and catastrophic at worst. Many firms have faced a recent example of this problem with the implementation of new e-mail policies. Resistance will exist and must be overcome.

Implementing new procedures in support of a new policy will require employees to follow very specific rules, and success of the records management program will depend on compliance with those rules. Even when user resistance is minimal, the reality is that many lawyers, secretaries, and paralegals regard records management duties as being low priority. Even when employees attend initial training, some follow-up training and ongoing education will be necessary. Records management policies usually put forth specific terms about the ownership and use of information and the responsibilities of firm staff.

Education and Training

Success in achieving a high degree of compliance and conformance necessitates not just orders about *what* and *how,* but real education about *why.* Passive publication of a policy or procedure by e-mail or memorandum is a sure path to noncompliance. Many personnel will not read it at all, and most that do will pay cursory attention to its implications or detail. Education and training can take many forms. The key is to target separate audiences with customized messages that get their attention and to use tools that reach as many people as possible without shutting down the department or the firm.

Education First

Tell people what is going on and why; get their undivided attention and explain the business and legal rationales for the program *("If we don't do this right it can cost us a lot of money and we can get in serious trouble with our clients and the bar association!"*). A new set of procedures presented as an arbitrary fiat is likely to be much less well-received than the same policy presented as a necessary step for good reasons. When employees understand the need, and particularly if they are given to realize that compliance will also yield tangible benefits such as increased ability to find information and better serve clients, resistance to the new policies is likely to be lower.

- *For Partners.* Raise the issue of a new RM system at retreats and partnership meetings as a matter of productivity, client service, competitiveness, ethics compliance, risk management, and cost containment.
- *For Summer and New Associates.* Make sure they know that the firm has an existing service model and that adherence is a way to build and share work product and to keep the partners happy.
- *For Laterals.* Inform them during orientation and in-processing about services and training, the importance of compliance, and the dangers of going it alone and following their own path.
- *For Paralegals.* Many firms have annual luncheons or meetings for paralegals to introduce new policies, changes to their duties, and upgrades in technology. This is a good opportunity to deliver the message, particularly if it is supported by individual mention of the importance of the new system by the partners with whom they work.
- *For Secretaries.* This group often presents the greatest challenge since many secretaries consider records management as a low-interest filing task that gets done last. Some secretaries still have a strong allegiance to a single partner or lawyer and are loath to change their current processes. They must get the message that the changes are important to and expected by the lawyers.
- *Administrative and Support Departments.* This actually tends to be the easiest group to train and manage during implementation. Records are usually already maintained in some consistent format, and staff from the same function (accounting, human resources, etc.) tend to have a common perspective on and understand the problems with current operations.

Training Approaches

The traditional lecture and PowerPoint session as an education tool remains popular and has the advantage of permitting question-and-answer sessions. This serves well in *educational* situations but has its limitations when *training* users in the use of new technology. The downside of lecture and slides in training is that group gatherings require the physical presence of trainer and trainees in a single location. This may to some extent be ameliorated by use of video conferencing technology—particularly if personnel are in different locations—but even this requires simultaneous participation. An increasingly popular alternative is the use of interactive, computer-based training supported by a knowledgeable proctor at each site. Prepared sessions walk attendees through topics using WebEx or some similar tool. Well-designed and professionally prepared, these presentations can be as detailed and targeted as they need to be. They can also track attendance, administer tests, and record the results, all without the need to incur the overhead of repeatedly assembling all trainees in a single room. There is, of course, the question of ensuring that the attendee is actually paying attention and not reading a magazine during the session (an issue that is not entirely absent from live sessions), but this can be protected against, at least to some extent, by making the sessions interactive and forcing attention. Specialized training consultants are worth considering. They can prepare more comprehensive and elaborate training materials than all but the largest firms can realistically prepare in-house.

A good deal of records management education and training will focus on relatively low-level and mundane procedures: the correct way to pack and label a box for storage, the proper labeling of a file, the correct way to read and use a retention schedule, and so on. The value and importance of this training should not be underestimated. Failures in areas such as these are far more common than failures to comply with things such as information ownership policies, and if widespread, can have severe repercussions: poor box packing and labeling and poor file labeling are among the more common failings found in law firms and are among the most difficult and expensive problems to repair if they are widespread and longstanding. Graphic displays showing, for example, exactly how a box label is filled out and exactly where on the box it is to be placed sound simple but are very useful.

Physical Files

Implementing the hard-copy portion of the records management program will have several components and may include:

- Creating the records retention schedules;
- Conversion from vertical or lateral file cabinets to open-shelf filing;
- Converting active file maintenance from decentralized to centralized operations;
- Changing from legal to letter-size paper and filing supplies;
- Restructuring of the filing and indexing system to conform to a new scheme;
- Changing from alphabetic to numeric sequencing of shelved files;
- Implementing bar coding or other automated tracking technology (such as RFID);

- Entering data about files into records management software;
- Moving on-site closed or inactive records to less expensive off-site storage; and
- Purging and record destruction.

Remember, a cost is incurred each time an object is touched. With so many tasks in play, each requiring multiple steps, the watchword in making an implementation work is *efficiency*. A properly managed and streamlined conversion process will minimize the number of times each object must be handled. How quickly, efficiently, and accurately the process moves along is directly related to the elegance of the workflow processes for handling the objects. A streamlined physical file conversion to a new labeling system with bar codes in conjunction with a move to a central file room will, for example, involve taking files off shelves, loading them on carts, moving them to a processing area, unloading them, relabeling existing folders or entirely refoldering and relabeling them, loading them back on a cart, moving them to the new filing area, and unloading and resequencing the files on the shelves. If metadata on the files are to be entered into a records management software system, the data entry for this must also occur somewhere along the way. Make the capture and data entry part of the conversion, rather than a separate and more expensive step.

Efficient throughput in this system is dependent upon a large number of factors: the kinds, capacities, and numbers of bins and carts available to transport the folders; the order in which items are placed in bins for transport; the area and layout of sorting and refiling tables; the ergonomic relationship between equipment and personnel (e.g., is it easy or difficult to move completed files back into a cart?); the precise equipment used (e.g., are sorting bins and other devices designed for these tasks being used?); and the precise sequence and layout of the relabeling or refiling tasks. How well these tasks are thought out can have a dramatic impact on the efficiency and cost of the entire process. If a variety of changes to the physical filing system are contemplated, careful consideration should be given to the sequence of all of the tasks involved, and each step in the process should be tested with the idea of reducing the number of times objects must be handled, transported, or touched. The objective is to accomplish as much as possible in a single pass through the system. Each pass costs money (direct costs) and may well disrupt business processes (an indirect cost). To the extent that some tasks can be paired, the total number of tasks can be reduced, and the number of passes reduced, pain and expense will be minimized and overall start-to-finish disruption time and cost reduced.

As with many other aspects of an implementation, there are no hard-and-fast rules; each implementation is unique since tasks, situations, physical space, and other variables will differ. Parameters for necessary activities may be constrained by the nature of current storage arrangements, room available for work areas, the need to make some files continually and immediately available, and to avoid disrupting business and other factors. Leaving planning aside and taking an ad hoc approach to implementation will always cost more, take longer, and result in fewer economies and a less efficient system than taking a well-structured approach. Detailed implementation planning should not be overlooked.

If internal resources are not available or are otherwise occupied, consider using a workflow specialist or consultant, or even outsourcing portions of the implementation. Poorly designed workflows can result in time and labor inputs of up to several times what a well-designed process would have required, and may drag on far longer than anticipated. An experienced and knowledgeable leader must be in charge of and responsible for the process.

Managing Electronic Records

One of the most frequently asked questions is, *"Now that we have our plan and process in place for managing the hard-copy files, what kind of systems, rules, and tools are we going to need to manage our electronic records and digital media?"* The good news here is that most of the basic processes, rules, and tools developed for hard copy also apply to electronic records:

- ◆ Retention Schedules. Medium does not matter. The same legal and ethics rules apply to paper and to nonpaper records, including word processing documents, Web content, e-mail, and databases. If the retention period for a hard-copy document is seven years, the retention period for its official digital replacement will be the same.
- ◆ Filing Schemes. The organization of hard-copy and digital records should be the same. Users are still going to want *correspondence* in date order, *depositions* grouped together, well-indexed *pleadings,* and so on.
- ◆ Software. If you are using or plan to use one of the legal-specific records management software applications, and that software has been DoD5015 certified, it will likely include substantial functionality for managing both hard-copy and electronic records. Some additional costs may be incurred for integration with other applications, but completely new technology is usually not required just to manage e-mail and other electronic records.

There will, however, be some tasks that are unique to dealing with electronic records. Beyond the introduction or modification of policies and procedures that affect various types of electronic information and records, implementation of a records management program in an electronic records environment may require additional work in three basic areas:

1. Extended configuration of records management software and integration with workflow, document management, conflicts checking, docketing, financial, litigation support, and possibly other firm applications like marketing;
2. Entry of data into the software and conversion of old data; and
3. Education and training of both records management and end-user staff.

If imaging or microfilming are being implemented as part of the flow, or if data conversion is being effected from multiple sources and datasets, they may take place concurrently.

Records Management and Document Management Software

Who is likely to be involved? Installation of records management software and integration with other applications will typically involve a considerable amount of behind-the-scenes work by some mix of IT staff, systems integrators, the vendor's professional services personnel, and consultants to install, test, and configure the software, ensure hardware compatibility, design and deploy a smooth integration with other applications, create and deploy a solid user interface, and deal with other technical issues. At some point, these will be resolved, and the software will be up and running in the records department and the pilot department. At this point, use of the records management software can begin.

Configuration

Good law firm–specific records management software is highly configurable with respect to screen display, data fields, and similar matters. This gives the firm great flexibility in designing it to meet the different needs of multiple user groups, but also requires significant effort to utilize effectively. For example, a given software package might give the user a choice of any of a dozen or more data entry and display fields to use with any record type, and most or all may be renamable. These might include fields for index entries or topics, keywords, notes fields, and more. In addition, other information such as document author might be recorded or even captured automatically. There are likely to be a good many other choices as well. The issue is to make standard as many of those as possible across the enterprise and to identify those that should be reserved for customizing within and according to the needs of specific departments and/or practices.

First Things First—Confidentiality and Security

Maintenance of confidentiality and security are of major importance in all law offices. Early on in the process of developing the criteria for software configuration, you will need to make a list of the matters, topics, and files that require limited access and close controls. Among the types of issues that will have to be considered are office-internal personal matters such as staff divorces, HIPAA requirements for protecting medical records if your office deals with physicians or insurance companies, confidential pre-merger or corporate information, and sensitive intellectual property records that may be of interest to those involved in corporate espionage. Document who should have access to which files, documents, and information by topic, matter, and name and carefully protect the listing. It will be critical to configuring the software in a fashion that meets the security and confidentiality needs of the firm and the clients it serves.

Other Configuration Issues

Other early configuration tasks are the assignment of user access rights, creation of practice-specific profiles, loading of the records retention rule set, and selection and report design. Decisions must also be made as to which fields will actually be used and how those fields will be titled. This will require consideration of what data is actually needed for various retrieval purposes. With all of this planning going on, it is a good idea to create and maintain a series of profiling documents that show what decisions were made, based on which rules, and when those decisions were made. Maintenance of a detailed project plan with each deliverable identified and careful documentation of your decisions will save a lot of grief.

Data Conversion

Data conversion is a conceptually simple process: the data are imported from one electronic system into another. In records management, this means that information objects and their associated metadata are exported from one system and imported into another. The objects in question could be any of a number of things—images and their associated indices, file folder listings, electronic documents, and box inventories are a few examples. The old system could be records management software, document management software, an old in-house designed database, an imaging system, or even spreadsheets.

In each case, the object exists in a data structure in the old system, and its metadata exist as cells and rows of data in the tables of a database in the same system. Each cell of a row contains a particular datum about its associated information object, for example a date or an index entry. Each column in the table contains that same data point for each object represented in the table. Fundamentally, all that is required is to determine which columns in the old database correspond to the columns in the tables in the new database. The data is then exported, either directly from one system to another or to a flat file such as a spreadsheet or delimited text file, from which it can be imported into the new database. In practice, however, things are not so simple, and data conversion can be an extremely problematic process.

The system will not work without good data. When preparing for data conversion, legacy datasets the firm may be importing from other applications and repositories must be mapped from the existing to the new table structures. We have already discussed the need to clean up the datasets you will be moving to the new software's data repositories. It is critically important that this task be completed for each dataset that will be moved to the new system. It is also very important to set up a master data profile for the new repository and to make sure, if you are combining a number of datasets into one new collection, that like data from the different source datasets are consistent in format and mapped to the same fields.

The first issue that commonly arises is that the old data is full of errors. For example, an index field could inadvertently contain other information such as a name, or a numeric field might contain alphabetic text rather than numerals. Assuring consistency and integrity in existing data structures complicates and extends the time and cost of data conversion. If errors such as these exist, the structures created by importing this data will have the same faults.

Even if the data does not contain outright errors (a highly unlikely possibility in any large dataset), other issues such as inconsistency of format will cause problems. For example, a name might be entered as John J. Smith in one record, Smith, John J. in another record, John Smith in yet another, and Smith, John James in still another. Where possible, these must be found and corrected. If the old database had a single field for [John J. Smith] and the new database splits these into three fields [John] [J] [Smith], not only must the three entries be corrected, but they must also be parsed out so that each part of the name goes into the correct field in the new database. Even the comma may cause a problem. If the output from the old database is a comma-delimited text file (a text file in which the separate data points are separated by commas, which are recognized by the new program as the start and end points of each data point), the output will be [Smith,,John,James] without the comma, [Smith, John,James] with the comma. The new program will read the extra comma as a blank field, and insert all subsequent data in the wrong place.

Once all of the errors and inconsistencies are identified and corrected, the data from the old system must be mapped to the new system. If there is not a one-to-one match between the structure of the default tables in the new system and the output of the old system, either the data must be massaged to fit the new system, or the new system must be altered to accept the data from the old.

Formats may be an issue as well. Older data such as images may not be in standard formats such as JPEG or TIFF and may instead be encoded into a proprietary format that cannot be read by the new system. If so, a translation routine must be created. The output from the old software may also be a problem. It is not unheard of for software vendors to make their output intentionally difficult to export to other programs to discourage changing vendors.

These are only a few examples of the many problems associated with a data conversion. If multiple systems are being converted, any or all of them may be present for each system. Depending on which of them are present, and to what degree, a data conversion can be a complex and drawn-out process. In most cases involving large datasets, particularly older datasets that have not been rigorously controlled, errors, inconsistencies, and mapping issues are present, and may be severe. A significant period of testing and error correction is therefore to be expected, involving as many as three data conversion passes, prior to a full and successful data conversion, and timelines should reflect this reality.

User Interface

One of the primary benefits of good software is the ability to configure the user interface—how the screen looks to individual users—so that it suits the specific needs of individual departments or practice groups. This requires optimizing the look and feel for the individual group or department in a way that is the most meaningful to them, laying out the screen so that they can search for and retrieve records easily, request files and access digital records (most commonly e-mail and word processing documents), request new folders be created, and other common user tasks. One of the key issues here is to create an interface that supports the needs of both the neophyte and the experienced computer user within each group. There is a tendency among those users who consider themselves techies to overstate the amount of information to which they will need access and to end up driving the creation of complex user interfaces. Start with a minimalist approach. Minimize screen clutter and provide only what the user absolutely needs; hide anything that is not necessary. Most users really need only a few functions. Concentrate on clarity and intuitiveness.

How About Workflow?

If the software is capable of managing (through its own functionality or by integration with other software) workflow by routing electronic documents between personnel, routing schemes must be devised and set up for each process, decision-making rules must be defined based on data pulled from multiple sources, and rules about timing and alternative decision paths must be established. All of this can get very complex. Trying to pilot and roll out records management software at the same time that you are designing, testing, and integrating a workflow solution is not a good idea. Make sure the records management solution works well, design and vet your processes, decisions, and rules for workflow, but do not try to test them simultaneously.

Classification Structures, File Plans, and Records Retention Schedules

Before you start testing the software, classification schema, file plans, indices, retention schedules, and other data structures have been developed. These must be loaded into the system, and like data entry fields, must be configured. Indices, profiling terms, and standard folder titling schemes may be displayed by drop-down menus, trees, and other displays, and like data entry fields, can be matched to individual departmental needs. Thus, for example, a particular user may only need to see a small part of the index related to her work, rather than the entire index. In similar manner, the retention schedule may be displayed to all or some users, or perhaps to no one—retention rules can sometimes be automatically assigned when an item is indexed. The goal of this entire process is to minimize the amount of effort required to either classify or retrieve a data object accurately. Most users, particularly lawyers, have a low tolerance for the intrusion of records management activities in the form of substantial administrative overhead into their daily routine. If using the software is too difficult, too confusing, or requires too many clicks of the mouse, they will do it incorrectly—or not at all.

Successfully managing configuration requires an intimate understanding of the actual needs of the firm and the user community. This in turn requires reference back to any data capture activities conducted earlier in the initiative. Ideally, earlier data gathering will have provided a substantial background in user needs and workflows, but it may be necessary to supplement it with further data gathering and analysis. Installing, testing, and configuring a new records management software solution is not a strictly linear process. The process presents multiple opportunities to confirm your original assumptions, make adjustments (*all carefully documented, of course*), identify new opportunities, and refine your processes and controls for bringing value to the end-user.

Take advantage of your original data gathering and documentation and continue your analysis during the testing phase. Software will not yield the results you want unless it is configured to meet the specific needs of your different user groups. Adequate attention to the configuration and setup will make operation intuitive and greatly minimize inconvenience and shorten the learning curve.

Imaging and Microfilm

Microfilming and imaging systems are two types of content management systems. In the past they have been minimally deployed in law offices, the primary exception being the use of database-driven imaging systems to support large and complex litigation support needs. In almost all cases these systems have operated mostly in stand-alone mode, without benefit of integration with other applications. With the possibility of creating large sets of content that have value across the enterprise or within specific practices or departments, these applications and others are being deployed as important components of knowledge management systems.

These systems will not be discussed in depth here, but a few comments are appropriate. First, neither an imaging application nor a knowledge management system nor any content/document management system is a replacement for a records management system. They are designed to address very different needs. Second, the value and ease of use can be significantly extended by careful integration with records management technology. In many cases, it makes good sense to integrate existing or planned imaging systems and those legacy microfilming systems, through their databases, with the new records management system. Doing this requires some planning and care.

To maintain productivity and justify the investment, imaging systems are rated by throughput in terms of documents per hour or some similar metric. This is, however, a measurement (generally a very optimistic one) of the ability of the scanners and software to feed documents through, and assumes all other processes are adequately efficient. Imaging is not merely a process of feeding documents through a scanner. Prep work in the form of removing staples and paper clips and repairing torn documents is required, and each document must then be scanned, indexed, and image quality checked. After scanning, documents and files must be reassembled and sent to storage or staged pending final release for disposition.

All of this requires efficient workflow if the required throughput is to be achieved at a reasonable cost in labor and equipment. It requires an efficiently designed work area and workflow procedures, as well as competent and trained staff. If the scanned images are to be retrievable, indices and other data structures must be fully developed and effective as well. Most of this must be designed before implementation.

Each of these issues must be carefully considered, and solutions crafted and tested, before any imaging for operational purposes is done. Imaging installations commonly fail to perform as anticipated or fail outright, and when they do it is rarely because the hardware or software did not perform adequately. The fault can almost always be traced to inadequate design up front, inattention to workflow, poor quality control, inadequate training, or a system bogged down with a large volume of useless images.

Proponents of imaging sometimes state that microfilming is a technology that no longer has value. There are, however, values to using microfilming instead of imaging in some situations. Microfilm is very stable, and over the long-term, quite inexpensive; and its retrieval and readability is essentially unaffected by technology changes. In contrast, imaging technology changes rapidly, as does the computer technology that serves as its infrastructure. Keeping images on a computer system for any length of time therefore requires periodic migration to new formats and changes in hardware and software if content is to continue to be accessible.

It remains true that while the ideal imaging candidate is a document with high retrieval rates but a relatively short useful life, the opposite is true of microfilming. Retrieval of either microfilm or microfiche works well for consistent, low-cost, rapid retrieval, and it has great value as an archival medium.

Some planning and processing requirements are common to the effective deployment of both image and microform-based systems. Beyond the issues briefly addressed above, a subset of specific considerations applicable to imaging applies. Quality control for the images is critical, as is the presence of a well-structured indexing system within which to catalogue the images: improperly or unindexed microform and digitized images may well be lost. Finally, throughput and workflow issues, and staff training, are virtually identical when using either technology. A poorly designed system will result in serious processing bottlenecks, reduced economy, and limited usability.

Summary

- ◆ Plan the Project—Planning and executing the installation, testing, and roll-out of records management software is a process that requires control. Create a detailed project plan: identify tasks and subtasks, assign responsibility for each one, define the deliverables that will serve as your indication that the task is complete, and know your critical paths.
- ◆ Get Good Help—Tap internal and external resources to do the job right. Even a small office or a solo lawyer can benefit from the selective use of experienced professionals who have done it before.
- ◆ Pay Attention to the Details—Write it down and check it multiple times. Document your assumptions, your processes, and workflow.

- Keep It Simple—Make it easy for the users. Cater to their needs but do not give them more functionality than they need to get started and to perform their basic functions. You can always go back and add more functions to their view of the system later on.
- Integration Works—Know what other applications the system needs to talk to and how that will bring value to the new operation. Any information that can be loaded from another repository or system in clean form does not have to be keyed in and is not subject to further human error in the process. Leverage your financial and content management systems first.
- Install One at a Time—Test, prove, and deploy your records management system first. Then add in other new systems. It is hard to analyze and rectify a problem when more than one system and set of assumptions is in play.
- Educate the Users—Tell everyone involved what you are doing and why. Your different user groups are more liable to pay attention and give the new records program a fair chance if they understand why it is important and how it will help them.
- Give Good Training—The best tools do not give value unless users know how to use them. After you have trained them, follow up and see if they need more training.

Appendix 1

SAMPLE RECORDS MANAGEMENT DEPARTMENT CHARTER

The Department

As a reflection of its role, the department responsible for supporting the firm's records management needs will be known as Records Services.

Service and Scope

Records Management is defined as the management of firm information from initial receipt or creation, during its active life, through secure inactive maintenance, to its ultimate disposition according to established firm policy, retention schedules, and procedures. The level of records management support and services will be consistent across the firm so that the lawyers and other staff at [Law Firm Name] can rely on the quality and integrity of records in all locations where the firm does business.

Firm Support

Records Services is charged with the appropriate application of policy and procedure to support the firm's information and records management, client service, risk management, and cost-containment initiatives.

User Support

Records Services is charged with the appropriate application of technology and process to support all authorized firm users in the identification, management, tracking, and disposition of hard-copy and electronic records. Records Services will provide a combination of user education, training, and hands-on support to make sure users can find and access the information they need, when they need it, in a manner consistent with conformance to legal ethics requirements, a superior level of client service, and minimizing risk to the client and the firm.

Strategy and Direction

Records Services will monitor changes in the records management discipline to make sure that as new issues and challenges emerge, and as tools and technology evolve, appropriate changes are recommended for incorporation into the firm's records management infrastructure and services.

Appendix 2

SAMPLE RECORDS MANAGEMENT POLICY STATEMENT

Policy No.:	Subject:	Records Management
Policy Date:	Supersedes:	Initial Issuance
Date Approved:	Approved by:	

1. POLICY STATEMENT

   [Law Firm Name] is committed to firm-wide compliance with records management policies and procedures. In keeping with this commitment, it is important that all partners and employees understand and support the firm's commitment.

2. SCOPE

   This policy applies to all partners and employees, including associates, support staff, legal assistants, and summer, temporary, and contract employees at all locations.

3. DEFINITION

   Records Management is defined as the management of firm information from active use through secure inactive maintenance to its ultimate disposition according to established policy and procedures.

4. PROCEDURE

   A. Ownership of Records—All records created, received, or maintained by [Law Firm Name] personnel in the performance of their duties are the property of the firm. Partners and staff may not create copies in any medium for persons or entities outside of the routine performance of their duties, or create and maintain copies of firm records at locations other than those approved by the firm.

   B. Procedures—Inactive records maintenance shall be governed by procedures set forth in the most current version of the Records Services Manual.

   C. Records Retention and Disposition—The firm's official policy on records retention scheduling and disposition procedures, controls, and exception management are set forth in the Records Retention Schedules and supporting Records Services Manual.

5. ADMINISTRATIVE RESPONSIBILITY

   It is the responsibility of all personnel to uphold the firm's records management policy. Questions regarding the content of or changes to records retention policy, interpretation of a Records Retention Schedule (RRS), or procedures supporting the schedules should be directed to the Records Manager.

I have read and understand the above policy and agree to abide by its terms.		
Name:	Signature:	Date:

Appendix 3

RECORDS MANAGEMENT READING LIST

General Resources

Records Management in the Legal Environment: A Handbook of Practice and Procedure; *Barr, Jean, CRM; Chiaiese, Beth, CRM; and Nemchek, Lee R., CRM* (2003).

> An authoritative, exhaustive, and recent handbook for records management practitioners about law practice records management by three well-respected practitioners. Highly recommended for those seeking in-depth guidance on the detailed operations aspects of law firm records management.

Records and Information Management: Fundamentals of Professional Practice; *Saffady, William* (2004).

> A very good general resource by a highly respected authority.

General Resources for Small Firms

At Your Fingertips in the Office: Information Management for the Small Business; *Bradley, Alexandra, and Dale, Denise.*

Organize Your Office: A Small Business Survival Guide to Managing Records; *Mark, Teri, CRM* (2003).

Filing Systems and Indexing

Establishing Alphabetic, Numeric and Subject Filing Systems; ANSI/ARMA 12-2005 (2005).

E-mail and Electronic Records

E-Mail Rules: A Business Guide to Managing Policies, Security, and Legal Issues; *Flynn, Nancy, and Kahn, Randolph Esq.* (2003).

Electronic Document Imaging: Technology, Applications, Implementation; *Saffady, William* (2001).

Electronic Records Retention: New Strategies for Data Life Cycle Management; *Stephens, David O., CRM, FAI; and Wallace, Roderick C., CRM* (2003).

Instant Messaging Rules; *Flynn, Nancy L.* (2004).

Framework for Integration of Electronic Document Management Systems and Electronic Records Management Systems (ANSI/AIIM/ARMA TR48-2004) (2004) (electronic publication).

Requirements for Managing Electronic Messages as Records, ANSI/ARMA 9-2004 (2004).

Legal Issues

Access Rights to Business Data on Personally Owned Computers; *Montaña, John C., J.D.* (2004) (electronic publication).

Retention Schedules

Records Retention Procedures; *Skupsky, Donald S., J.D., CRM* (1995).

Report on Issues Surrounding Retention of Client Files in Law Firms; *Andrews, Helen; Holloway, Phillip L.; Ledwith, Clare M.; Mutchler, K. Anne; Shea, Roseanne M.; and Zimmerman, Gloria* (1993).

Appendix 4

RECORDS AND INFORMATION MANAGEMENT
ASSOCIATIONS AND ORGANIZATIONS

National Professional Organizations with a Records Management Focus

AIIM (The Association for Information and Image Management)
1100 Wayne Ave., Suite 1100
Silver Spring, MD 20910
(301) 587-8202; (800) 477-2446; fax: (301) 587-2711
www.aiim.org
e-mail: aiim@aiim.org

ARMA International (Records Managers Professional Organization)
13725 W. 109th St., Suite 101
Lenexa, KS 66215
(913) 341-3808; (800) 422-2762; fax (913) 341-3742
www.arma.org
e-mail: hq@arma.org

NAID—National Association for Information Destruction
3420 E. Shea Blvd., Suite 115
Phoenix, AZ 85028
(602) 788-6243; fax (602) 788-4144
www.naidonline.org

PRISM—Professional Information and Records Services Management (Records Storage)
Int'l HQ: 131 U.S. 70 West
Garner, NC 27529
(800) 336-9793; (919) 771-0657; fax (919) 771-0457
www.prismintl.org

The Sedona Conference
180 Broken Arrow Way South
Sedona, AZ 86351
(866) 860-6600; (928) 284-2698; fax (928) 284-4240
www.thesedonaconference.org
e-mail: tsc@sedona.net

Society of American Archivists
527 South Wells St., 5th Floor
Chicago, IL 60607
(312) 922-0140; fax (312) 347-1452
www.archivists.org
e-mail: info@archivists.org

Local Legal-Specific Records Management Organizations

(Note: There are other local groups in addition to those listed below; the contact names change with some frequency, and not all groups meet regularly.)

Atlanta Legal Records Managers (ALRM)
Mary Mulinix, Records/Client Information Manager
Alson & Bird, LLP
1149 Logan Circle NW
Atlanta, GA 30318-2854
(404) 881-7401 phone
(404) 352-9305 fax
mmulinix@alston.com

Boston Legal Records Managers Group
Sandra Taylor, Records Manager
Palmer & Dodge LLP
111 Huntington Ave.
Boston, MA 02199
(617) 239-0241 phone
(617) 227-4420 fax
staylor@palmerdodge.com

Boston Conflicts Administrators Group
Mark C. Robinson CRM, Record Center Manager
Choate Hall & Stewart
Exchange Place
53 State St.
Boston, MA 02109
(617) 248-5137 phone
(617) 248-4000 fax
mrobinson@choate.com

Chicago Legal Association for Records Managers and Administrators (LARMA)
Jerry Brandes, Records Supervisor
Jenner & Block
One East IBM Plaza #RC43
Chicago, IL 60611
(312) 222-9350 phone
(312) 527-0484 fax
jbrandes@jenner.com

Dallas Downtown Legal Records Group
Laura Livingston, Records Manager
Fulbright & Jaworski LLP
2200 Ross Ave., Suite 2800
Dallas, TX 75201-2784
(214) 855-8370 phone
(214) 855-8200 fax
llivingston@fulbright.com

Denver Legal Records Managers Group
Bonnie Clarke
McGeady, Sisneros
1675 Broadway #2100
Denver, CO 80202
(303) 592-4369 phone
(303) 592-4385 fax
bclarke@mcgeadysisneros.com

District of Columbia Conflicts Roundtable
Robert K. Oaks
Director of Global Information Resources
Latham & Watkins
555 11th St. NW, Suite 1000
Washington, DC 20004-1304
(202) 637-2294 phone
(202) 637-2201 fax
bob.oaks@lw.com

Greater Kansas City ARMA Legal ISG
Shawn T. Sourk, Director of Records
Lathrop & Gage L.C.
2345 Grand Blvd., Suite 2700
Kansas City, MO 64108
(816) 460-5759 phone
(816) 292-2001 fax
sourkst@lathropgage.com

Downtown Los Angeles Legal Records Managers Networking Group
Lee R. Nemchek CRM, MLS
Morrison & Foerster LLP
555 W. Fifth St., Suite 3500
Los Angeles, CA 90017
(213) 892-5359 phone
(213) 892-5454 fax
lnemchek@mofo.com

Legal Records Management Association (LRMA),
Westside Los Angeles Chapter
Patricia Merdan CRM, Membership Chair
Pircher, Nichols & Meeks
1925 Century Park East, Suite 1700
Los Angeles, CA 90067
www.goclubexe.com/clubportal

Appendix 5

LEGAL-SPECIFIC RECORDS MANAGEMENT SOFTWARE VENDORS

Functionality alone does not tell the tale. Selection of software should be based on all aspects of a vendor's offerings: frequency of updates, responsiveness, hours and timeliness of support, and service ratings, as well as their general reputation on the street.

A place on this list implies no endorsement by the authors or by the ABA. The presence on this list of any vendor indicates only that they (a) have one or more software products that deal directly with records management and (b) are fairly widely installed among law firms and law offices.

Accutrac
University Research Park
5251 California Avenue, Suite 170
Irvine, CA 92617 USA
(949) 854-0382 phone
(800) 578-9361 toll free
(949) 854-0390 fax
www.accutrac.com

Elite Information Systems
5100 West Goldleaf Circle, Suite 100
Los Angeles, CA 90056-1271 USA
(323) 642-5200 phone
(323) 642-5400 fax
www.elite.com

Interwoven
803 11th Avenue
Sunnyvale, CA 94089 USA
(408) 774-5800 phone
(408) 774-2002 fax
info@interwoven.com

Hummingbird

1 Sparks Avenue
Toronto, Ontario M2H 2W1 Canada
(416) 496-2200 phone
(877) 359-4866 toll free
(416) 496-2207 fax
www.hummingbird.com

MDY Advanced Technologies

21-00 Route 208 South
Fair Lawn, NJ 07410 USA
(888) 639-6200 phone
(201) 797-6852 fax
www.mdy.com

Appendix 6

DESTRUCTION CERTIFICATION MEMORANDUM

This sample memo is used to document that files were destroyed at the end of the Retention Schedule Implementation Process. The assumption by most clients is that a commercial records storage or disposition service actually executes the destruction. *Destruction certificates from vendors are, however, usually not specific to the necessary level of detail required to document a firm's actions. This information (along with the destruction vendor's certificate) should be kept in electronic/digital format wherever possible.*

To: **Records Destruction Project Control File**

From: **(Project Team Member/Records Manager)**

Date:

Subject: **Records Destruction**

Records were destroyed on this date relating to the official firm file on the following:

CLIENT NO.	CLIENT NAME
MATTER NO.	MATTER DESCRIPTION

Appendix 7

CLIENT FILES REVIEW AND DOCUMENTATION PROCEDURES

This draft procedure is designed to support the processes that should take place when reviewing old client files in anticipation of their disposition. It takes the user through the processes of preparing for attorney review and client contact, segregating out work product you know you want to keep, and dealing with the occasional need to return a file to a client. All of this supposes the files can be identified accurately and linked to a client. Remember, this is a sample process and a starting point for creating your own procedures and controls. None of this should be started without first checking on the ethics requirements in your particular state and making sure that the processes work in that context.

KEY:

OPS – Operations Staff
DE – Data Entry Staff
KM – Knowledge Management
RA – Responsible Attorney

RMS – Records Management Software (or listing)
SASE – Self Addressed Stamped Envelope
SOL – Statute of Limitation

Task   **Responsible Party**

1. Select closed matters past their retention lifetime   OPS
   a. Start the Client Files Tracking Form (CFT)

CLIENT FILES TRACKING FORM			
Attorney Name:	Box Number/Identification:		Date Closed:
CLIENT Number:	MATTER Number:		
Inventory By:	Date:	Quality Check By:	Date:
☐ OK to Return or Destroy	☐ Keep Until _____	☐ Other (see comments)	
Sent to Client By:	Date:	Client Return Confirmed By:	Date:
☐ Destroyed on _____	☐ Returned _____	☐ Other (see comments)	
Comments:			

SABRM01/26/2005

b. Attach CFT to boxes, files

Use carton lids to move the small, one and two file matters; use the cartons and carts for larger collections. Mark them with client matter number on large Post-its®.

2. Establish a matter close date.   **OPS**
    a. Close date in RMS—all matters inactive before //insert date// should have a close date.
    b. Date of last time charged to the code
3. Update RMS with new closed date if appropriate   **OPS**
4. Segregate known valuable firm work product for review and indexing.   **OPS**

    Some samples (certainly not inclusive):
    a. Expert Witness (see Handbook item xx)
    b. Legal Opinions and Memoranda of Law (see Handbook item xx)
    c. Closing binders from RE, financial deals, etc.
5. List the files for attorney review   **DE**
    a. Generate file index/listing
    b. Generate cover memo to attorney
    c. Duplicate and file (digital/hard copy) of both, by attorney name
    d. Send hard copy of both cover memo and file index report to attorney for his/her reference
    e. Stage files for next step
6. Confirm Client Contact Information
    a. Check RMS for address and last contact date
    b. Determine situations where there will be no information in RMS
    c. If part of the //insert date// group, the address may be old but we will send the letter anyway.

    Note: Consider starting this process while the attorney is doing his/her review as a way of saving time.

7. Review by Responsible Attorney   **RA**
    a. Flag any additional documents as possible work-product/KM resources
    b. Sign-off on files that qualify for disposition
    c. Document any exceptions to disposition process
    d. Send form back to RM
8. Initiate Client contact   **DE**
    a. *Contact Attempt 1*—by registered mail, return receipt requested. The letter reminds the client that if they select disposition, such disposition should be in compliance with client's records retention schedule and sound records management practices. Letter should specify payment responsibility—and offer
        i. Secure Destruction
        ii. Return of file

       iii. Continued Firm storage

Note: If you have the staff and volume to warrant it, consider having one person handle the preparation of the letters and a second person handle the mailing, filing and tracking of responses. The second individual could qualify check the first on the mailings and the first could be the back up for the second in case of absenteeism.

  b. *Contact Attempt 2*

     i. Validate contact information

    ii. Verify close date and failed contact information

   iii. Library check for new name or location (set up a standard e-mail)

   iv. Send new letter

    v. Get hard-copy results of library efforts and file them

Note: A process needs to be developed for involving the Library staff to do some of the research for instances when the department is unable to identify a client contact address.

  c. *Contact Attempt 3*

     i. Determine last valid address

    ii. Identify local newspaper

   iii. Post newspaper advertisements and file a copy

Allow 30 days after posting for response.

9. Client Response   **DE/OPS**

  a. Disposition OK per client

     i. File admin and contact documents

       1. Attorney OK

       2. Update destruction batch list documentation that had not been set aside during attorney review may be destroyed with the exception of the Client file, as stated in the Records Retention Schedule.

    ii. Destroy the records; and

   iii. Document the destruction in the RMS Records Management Program and file the documentation with the contact letters in the Client file.

Note: You may want to keep either hard-copy or electronic copies of the destroyed files indices.

  b. Return OK per client

     i. Retrieve and clean up file

    ii. Print index and attach to cover letter

   iii. Duplicate and file index and cover letter in the client contact file

Q: Is this step necessary? In the rare instances when a client actually wants the file returned, prudence dictates you cover the firm by keeping the documentation on what you did for a time period sufficient to cover the SOL for professional liability.

   iv. Update RMS

    v. Package and ship the file and a receipt with a SASE

c. Client requests that we keep the file!
  i. Review and consolidate the file (see above)
  ii. Update index in RMS with reason (their retention requirements, historical significance, etc.)
  iii. Send client a copy (or notify them via e-mail that one is available, of the index)

Appendix 8
CLIENT FILES REVIEW ANNOUNCEMENT

This memo has been designed to serve as a model for all sizes of law offices. Customize it to meet your needs and to reflect your review process and timing. If yours is a solo practice, then turn it into a document explaining your process.

To: All Attorneys
From: (Managing Partner)
CC:
Date:
Re: Records Retention Project

Project Status

As you are aware, the Firm has recently completed the development and adoption of Client Files Records Retention Schedules. With Executive Committee approval, this schedule is now official firm policy. The retention schedule supports the firm's strategy of containing costs while meeting risk management and legal compliance requirements in all U.S. locations where the firm has offices.

Implementation

We are now preparing to implement the new schedule. This major undertaking will involve the review of all boxes of records stored in off-site facilities, some records maintained on-site, and the disposition of those records that fall outside the time frames listed on the retention schedules. We plan to start the review in the next month using teams of trained personnel led by members of the in-house Records Management department. //insert name//, firm-wide //insert title//, will lead the project.

As part of our review, we will be indexing and setting aside selected documents with research value.

Responsible attorneys will receive sign-off memoranda referencing files that qualify for disposition. Reports listing appropriate client and matter descriptions, closing dates, and file indices will be attached to these memoranda. Records will not be disposed of without appropriate attorney authorization. As a further reminder, in accordance with ethics requirements, we will be notifying clients of our intent to dispose of the files unless they indicate otherwise.

A bonded company that specializes in secure records destruction, with which the firm has done business for many years, will process the records.

Timing

We are currently finalizing our review procedures and checklists. Our focus in the xxx quarter is to assemble and train our review teams and thoroughly test the procedures. We expect to start the actual review on //insert date// so the first sign-off memoranda should be issued starting //insert date//.

Thank you for your participation and assistance with this important initiative. If you have any questions, please contact //insert name and extension here//.

Appendix 9

CLIENT FILES REVIEW AND SIGN-OFF MEMO

This memo has been designed to serve as a model for all sizes of law offices. Customize it to meet your needs and to reflect your review process and timing. If yours is a solo practice, then turn it into a document explaining your process.

To:
From:
CC:
Date:
Re: Records Disposition

Client Files
The client files on the attached list are candidates for destruction according to the firm's records retention policy. Please review the listing and initial in the space provided to indicate your authorization to proceed with disposition. File titles are listed to facilitate your review.

Documents with Research Value
The review team that assembled this list is already identifying selected documents for continued maintenance because of potential work product or research value. Disposition of additional specific documents in the remainder of the file will be delayed only in situations where the records are required for current client service. If you believe some of the files on the attached list contain documents that qualify for continued retention, indicate them clearly in the space below.

REQUEST FOR EXCEPTION FROM STANDARD DISPOSITION			
Matter No.	File/Document	Rationale	Expected Time Period

Client Notification

As a reminder, in accordance with ethics requirements and firm policy, we will be notifying clients of our intent to dispose of the records unless they indicate otherwise.

If you wish to review the file before authorizing disposition, please contact //insert name and extension// to arrange a time to visit the records center. Return the completed form to //insert name and extension// by //insert date//.

Appendix 10
CLIENT NOTIFICATION LETTER

This letter has been designed to serve as a model for all sizes of law offices. Customize it to meet your needs and to reflect your review process and timing and make sure it works in context of the ethics opinions of your state.

Dear:

Please be advised that the Firm is purging its files of records pertaining to matters that have been closed beyond xxx years. Our policy is to contact our clients and notify them of our intention to destroy the records unless they wish them returned.

Since these dead files pertain to matters that were concluded years ago, you may not wish for their return. However, we will make these files available to you upon your written request. Please indicate your preference for destruction or return of the files on the attached listing and return it in the enclosed, self-addressed stamped envelope.

Destruction of Files
If you select destruction, the files will be physically destroyed by a bonded organization. There is no charge for this service.

If we are notified that you have received this letter, but we receive no response within six weeks of your receipt, we will assume that you wish the file(s) to be destroyed.

Returning Records
If you wish the records returned, we will pack and ship them to the individual and the address you specify on the attached listing. We will bill for the cost of handling and shipping the files to you. If you wish the invoice sent to a different address, please let us know.

If you have questions, please address them to //insert name and title// at the address in the letterhead, or by e-mail at //insert e-mail address//.

As always, we greatly appreciate your business and hope to continue working with you. Thank you for your assistance. You may receive additional correspondence regarding closed files for other work we have done on your behalf.

Sincerely,

Index

Selected Books from . . .
THE ABA LAW PRACTICE MANAGEMENT SECTION

Electronic Evidence and Discovery Handbook: Forms, Checklists, and Guidelines
By Sharon D. Nelson, Bruce A. Olson, and John W. Simek
This comprehensive book provides lawyers with the templates they need to develop an effective E-Discovery strategy, and to frame appropriate E-Discovery requests. In addition to the ready-made forms (included on the accompanying CD-ROM), the authors also supply helpful information and commentary to bring you rapidly up to speed in the electronic discovery field.

The Lawyer's Guide to Creating Persuasive Computer Presentations, Second Edition
By Ann Brenden and John Goodhue
This book explains the advantages of computer presentation resources, how to use them, what they can do, and the legal issues involved in their use. You'll learn how to use computer presentations in the courtroom, during opening statements, direct examination, cross examination, closing arguments, appellate arguments and more. This revised second edition has been updated to include new chapters on hardware and software that is currently being used for digital displays, and all-new sections that walk the reader through beginning skills, and some advanced PowerPoint® techniques. Also included is a CD-ROM containing on-screen tutorials illustrating techniques such as animating text, insertion and configuration of text and images, and a full sample PowerPoint final argument complete with audio, and much more.

The Lawyer's Guide to Adobe® Acrobat®, Second Edition
By David L. Masters
This book will show you the power of using the Adobe Acrobat system and how to utilize its full potential in your law practice. Author David Masters takes readers step by step through the processes of creating PDF documents and then working with these documents. In subsequent chapters, Masters covers adding document navigation aids, commenting tools, using digital signatures, extracting content from PDF documents, searching and indexing, document security, saving Web pages to PDF, plug-ins, display mode, e-briefs, using Acrobat in the paperless office, and more.

The Lawyer's Guide to Fact Finding on the Internet, Third Edition
By Carole A. Levitt and Mark E. Rosch
Written especially for legal professionals, this revised and expanded edition is a complete hands-on guide to the best sites, secrets, and shortcuts, for conducting efficient research on the Internet. Useful for investigations, depositions, and trial presentations, as well as company and medical research, gathering competitive intelligence, finding expert witnesses, and fact checking of all kinds. An accompanying CD-ROM includes the links contained in the book, indexed, so you can easily navigate to these Web sites without typing URLs into your browser.

The Lawyer's Guide to Extranets: Breaking Down Walls, Building Client Connections
By Douglas Simpson and Mark Tamminga
An extranet can be a powerful tool that allows law firms to exchange information and build relationships with clients. This new book shows you why extranets are the next step in client interaction and communications, and how you can effectively implement an extranet in any type of firm. This book will take you step-by-step through the issues of implementing an extranet, and how to plan and build one. You'll get real-world extranet case studies, and learn from the successes and failures of those who have gone before. Help your firm get ahead of the emerging technologies curve and discover the benefits of adopting this new information tool.

The Lawyer's Guide to Marketing on the Internet, Second Edition
By Gregory Siskind, Deborah McMurray, and Richard P. Klau
The Internet is a critical component of every law firm marketing strategy—no matter where you are, how large your firm is, or the areas in which you practice. Used effectively, a younger, smaller firm can present an image just as sophisticated and impressive as a larger and more established firm. You can reach potential new clients, in remote areas, at any time, for minimal cost. To help you maximize your Internet marketing capabilities, this book provides you with countless Internet marketing possibilities and shows you how to effectively and efficiently market your law practice on the Internet.

The Lawyer's Guide to Effective Yellow Pages Advertising, Second Edition

By Kerry Randall and Andru J. Johnson

Although Yellow Pages advertising should be a major profit-building business marketing strategy for many law firms, the harsh reality is that most ads simply don't work. This book will provide you with the information you need to create effective, powerful Yellow Pages ads and drive your client development programs forward. You'll find information on identifying and focusing on your target market, as well as how to plan and design the perfect ad that not only reaches potential clients, but motivates them to call.

The Lawyer's Guide to Balancing Life and Work, Second Edition

By George W. Kaufman

Updated and revised, this Second Edition is written specifically to help lawyers achieve professional and personal satisfaction in their career. Writing with warmth and seasoned wisdom, George Kaufman examines the roots of stress, including how the profession has changed over the last five years (what's better and what's worse), then offers philosophical approaches, practical examples, and valuable exercises to help lawyers reconcile their goals and expectations with the realities and demands of the legal profession. You'll find information on empowering yourself to take charge of your environment and how to achieve your plan for personal growth. Interactive exercises are provided throughout the text and on the accompanying CD, to help you discover how stress is affecting you. New lawyers, seasoned veterans, and those who have personal relationships to lawyers will all benefit from this insightful book.

Compensation Plans for Law Firms, Fourth Edition

Edited by James D. Cotterman, Altman Weil, Inc.

In this newly revised and updated fourth edition, you'll find complete and systematic guidance on how to establish workable plans for compensating partners and associates, as well as other contributors to the firm. Discover how to align your firm's compensation plans with your culture, business objectives, and market realities. The book features valuable data from leading legal consulting firm Altman Weil's annual and triennial surveys on law firm performance and compensation, retirement, and withdrawal and compensation systems. You'll see where your firm stands on salaries and bonuses, as well as benefit from detailed analyses of compensation plans for everyone in your firm.

Paralegals, Profitability, and the Future of Your Law Practice

By Arthur G. Greene and Therese A. Cannon

This is your essential guide to effectively integrating paralegals into your practice and expanding their roles to ensure your firm is successful in the next decade. If you're not currently using paralegals in your firm, you'll learn why you need paralegals and how to create a paralegal model for use in your firm—no matter what the size or structure. You'll learn how to recruit and hire top-notch paralegals the first time. If you are currently using paralegals, you'll learn how to make sure your paralegal program is structured properly, runs effectively, and continually contributes to your bottom line. Finally, eight valuable appendices provide resources, job descriptions, model guidelines, sample confidentiality agreements, sample performance evaluations, and performance appraisals. In addition, all the forms and guidelines contained the appendix are included on a CD-ROM for ease in implementation!

The Lawyer's Guide to Marketing Your Practice, Second Edition

Edited by James A. Durham and Deborah McMurray

This book is packed with practical ideas, innovative strategies, useful checklists, and sample marketing and action plans to help you implement a successful, multi-faceted, and profit-enhancing marketing plan for your firm. Organized into four sections, this illuminating resource covers: Developing Your Approach; Enhancing Your Image; Implementing Marketing Strategies and Maintaining Your Program. Appendix materials include an instructive primer on market research to inform you on research methodologies that support the marketing of legal services. The accompanying CD-ROM contains a wealth of checklists, plans, and other sample reports, questionnaires, and templates—all designed to make implementing your marketing strategy as easy as possible!

The Complete Guide to Designing Your Law Office

By Suzette S. Schultz and Jon S. Schultz

Here's the information you need to create an impressive, efficient law office that meets your business requirements. Learn the best approaches for designing every area in the law office, including offices and work stations, conference rooms and reception areas, and more. You'll be guided through every step of the process, from determining your optimal square footage, to selecting the right security systems and technology, to hiring and working with movers. In addition, helpful checklists, schedules, forms, and letters are included on an accompanying CD-ROM to make your renovation or relocation as easy as possible. For anyone contemplating a new or redesigned office, this is the book that covers all the details.

ABA LawPracticeManagementSection

MARKETING • MANAGEMENT • TECHNOLOGY • FINANCE

30-Day Risk-Free Order Form
Call Today! 1-800-285-2221
Monday–Friday, 7:30 AM – 5:30 PM, Central Time

Qty	Title	LPM Price	Regular Price	Total
_____	Compensation Plans for Law Firms, Fourth Edition (5110507)	$ 79.95	$ 94.95	$_____
_____	The Complete Guide to Designing Your Law Office (5110537)	99.95	129.95	$_____
_____	The Lawyer's Guide to Adobe® Acrobat®, Second Edition (5110529)	49.95	59.95	$_____
_____	The Lawyer's Guide to Balancing Life and Work, Second Edition (5110566)	29.95	39.95	$_____
_____	The Lawyer's Guide to Creating Persuasive Computer Presentations, Second Edition (5110530)	79.95	99.95	$_____
_____	The Lawyer's Guide to Effective Yellow Pages Advertising, Second Edition (5110538)	54.95	69.95	$_____
_____	The Lawyer's Guide to Extranets (5110494)	59.95	69.95	$_____
_____	The Lawyer's Guide to Fact Finding on the Internet, Third Edition (5110568)	84.95	99.95	$_____
_____	The Lawyer's Guide to Marketing on the Internet, Second Edition (5110484)	69.95	79.95	$_____
_____	Electronic Evidence and Discovery Handbook (5110569)	99.95	129.95	$_____
_____	Paralegals, Profitability, and the Future of Your Law Practice (5110491)	59.95	69.95	$_____
_____	The Lawyer's Guide to Marketing Your Practice, Second Edition (5110500)	79.95	89.95	$_____

*Postage and Handling	
$10.00 to $24.99	$5.95
$25.00 to $49.99	$9.95
$50.00 to $99.99	$12.95
$100.00 to $349.99	$17.95
$350 to $499.99	$24.95

**Tax
DC residents add 5.75%
IL residents add 9.00%

*Postage and Handling	$_____
**Tax	$_____
TOTAL	$_____

PAYMENT

❏ Check enclosed (to the ABA)

❏ Visa   ❏ MasterCard   ❏ American Express

Account Number   Exp. Date   Signature

Name _____ Firm _____

Address _____

City _____ State _____ Zip _____

Phone Number _____ E-Mail Address _____

Guarantee
If—for any reason—you are not satisfied with your purchase, you may return it within 30 days of receipt for a complete refund of the price of the book(s). No questions asked!

Mail: ABA Publication Orders, P.O. Box 10892, Chicago, Illinois 60610-0892
♦ **Phone: 1-800-285-2221** ♦ **FAX: 312-988-5568**

E-Mail: abasvcctr@abanet.org ♦ **Internet: http://www.lawpractice.org/catalog**

About the CD

The accompanying CD contains the text of the Appendices from *The Lawyer's Guide to Records Management and Retention*. The files are in Microsoft Word® format.

For additional information about the files on the CD, please open and read the "**readme.doc**" file on the CD.

NOTE: The set of files on the CD may only be used on a single computer or moved to and used on another computer. Under no circumstances may the set of files be used on more than one computer at one time. If you are interested in obtaining a license to use the set of files on a local network, please contact: Director, Copyrights and Contracts, American Bar Association, 321 N. Clark Street, Chicago, IL 60610, (312) 988-6101. **Please read the license and warranty statements on the following page before using this CD.**

ABA
Defending Liberty Pursuing Justice

...ment

WARNING: Open _____ ...ce of the following Terms and Conditions.

READ THE FOLLO _____ ...ALED PACKAGE. IF YOU
DO NOT AGREE W _____ ...TO EITHER THE PARTY
FROM WHOM IT W _____ ...ND YOUR MONEY WILL
BE RETURNED.

The document files _____ ...r Association and are
protected by Copyri _____ ...d ownership of these
files.

License
You may use this set _____ ...ther computer, but
under no circumstance _____ ...the same time. You
may copy the files eith _____ ...or for backup purposes. If you are interes _____ ...twork, please contact: Director, Copyrigh _____ ...treet, Chicago, IL
60610, (312) 988-6101.

You may permanently tra _____ ...es to accept the
terms and conditions of t. _____ ...ust at the same
time transfer all copies of _____ ...d. Such transfer
terminates your license. Yc _____ ...xcept as stated
in this paragraph.

You may modify these files _____ ...nent. You may
not redistribute any modifie _____

Warranty
If a CD-ROM in this package i _____ ...ve, the American Bar Association will replace it at no charge if the defective diskette is returned to the American Bar Association within 60 days from the date of ac-quisition.

American Bar Association warrants that these files will perform in substantial compliance with the documentation supplied in this package. However, the American Bar Association does not warrant these forms as to the correctness of the legal material contained therein. If you report a significant de-fect in performance in writing to the American Bar Association, and the American Bar Association is not able to correct it within 60 days, you may return the diskettes, including all copies and documen-tation, to the American Bar Association and the American Bar Association will refund your money.

Any files that you modify will no longer be covered under this warranty even if they were modified in accordance with the License Agreement and product documentation.

IN NO EVENT WILL THE AMERICAN BAR ASSOCIATION, ITS OFFICERS, MEMBERS, OR EMPLOYEES BE LIABLE TO YOU FOR ANY DAMAGES, INCLUDING LOST PROFITS, LOST SAVINGS OR OTHER INCIDEN-TAL OR CONSEQUENTIAL DAMAGES ARISING OUT OF YOUR USE OR INABILITY TO USE THESE FILES EVEN IF THE AMERICAN BAR ASSOCIATION OR AN AUTHORIZED AMERICAN BAR ASSOCIATION REP-RESENTATIVE HAS BEEN ADVISED OF THE POSSIBILITY OF SUCH DAMAGES, OR FOR ANY CLAIM BY ANY OTHER PARTY. SOME STATES DO NOT ALLOW THE LIMITATION OR EXCLUSION OF LIABILITY FOR INCIDENTAL OR CONSEQUENTIAL DAMAGES, IN WHICH CASE THIS LIMITATION MAY NOT APPLY TO YOU.